Media, Myth, and Millennials

Media, Myth, and Millennials

Critical Perspectives on Race and Culture

Edited by
Loren Saxton Coleman
and Christopher P. Campbell

LEXINGTON BOOKS
Lanham • Boulder • New York • London

Published by Lexington Books
An imprint of The Rowman & Littlefield Publishing Group, Inc.
4501 Forbes Boulevard, Suite 200, Lanham, Maryland 20706
www.rowman.com

6 Tinworth Street, London SE11 5AL

British Library Cataloguing in Publication Information Available

Library of Congress Cataloging-in-Publication Data

ISBN 978-1-4985-7735-9 (cloth : alk. paper)
ISBN 978-1-4985-7737-3 (pbk : alk. paper)
ISBN 978-1-4985-7736-6 (electronic)

∞™ The paper used in this publication meets the minimum requirements of American National Standard for Information Sciences Permanence of Paper for Printed Library Materials, ANSI/NISO Z39.48-1992.

Contents

Introduction

Media help us make sense of our world and everyday experiences. Media often use myth, archetypal stories, to help people organize and simplify complex information (Lule, 2001). In Lule's (2001) book that explores news as myth, he argued that news and myth both function to instruct and inform by using narrative structures, with distinct beginnings, middles and ends. Yet, these myths are often embedded with racist and stereotypical representations of marginalized groups, and the stories told via various media outlets are often incomplete.

For example, the "post-racial myth" emerged after the election of the first African-American president, Barack Obama (Dawson & Bobo, 2009; Squires, 2014). This myth tells the story that President Barack Obama signified that America had eradicated and overcome racism. Yet, as Squires (2014) highlighted, racial inequalities persist, and in many cases, have increased, across social, political and economic life. "The gap between the aspirational post-racial discourse and the brutal realities of poverty, police profiling, anti-immigration vitriol, and mind boggling incarceration rates for blacks and latinos/as is wide," she writes (p. 12).

A post-racial society is indeed a myth, in that it helps perpetuate a narrative that largely ignores ongoing institutional and systemic practices of racism and provides a false sense of comfort and triumph of America overcoming its violent history of racism. This myth also makes it difficult to call out, critique, and work to dismantle systems of racial oppression, because it perpetuates the idea that racism "ended" with President Obama's election in 2008. *Media, Myth, and Millennials: Critical Perspectives on Race and Culture* explores both the proliferation and the subversion of this myth among millennial media consumers and producers.

Many of our contributors cited specific ranges of birthdates to define millennials. It is often difficult to precisely define the ages of any generation, and this seems particularly true for millennials. Rather than an emphasis on the age range, our text draws attention to this generation as digital natives. As digital natives, our volume highlights how the millennial generation has grown up since the emergence of the internet and has embraced a variety of digital technologies, including cell phones, smart phones, text messaging, video games and instant messaging (Considine et al., 2009). Millennials have the distinct characteristic of having access to more information than any prior generation; indeed, they are immersed in Information Communication Technology (Considine et al., 2009).

The millennial generation is the most ethnically and racially diverse in American society (Milkman, 2017). Although growing up in an alleged "post-racial" society, Milkman (2017) argued that millennials are more likely to confront persistent racism. Our edited volume explores the intersections of media, myth and millennials, with a specific emphasis on issues of race and culture. Our text investigates the following questions: How are millennials engaging with media that perpetuate the post-racial myth? How are millennial audiences commodified? And how are millennials producing counter-narratives that not only dispel the post-racial myth, but also provide alternative representations that challenge dangerous and crippling representations of marginalized groups?

Media, Myth, and Millennials is divided into two parts—The Commodification of the Millennial Audience and Representation as Resistance. Chapters in The Commodification of the Millennial Audience provide evidence of the persistence of racism and racist representation across media forms, and also critically examine how media engage with millennial audiences on issues of race, racism and racial equality.

Christopher P. Campbell, in "Commodifying the Resistance: Wokeness, Whiteness and the Historical Persistence of Racism," analyzes advertising and other media that appeals to progressive millennial audiences and how it reflects the persistence of the kind of racism that was found in media produced before the supposed enlightenment of a "post-racial" America. It discusses Nike's use of the controversial NFL football player and social justice advocate Colin Kaepernick and includes an analysis of a curious Pepsi ad that featured celebrity/model Kendall Jenner at a street protest. The chapter argues that the racial messages in millennial media reflect similar problems to those in media produced by white Baby Boomers and Gen Xers. It uses a recently developed political science theory of "historical persistence" to explain the persistence of white supremacist notions in contemporary media.

The chapter by Natalie Hopkinson and Sharifa Simon-Roberts, "Tweet Black-*ish* to Make Black Lives Matter: Race and Agenda Setting in the Age of Millennials," analyzes inter-media agenda setting by examining the public discourse around racial violence and inequality in the public sphere launched by the millennial-led Black Lives Matter (BLM) movement. Their piece is a comparative analysis of BLM discourse across a selection of media—a scripted television comedy program, major network news, and Twitter—in a single week in 2016 during a key primary in the U.S. presidential elections. The authors found that the comedy show *Black-ish* and #BlackLivesMatter social media campaigns were effective in putting the loss of black life on the public and policy agenda and linking it to the long struggle of racial inequality. However, this framing clashed with television news narratives that either emphasized the political "horse race" coverage or perpetuated deeply ingrained myths and dehumanizing narratives of aggressive and problematic black youth.

In "Reading Race and Religion in Aziz Ansari's *Master of None*," Nadeen Kharputly provides an analysis of the show and examines the different responses that Muslim Americans have to the portrayal of Islam on the show, focusing on the "Religion" episode in particular. The tensions between Aziz Ansari's depictions of Islam in *Master of None* and the Muslim American responses to those depictions highlight both the burden of responsibility placed on Ansari and the expectations demanded by Muslim-American audiences.

Robert D. Byrd, Jr., in "Quaring Queer Eye: Millennials, Moral Licensing, Cleansing and the *Queer Eye* Reboot," looks at the 2018 Netflix revival of the 2003 reality makeover show *Queer Eye for the Straight Guy*. *Queer Eye*, the new show, like many other television show revivals or reboots, allows previous fans of the show a new outlet to watch and continue their fandom, but, probably more importantly, it opens the show to a new generation of fans. This chapter, however, is not about the success of television reboots and revivals. Byrd examines the *Queer Eye* reboot through a quare theory lens to problematize the neoliberal, heterosexist and racist representations of race, racism and queer identity in the 2018 iteration of the show. He argues that *Queer Eye*, in an effort to present all walks of life and all views, actually creates an outlet for moral licensing and cleansing for its viewers—giving its viewers the moral high ground to support and promote issues, politicians and points of view detrimental to LGBTQ people of color—specifically black LGBTQ people.

In "#BaltimoreUprising: Race, Representation and Millennial Engagement in Digital Media," Cheryl Jenkins examines the consistent lack of minority representation in mainstream news media and how minority groups have often had to find alternative ways to tell their stories. Digital news and other online options have provided a way for African-American and other minority journalists to tell stories that are unique to their particular communities in ways often not impeded by traditional journalistic tenets. These digital platforms are most popular with the large millennial population in the country and, as a result, connect underrepresented journalists to an influential and socially active group of citizens. As such, this chapter examines how minority news producers, including those who used social media to critique police violence in Baltimore, have capitalized on alternative and digital media formats as a result of mainstream media's failure to incorporate more diversity in their newsrooms. It also analyzes the growing influence of digital media, specifically social media, on the large millennial population and how African-American millennials in particular have been able to use the platform to add more diverse perspectives to news stories that tackle complex and sensitive subject matter like police brutality and racism.

Jenkins' chapter serves as the bridge between the two parts of this book. Her chapter's emphasis on the lack of diversity highlights the persistence of racial inequality and racism in the newsroom and offers a path forward for minority journalists—digital and social media storytelling. In Part Two, Representation as Resistance, authors provide evidence of how millennials produce counter-hegemonic representations across various media forms. In this section, authors problematize the production of counternarratives in digital and social media and highlight how media consumers and producers are challenging and subverting cultural appropriation, (mis)representation and displacement.

In "The Role of Parody in Decoding Media Text: *Saturday Night Live* and the Immigration Narrative," Daleana Phillips analyzes *Saturday Night Live*'s "Caravan Cold Open" (the program's opening skit) and how the program increasingly uses celebrities, music, popular culture and political humor to expose dominant political ideology. Using Stuart Hall's encoding/decoding framework, the chapter investigates how political humor, such as satire, negotiates dominant narratives of illegal immigration, asylum seekers and U.S. immigration policy by poking holes in hegemonic ideologies that are perceived to be incongruous with lived experiences. With a growing increase in popularity and consumption of "infotainment" and "partisan news" among millennials, Phillips argued that parody creates conditions for the subversion of dominant ideologies and the reinforcement and perpetuation of restrictive metaphors in discourse about immigration in the United States.

Loren Saxton Coleman, in "#DCNative: Examining Community Identity, Representation and Resistance in Washington, D.C.," examines how black native Washingtonians pursued spatial justice via media practice. This critical textual analysis investigates how Instagram was used to challenge monolithic representations of urban authenticity that centered on white millennials and to create alternative geographies that celebrated black life and culture amidst swift practices of urban revitalization. This chapter calls on scholars to prioritize the communities, counter narratives *and* cultural geographies in the periphery that are engaging in media practice in the pursuit of social justice.

In "Calling out Racism for What It Is: Memes, BBQ Becky and the Oppositional Gaze," Jessica Maddox interrogates the intersection of race and internet memes in order to understand how these popular digital image macros can simultaneously be tools of entertainment and resistance. She examines the widely viewed "BBQ Becky" meme through the lens of bell hooks' oppositional gaze (1992) as social commentary about racism and race relations in America. This chapter explores questions of race, space and place, and how black millennials and black meme-makers can wield memes to actively comment on and critique a dominant whiteness that seeks to regulate black individuals to social margins. Ultimately, Maddox argues that the meme speaks truth to power, as meme makers creatively resist, comment on, and point out the failings of dominant whiteness.

In "Latina/o Millenials in a Post-TV Network World: Anti-Stereotypes in the Transmedia Edutainment Web TV Series *East Los High,*" Celeste González de Bustamante and Jessica Retis identify the emergence of "anti-stereotypes" and analyze Latina millennial representations in *East Los High* by paying specific attention to the topic of teen pregnancy. The chapter also examines the potential for collective action among producers and actors of *East Los High* through the process of "scale-shifting." The authors focus their attention on the structural issues involving the entertainment industry and the ability of Latina/o producers and actors to circumvent traditional power structures to contribute to collective-action to effect social change. They ask if, in this post TV-network era, whether approaches involving transmedia and edutainment strategies and the use of social media by celebrity activists may contribute to create a sense of collective action.

Ashley Cordes and Debra Merskin, in "#DontTrendOnMe: Addressing Appropriation of Native Americanness in Millennial Social Media," explore representations of woman Native Americanness at the 2018 Coachella Valley Music and Arts Festival (CVMF). The authors consider the politics of representation and cultural appropriation as well as the lived and "felt" experiences and responses to these displays from Native American people and their allies. They textually analyze Instagram images that illustrate the "Coachella look." This look consists of hypersexualized outfits paired with bricolages of headdresses, tribal hairstyles, feathers, beads, war paint, and other markers of Native Americanness. Although millennials are proclaimed to be "woke" to issues of race and gender, the widespread appropriation of Native Americanness at CVMF suggests that this generation has blind spots to these issues. At the same time, the authors celebrate a new wave of Native and ally millennials that speak back to these racial and cultural "rip offs" that are experienced as "felt" attacks on Indigenous cultures and identities. To demonstrate these acts of resistance, the authors describe memes, hashtags and blogs on social media platforms that aim to re-articulate and revise the problem. The authors find that these are useful digital terrains for decolonial views to uniquely speak to and against racist performances of Native identities.

In "(Un)covering *International Secret Agents:* Constituting a Post-Network Asian American Identity through Self-Representation," Vincent N. Pham and Alison Yeh Cheung theorize a post-network Asian American millennial audience by looking at them on YouTube, one of the platforms that cultivates such audiences. By focusing on International Secret Agents (ISA) and their Youtube channel, ISAtv, the authors contextualize millennials' efforts within a long-standing history of Asian American media-making that have longed for "self-representation" in response to mainstream media representations. Through an examination of ISAtv's content and circulation of ISAtv, they argue that ISAtv locates the endeavors and possibilities of discursively constructed yet geographically dispersed Asian American millennial audiences within the necessity of community-based Los Angeles spaces. The authors argue that, in doing so, the International Secret Agents see Asian American millennial audiences' future as dependent on self-representation.

In "Being Black at Southern Miss": The Mythology of the African-American True Believer," Marcus Coleman discusses the use of public appeals by millennials to overcome subversive racial practices. In this chapter, Coleman assesses the use of African-American mythoforms as a way of decomposing the *relational tension between publics* to illustrate the function of myth. To do so, Coleman first inductively analyzes the appeals made in letters written by one of the first African Americans to attempt to enroll at all-white Mississippi Southern College (now the University of Southern Mississippi). In examining Clyde Kennard's correspondence in 1958, 1959 and 1960, Coleman finds that Kennard employed dialectics as a strategy to undermine white supremacy via public appeals for racial equity. Next, through the lens of dialectics, Coleman assesses a 2015 video, "Being Black at USM," produced by millennial students at the University of Southern Mississippi. The analysis suggests that there is an understudied black mythoform characterized as a true believer, in other words, the black patriot.

In the final chapter, Jayne Cubbage offers a pedagogical approach to teaching concepts of race, media literacy and media production in the college classroom. In "Making Meaning of the Messages: Black Millennials, Film and Critical Race Media Literacy," Cubbage explores the themes of race and millennials and their understanding of contemporary film and targeted messaging in films directed at black millennials. Her chapter, which explores student responses to *Black Panther*, *Get Out*, and *Dear White People*, highlights the necessity for the insertion and prioritization of race and other intersections within media literacy education. This chapter provides practical pedagogical tools to help students engage in critical and active consumption of films, particularly those with a heavy dose of race-based themes and non-white characters.

—Loren Saxton Coleman and Christopher P. Campbell

REFERENCES

Bialik, K., & Fry, R. (2019, Feb. 14). Millennial life: How young adulthood compares with prior generations. http://www.pewsocialtrends.org/essay/millennial-life-how-young-adult-hood-today-compares-with-prior-generations/.

Considine, D., Horton, J., & Moorman, G. (2009). Teaching and reading the millennial generation through media literacy. *Journal of Adolescent & Adult Literacy, 52*(6), 471–481.

Dawson, M. C., & Bobo, L. (2009). One year later and the myth of a post-racial society. *DuBois Review, 6*(2), 247–249.

Lule, J. (2001). *Daily news, eternal stories: The mythological role of journalism.* New York: The Guilford Press.

Milkman, R. (2017). A new political generation: Millennials and the post-2008 wave of protest. *American Sociological Review, 82*(1), 1–31.

Squires, C. (2014). *The post-racial mystique: Media and race in the twenty-first century.* New York: NYU Press.

Part I

The Commodification of the Millennial Audience

Chapter One

Commodifying the Resistance

Wokeness, Whiteness and the
Historical Persistence of Racism

Christopher P. Campbell

When Nike in September of 2018 announced that Colin Kaepernick would be the face of the 30th anniversary of its "Just Do It" advertising campaign, sparks, predictably, flew. Kaepernick, who lost his job as an NFL quarterback after launching a campaign in which NFL players knelt during the National Anthem to protest racial inequality and police killings of African Americans, was a controversial choice. The digital poster that Nike posted on social media showed a close-up of Kaepernick's face, with these words superimposed: "Believe in something. Even if it means losing everything. Just do it." The internet exploded, and Nike surely knew the post would generate disparate reactions. Those opposed to the ad and the NFL protests (including President Donald Trump) considered Kaepernick and the other protesters unpatriotic, and the protests left the NFL in the unenviable position of trying to limit the damage. For many NFL fans, the protests were a slap in the face to the police and military; to others, the protests represented a welcome challenge to the persistence of white supremacy in the United States. For Nike, the controversy represented an intriguing marketing opportunity, and the company chose to side with the protesters.

Fallout from the launch of the campaign was widespread and immediate. Social media sites were flooded with both praise and scorn for Nike. Some pundits observed that Nike had done its homework and decided to use Kaepernick to symbolize the company's alliance with its millennial customers who, Nike suspected, mostly sided with the NFL protesters. As *Washington Post* columnist Sally Jenkins (2018) observed, "What (Nike) sees in Kaepernick is not just a digital poster but the face of an entire new wave. In that sense, Nike's campaign is not radical. It's the furthest thing from it. It's just the future." At the Emmy Awards ceremony that closely followed the campaign's launch, African American actress Jennifer Lewis wore a Nike sweater on the red carpet, explaining, "I am wearing Nike to applaud them for supporting Colin Kaepernick and his protest against racial injustice and police brutality . . . [and] to say thank you for leading the resistance" (Bieler, 2017).

A day after the campaign was launched, the value of the flood of social media exposure related to the digital poster was estimated at $43 million (Novy-Williams, 2018). A few days later, the company announced that its online sales had increased by 31 percent (Raggs, 2018). Nike likely expected such a response, so its interests may not have been as much of a cultural touchstone as it was a marketing ploy by advertisers who knew that taking progressive stands on controversial issues could generate social media exposure and sales. This ploy has become a common one, and I'll argue here that it likely doesn't reflect the actual racial attitudes of the white, progressive millennials who were expected to embrace the message. If Nike was indeed "leading the resistance," the company and its leadership would certainly not have steered 78 percent of nearly $1 million in campaign donations in 2018 to conservative political candidates (Bery, 2018).

Advertising directed at millennial audiences has increasingly sought to link politically progressive ideas with all kinds of products. For the 2014 Super Bowl, Cheerios aired a much-discussed commercial as part of its "Wholesome" campaign that featured a nuclear family with an African American father, white mother and their young mixed-race daughter. For the 2015 Super Bowl, feminine-hygiene pad maker Always ran its "Like a Girl" campaign, which challenged stereotypes about girls and women. Anheuser-Busch in 2017 aired a pro-immigration ad during the Super Bowl that followed a contentious presidential election in which Trump used an aggressive anti-immigration stance as part of his appeal to white voters.

Traditional critical media analysis of advertising often follows the pattern described by Stuart Hall (1982) in his seminal essay "Encoding/Decoding." First is a description of the commercial's "preferred" message (directly or indirectly exhorting the value of the product, what Hall describes as the hegemonic code embedded in the encoding process) followed by a "negotiated" reading (the subtle ways the advertiser was appealing to audiences' baser instincts to buy the product, which Hall describes as the decoding process). Ultimately, critics analyze messages of racism, sexism or classism on the "oppositional" level, examining the problematic messages embedded beneath the surface of the ads.

But what I've noticed in many commercials directed at millennials is that the advertisers themselves seem to be *encoding* politically loaded messages as a means to sell products. Anti–white supremacy? Have some Cheerios. Pro #MeToo? Use Always hygiene products. Support the Dreamers? This Bud's for you. The millennial era seems to be one in which marketers believe they can tap into the Resistance—the progressive, anti-Trump political movement that embraces racial, gender and environmental activism—to sell products.

The ads beg this question: Are these companies really committed to the ideals in their commercials, or are they embracing those ideals to sell products? For instance, was Proctor and Gamble really invested in improved race relations as it would seem in its provocative online campaign called "The Talk," in which black parents explained to their teenage children how to deal with the perils of contemporary racism? Was Fiat Chrysler really supportive of Dr. Martin Luther King Jr.'s anti-capitalist message when it used out-of-context clips from his "Drum Major Instinct" sermon to sell Ram Trucks during the 2018 Super Bowl?

In this chapter, I'll ask if companies like Nike, Pepsi-Cola and others are really committed to cultural diversity and the Black Lives Matter movement. At least that seemed to be the message of Pepsi's strange, controversial (and largely ridiculed) 2017 Kendall Jenner "Jump In" ad. While it might seem like a rhetorical question, I believe it's worth unpacking Nike's and Pepsi's (and the advertising industry-at-large's) "woke" attempts to sell things in the age of Donald Trump. The purpose of this essay is to analyze advertising designed to appeal to progressive millennial audiences and how it reflects the persistence of the kind of racism that was found in media produced before the supposed enlightenment of a "post-racial" America. That is, I will argue here that the racial messages in millennial media reflect identical problems to those in media produced by white Baby Boomers and Gen Xers. I'll also argue that a recently developed "theory of historical persistence" (Acharya, Blackwell, & Sen, 2016), which explains how the centuries-old prevalence of slavery continues to have "a detectable effect on present-day political attitudes in the American South" (p. 621), may also explain the powerful persistence of the myth of post-racialism.

RACE AND MEDIA

The examination of race and media during the Baby Boom era largely focused on the notion of "symbolic annihilation," the general invisibility of people of color in all forms of media (Gerbner & Gross, 1976). As media portrayals of people of color increased, scholars looked at race in terms of *representation*. As Hall explains, the analysis of media representations is the key to unlocking the power of the media's dominant meanings—meanings that indirectly serve the interests of the wealthiest and most powerful members of a society. He described this critically informed notion of representation as

> a way of constantly wanting new kinds of knowledges to be produced in the world, new kinds of subjectivities to be explored and new dimensions of meaning which have not been foreclosed by the systems of power which are in operation. (quoted in Jhally, 1997)

Herman Gray's work is especially useful in looking at racialized media representations during the era that bridged the Baby Boomers and Gen Xers. For instance, he identified in 1986 the "twin representations" of African Americans in fictional and nonfictional television. He contrasted the upper middle-class life portrayed on the mega-hit sitcom *The Cosby Show* with the underclass black life portrayed in a 1985 PBS documentary titled *The Vanishing Family: Crisis in Black America*. Race as it is portrayed on fictional television, according to Gray, was consistent with The American Dream, and "appeals to the utopian desire in blacks and whites for racial oneness and equality while displacing the persistent reality of racism and racial inequality or the kinds of social struggles and cooperation required to eliminate them" (1991, p. 302).

Gray argued that the underclass black life on nonfictional TV, on the other hand, failed to "identify complex social forces like racism, social organization, economic dislocation, unemployment, the changing economy, or the welfare state as the causes of the crisis in (the urban underclass) community" (p. 300). Gray foresaw the problems posed by the notion of a "post-racial" America when he concluded that

> the assumptions and framework that structure these representations often displace representations that would enable viewers to see that many individuals trapped in the underclass have the very same qualities (of hard work and sacrifices as seen on *Cosby*) but lack the options and opportunities to realize them. (p. 303)

I made similar observations in my study of local television news (Campbell, 1995). That study identified three myths in stories about people of color: a myth of marginality, which reflected the general invisibility of non-white people in the news; a myth of difference, which described the impact of criminal images of black and Latino men that dominated local television journalism; and a myth of assimilation, which identified the cherished newsroom myth that represents people of color, especially in coverage of African Americans on the annual holiday honoring Dr. Martin Luther King, Jr., as having overcome racism and fully assimilated into the American mainstream, where equality has been achieved.

Like Gray, I recognized the potential consequences of dominant media messages that portray people of color as pathological criminals while also portraying a mythical world free of racism. If the world is a fair and just place and racism is a thing of the past, skin color becomes the explanation for the criminal behavior of people of color in poor communities, gives birth to bad public policy (like "three-strikes" criminal legislation) and confirms the attitudes of white supremacists.

Much recent examination of race and media is based on Critical Race Theory (CRT), which positions the notion of *whiteness* (and white privilege) at the center of discussions about race. CRT, a relatively recent theory that emerged out of legal studies, argues that racism functions institutionally, often without notice, among whites. The theory allows researchers to examine race by acknowledging the inherent privilege of whiteness and analyzing race from a perspective that recognizes that privilege. Mahoney (1995) explains that "part of white privilege is not seeing all we (white people) have and all we do, and not seeing how what we do appears to those defined as other" (p. 306). She continues,

> This country is both highly segregated and based on the concept of whiteness as "normal." It is therefore hard for white folks to see whiteness both when we interact with people who are not socially defined as white and when we interact with other white people, when race doesn't seem to be involved (p. 306).

LeDuff (2016) concurs:

> Critical Race Theorists saw the writing on the wall early on. In some ways the initial response of society and media coverage of life in the early years after the Civil Rights Movement gave the false impression that racism was over. The media perpetuated the myth by avoiding the stories that indicated the true price of oppression. Instead they focused on sensational stories to increase their viewership and for ratings. Unfortunately, hegemonic thoughts and practices in relation to race persisted and festered, and today it seems that many of the old challenges that society faced in pre-civil rights America are coming back to haunt us with a new and different twist. (p. 71)

LeDuff argues that millennial media have yet to provide significant evidence of more insightful and accurate representations in contemporary media, including what she has seen in social media: "This technology, which was once touted as being almost utopian, has instead become one of the places where we can witness first-hand the great divides among race and class in modern society" (p. 72).

My more recent work includes analyses of millennial media based in Critical Race Theory. In examining the hashtag campaign that followed the killing of Michael Brown, the young African American man shot by a white

Ferguson, Missouri, policeman in the summer of 2014, I found some hope in the power of social media to contradict the powerful myths of local television news. In the #IfTheyGunnedMeDown campaign, young African Americans posted two photos of themselves on Twitter and other social media sites; the images represented both positive and negative images of the participants, suggesting that the negative photos would be used by the news media if they happened to be shot by police. The campaign reached an audience of millions through social media as well as through coverage by national and international news organizations. My study observed that in the campaign "young African Americans perceptively and concisely identified the problems inherent in dominant media representations of Black men as pathological criminals" (Campbell, 2016, p. 195).

Ultimately, however, I argued that millennial social media campaigns like those connected to the Black Lives Matter and Occupy Wall Street movements were useful in raising awareness about issues, but that, ultimately, those campaigns would likely not trigger dramatic shifts in American public policy or in traditional media approaches. I argued that progressive white millennials remained generally indifferent to racial injustice and that news audiences would "continue to be bombarded with murder-of-the-day coverage of poor Black and Hispanic communities, and journalists will largely continue to ignore the context for the horrible realities of life in America's most impoverished communities" (p. 209). My analysis did suggest that there might be "good news":

> Audiences for traditional journalism are rapidly shrinking, and future generations of social media-savvy audiences will rely more heavily on media that have the potential to provide representations of people and communities of color that refute the mythical notions that have dominated news coverage for decades. (p. 209)

But when a year later I examined the racial humor of progressive white millennial comedians, I found their messages about race to echo the messages of previous generations:

> There doesn't seem to be much evidence that media produced by and for the millennial generation will be any different. It's difficult to be optimistic because the problem may be compounded as 1) millennials access video and other media primarily through the echo chambers of social media platforms and streaming services, where they will have less impact and 2) they continue to produce media that reinforces the attitudes of contemporary racism. (Campbell, 2017, p. 26)

WOKENESS, WHITENESS AND MILLENNIALS

The Kerner Commission, the landmark study that examined racism in America that was published in 1968, famously reported that America was moving toward two societies, "one black, one white—separate and unequal" (Kerner Commission, 1968, p. 1). Fifty years later, the Economic Policy Institute found that in many cases African Americans were no better off. The institute's study found that more African Americans were unemployed in 2017 than in 1968, that black home ownership had not increased and that the number of incarcerated black Americans had tripled, noting that "African Americans are 6.4 times as likely than whites to be jailed or imprisoned," worse than in 1968 (Jan, 2018). The institute found that median net worth of white families was 10 times that of black families, a gap that was increasing, and, as the Federal Reserve reported in 2017, "Nearly 1 in 5 black families have zero or no negative net worth—twice the rate of white families" (Jan, 2017). A study by the Brookings Institute found that in 2016 the median white family had a net worth of $140,000 while the median black family had a net worth of $3,400 (Ingraham, 2018).

Such findings make the notion of "post-racism" preposterous, though it remains to be a dominant myth among most white millennials, who, like most white Baby Boomers and Gen Xers, do not believe that racism is one of America's most pressing issues. Indeed, most white millennials believe that "discrimination against whites is as significant as discrimination against other groups," and most young white men believe they are more likely to be victims of discrimination than black people (Bump, 2018). Even millennials who hold progressive attitudes about same-sex marriage and socialism and identify as liberal Democrats don't consider racism to be a pressing problem (Lewis, 2017).

Michael Denzel Smith, the author of *Invisible Man: Got the Whole World Watching*, is among the observers of contemporary racism who believe that white millennials cling to a worldview not that different from previous generations:

> The education these young white people have received left them ill-equipped to understand the nature of racism and subsequently supplied them with analysis that won't address the problem. . . . They were taught by their elders, Baby Boomer and Gen-Xers, about how to think about race and racism . . . that racism is a matter of personal bigotry—racists hate people because of the color of their skin, or because they believe stereotypes about groups of people they've never met—not one of institutional discrimination and exploitation. (2015)

Similarly, Ali Michael, co-author of *Two-Faced-Racism*, explains, "It's clear that a lot of white families want to raise their kids not to be racist—

middle of the road or even liberal families who think that it's wrong to be racist." But, he adds, "They think that racism is like . . . KKK type racism . . . and they don't see the shades of microaggressions, or aggressive racism. They don't see that there is systemic or historic racism" (quoted in Love, 2016). So perhaps we shouldn't be surprised when media produced by and for millennials is unchanged in its representations of race.

RACISM, ADVERTISING AND PEPSI: THE CHOICE OF A NEW GENERATION?

Hall identified the ways in which media representations indirectly served the interests of Western culture's most powerful people—white, wealthy men. Hall (1980) described "decoding" media texts through at least two levels of analysis. Simply put, the first level is the denotative or preferred reading— that which was intended by the producer—and the second level is the connotative reading—the audience's negotiated or oppositional analysis—of the same message. According to Hall, such connotative readings require a recognition of the dominant ideology: "Negotiated codes operate through what we might call particular or situated logics: and these logics are sustained by their differential and unequal relation to the discourses and logics of power" (p. 137). In this way, the denotative, commonsense meanings of the texts are understood within the larger context provided by connotative, interpretive readings. Hall ultimately described "oppositional" readings of media messages in which audiences resist the preferred meaning and recognize deeper, problematic meanings. As he wrote, "One of the most significant political moments . . . is the point when events which are normally signified and decoded in a negotiated way begin to be given an oppositional reading. Here the 'politics of signification'—the struggle in discourse—is joined" (p. 138).

In Pepsi-Cola's controversial Kendell Jenner two-minutes-plus online ad (deemed by Pepsi to be a "short film"), we see the celebrity (who gained fame as a member of the Kardashian/Jenner family of reality TV notoriety) leave a modeling session to join a large group of street protestors, good-looking young people from a variety of ethnic backgrounds; simultaneously, an Asian cello player and hijab-clad photographer, both millennials, leave their work to join the protest (which curiously looks like a street party and the cellist joins a rock band on stage). Of course, bottles and cans of Pepsi are everywhere. The music in the background, a contemporary protest song, "Lions," by Skip Marley, the grandson of reggae superstar Bob Marley, hearkens back to Pepsi's 1980s-era "Choice of a New Generation" campaign. "We are the lions, we are the chosen," young Marley sings. "We gonna shine out the dark. We are the movement, this generation."

As she leaves her modeling session, Jenner wipes the bright red lipstick from her face and pulls off her long blonde wig. Still looking glamorous as a brunette in her new denim outfit, she grasps a Pespsi can from a tub of ice, cuts through the protestors to a line of police officers and hands a cop the can, which he accepts, and smilingly drinks, as the Muslim photographer smiles and snaps a shot. As the video and music fade out, the audience sees the Pepsi logo and these phrases: "Live Bolder, Live Louder, Live for Now."

The social media response was immediate, questioning Pepsi's attempt to hijack symbols from the Black Lives Matter movement to sell soda. After pulling it off the airwaves, the Pepsi-Cola Company described the commercial's preferred reading: "Pepsi was trying to project a global message of unity, peace and understanding." The ad, according to Pepsi, "reflects people from different walks of life coming together in a spirit of harmony, and we think that's an important message to convey" (Izadi, 2017). Its decision to pull the ad came only 24 hours after it originally aired. Among the many memes that mocked the commercial was one from Bernice King, the daughter of Martin Luther King, Jr. Below a photo of her father being manhandled as he faced down a line of riot police, she wrote, "If only Daddy had known the power of Pepsi" (quoted in Victor, 2017).

Despite Pepsi's efforts to appear to join the Resistance, many viewers immediately identified a "negotiated" meaning of the ad, that Pepsi was attempting to use the progressive political politics of millennials to sell its products. While there has been little backlash against other company's subtler efforts to do the same thing—for instance, Nike's Kaepernick poster or Proctor & Gamble's pro-black, pro-woman, pro-environment stances—Pepsi's ad was simply over the top. Of particular scorn was its appropriation of the iconic photograph of Ieisha Evans, the African American woman who confronted riot police during protests over police violence in Baton Rouge, Louisiana, which was captured by Reuters photographer Jonathan Backman. Beneath the juxtaposed images of Jenner and Evans, one commenter tweeted, "The best example of white and economic privilege/ignorance I've ever seen. Never forget Ieshia Evans" (quoted in Victor, 2017).

But it is at the oppositional level of analysis, where Stuart Hall encourages us to recognize "the politics of signification," the commercial's more meaningful, hegemonic implications can be found. That an ad agency and the Pepsi-Cola Corporation decided that this commercial would be an effective way to sell its product is telling, especially given the extensive market-based research that supports the creative efforts of ad makers. The producers clearly thought that young viewers would respond well to its embrace of cultural diversity and political protest. The commercial's version of progressive millennials is especially telling—the smiling faces of the diverse throng of beautiful young protestors suggests a world in which racism does not exist (and contradicting the idea that they are protesting police violence toward African

Americans!). This is a world not so different from the post-racial one on *The Cosby Show*, likely the most viewed media representation of African Americans for both Baby Boom and Gen X audiences. *Cosby* was a huge success during the Reagan era, when virtually all of the advances of The Great Society were undone, and the income, education and criminal justice gap between white and black Americans began widening.

It is easy for contemporary media producers to fall back on the mythology of post-racialism. That myth held sway beyond the *Cosby* era and grew exponentially during the presidency of Barack Obama, when the existence of a black president confirmed for many white Americans the country's victory over its racist past. Ironically, it was the election of Donald Trump that exposed the absurdity of the mythical world of racial harmony. The thinly veiled racism in Trump's campaign and in his policy-making made it clear that many white Americans—including white millennials, who supported Trump at about the same rate as their parents (Mosendz, 2016)—still held racist attitudes.

The Kendall Jenner ad was deemed a failure not because Pepsi's sales faltered or because it didn't attract a large viewership on social media; indeed, even the thousands of black millennials who ridiculed and shared the ad were subjected to multiple images of ice-cold Pepsi. It was deemed a failure because it lacked the authenticity that was lauded in Nike's appropriation of Colin Kaepernick's anti-racist message. Both ads, however, were constructed with the same idea, that young people, including white millennials, embraced black protest and that we are now living in a truly post-racial era. That the Nike ad was viewed as genuine makes it perhaps even more insidious; if white millennials believe that Nike (or corporate America in general) is sincere in its commitment to real social justice and an end to the enormous gaps in racial equity in the United States, the chance for actual progress becomes severely limited. Both ads found audiences in numbers that rivaled those of *The Cosby Show*, and like that iconic show, they reinforced mythic racial harmony during an era in which there is little evidence of true racial progress.

Like the Boomers, millennials in the advent of the 2020s are living through a turbulent political period, and movements from Occupy Wall Street to #MeToo to #NeverAgain might indicate that this is a generation that could successfully advance progressive political causes. Avowed socialist Bernie Sanders found surprisingly strong support from young people when he ran for president in 2016; several of the 2018 media awards TV shows—including the Emmys and the Oscars—spotlighted sexual harassment; high school kids from Parkland, Florida who were victimized by a school shooting led in 2018 a nationwide conversation on gun control. But my fear is embodied in the post-racial message of the Pepsi ad (and just below the surface of Nike's use of Kaepernick)—that white millennials have embraced racial justice. That is simply not the case. While some progressive causes may find receptive millennial audiences, anti-racism movements like Black Lives Matter or the pro-immigration DREAMERS appear stalled and have largely failed to gather the support of progressive white millennials.

Historian James Kirchick (2018), comparing millennials' efforts to advance gun control legislation to the advancement of LGBTQ rights, observed that American support of gay rights was likely because "allowing gay people to marry would have no detrimental effect on their own marriages or the institution of marriage itself." But, he said, it was unlikely that millennials would be able to advance American support for gun control, which "requires Americans to sacrifice something—access to firearms—which many of them consider to be as fundamental a freedom as the right to free speech." Likewise, because most white Americans, including white millennials, believe that discrimination against people of color is not a significant issue (and that whites are more likely to be discriminated against because of their race), it is doubtful that the United States will see significant advances in its long battle to overcome racism. Like the "historical persistence of racism" that has left much of the South still reeling from the effects of slavery, the dominant media myth of post-racialism persists, curtailing more sophisticated, accurate representations that might contradict white supremacist ideology. Meanwhile, the racial attitudes of white members of the current Pepsi Generation do not appear to have changed dramatically from those of their parents and grandparents.

WHITENESS, MEDIA AND HISTORICAL PERSISTENCE

The fact that Pepsi had the good sense to pull its Kendall Jenner commercial almost immediately after the social media backlash might give us some hope that the contemporary advertising industry has at least some sensitivity to racial politics. Plus, there is occasionally other evidence that woke, white millennials are willing to recognize their sense of privilege and resist the racial enmity of earlier generations. The financial and critical success of Jordan Peale's 2017 film *Get Out*, a horror flick in which evil is personified by the film's white suburbanites, points to a willingness of some young whites to identify with the victims of white supremacy. In his assessment of white audiences' acceptance of the film, Richard Benjamin, author of *Searching for Whitopia*, describes its depiction of "white racial innocence," which he says is not just a form of racism: "Rather, it's a belief that no longer advances the self-interest of whites, to the extent that it brutally backfires. Onscreen and in life, the welfare of white people feels decidedly yoked to the well-being of racial minorities" (Benjamin, 2017).

Occasionally, other moments in millennial popular culture indicate a similar wokeness. At the 2017 BET Hip Hop Awards, white rapper Eminem, whose fans included many young whites who supported Donald Trump, excoriated Trump's racist ideology and ripped those fans: "Any fan of mine/ who's a supporter of his/I'm drawing in the sand a line/you're either for or against," he rapped, lifting his middle finger to the camera and to those fans "who can't decide" (Shoe & Coscarelli, 2017). But most progressive, white millennial media stars seem to fail to recognize their privilege. Singer Taylor Swift weighs in on sexual harassment, but she ignores the use of her image by white nationalist organizations (Yahr, 2017). Lena Dunham's hit HBO show *Girls* was widely praised for its offbeat form of third-wave feminism, but the show was bashed for its near complete lack of racial diversity. Comedian Amy Schumer, a feminist, anti-gun activist, mocks Hispanics in her stand-up routines and films and blackness in Beyonce's "Formation" (Campbell, 2017).

The success or failure of late-night programs on the cable network Comedy Central may help explain the racial attitudes of progressive white millennials. Jon Stewart and Stephen Colbert, the white hosts of *The Daily Show* and *The Colbert Report*, were able to amass larger audiences of millennials to their decidedly progressive brand of irreverent humor than the combined audiences of the three major networks' evening newscasts. But when their timeslots were handed over to hosts Trevor Noah, a black South African, and Larry Wilmore, an African American comic who had frequently appeared on *The Daily Show*, the ratings of both programs plummeted, both shows losing close to 40 percent of their audiences (Brennan, 2015). Wilmore's show was canceled after 18 months. Both Noah and Wilmore's shows were more pointed in their critiques of racism. Stewart's producers admitted having a blind spot for racial issues, especially following a 2011 disagreement between Stewart and the show's only black writer, Wyatt Cenac (Itzkoff, 2015). And Colbert, whose right-wing persona frequently pointed out that he "didn't see color," a nod to the absurdity of post-racialism, never seemed at ease with racial humor and at one point was forced to defend a racist tweet; his tongue-in-cheek defense actually harkened the sentiments of Donald Trump: "I just want to say that I'm not a racist. I don't even see race. Not even my own. People tell me I'm white and I believe them because I just devoted six minutes to explaining how I'm not a racist!" (Savage, 2014).

Even an irreverent, progressive sitcom like *The Simpsons*, the long-running animated sitcom that has been viewed by Baby Boom, Gen X and millennial audiences, has demonstrated a blind spot when it comes to race. But it took a millennial comedian, Hari Kondabolu, to call out the program for the egregiously racist portrayal of Apu, the recurring character who owned the local Kwik-E-Mart. Kondabolu produced in 2017 *The Problem with Apu*, a documentary that aired on truTV. The documentary derides *The*

Simpsons, the longest-running sitcom in the history of television, for its stereotypical depiction of the Indian shopkeeper—his ridiculous, over-the-top accent (voiced by a white actor), his goofiness, his servility, his deviousness. Kondabolu told NPR,

> I remember watching "The Simpsons" as a kid. And I still love "The Simpsons." And I would always be taken out of the show a little bit when Apu would come on or there would be another racist stereotype 'cause it'd be like, oh, this wasn't for us. This was meant for someone else. And it matters now because I feel like we need to talk about the history of the past if we're going to move forward. You have to know how we got here, and we have to learn not to repeat mistakes. (quoted in Deggans, 2017)

The persistence of racism in the work of contemporary, white, progressive media producers is not so different from the kind of persistence that Achara, Blackwell and Sen (2016) have described in observing the long-term impact of slavery on the political attitudes of contemporary whites in the South. The overwhelming power of the historical media myths about people of color—painful, stereotypical representations as well as the problematic notion of post-racialism—will likely take decades to overcome.

Perhaps millennials of color who are working in the media will have more luck than previous generations at battling the problematic racial representations that have haunted the media throughout its history. As Kondabolu observed, "Racism doesn't just disappear. It mutates. It shows up in different ways." He says it's the job of the current generation of media makers to challenge the status quo: "We have to figure out what this is before it mutates and squash it" (quoted in Deggans, 2017). But this will be an uphill battle.

In describing their theory of the historical persistence of racist political attitudes, Achara, Blackwell and Sen (2016) point out that "historical institutions like slavery are significant in shaping American culture and politics, even if they no longer exist" (p. 639). The post-racial world that most white millennials believe they inhabit is one that has been historically mythologized by the media. That history is well documented in Marlon Rigg's 1991 documentary *Color Adjustment*, which describes the power of assimilationist programming in television history: In 1956 NBC aired the *The Nat King Cole Show* as if the Jim Crow South did not exist; during the racial turmoil of the 1960s, programs like *Julia* and *I Spy* comforted white audiences with the middle-class images of Diahann Carroll and Bill Cosby; in the 1980s, Cosby returned to star in one of the most popular programs in TV history just as the successes of the Civil Rights era were unraveling. For millennial audiences, popular programs with multicultural casts like those produced by Shonda Rhimes—*Grey's Anatomy, Scandal, How to Get Away with Murder*—all depict a post-racial world. Primetime TV producers throughout the medium's history have failed to provide audiences with accurate and complex portrayals of race; because of those programs' success, it's unlikely that change will come anytime soon. And that means the racial attitudes of white Americans (including progressive white millennials) and the social policies to which they show antipathy or indifference (the Black Lives Matter movement or immigration reform) will allow economic, social and political inequality to persist.

Pepsi Cola's absurd effort to sell soda by making a pathetic attempt to connect it with Black Lives Matter makes it an easy target; nevertheless, the sentiments of the ad are not so far removed from Nike's more "authentic" message, not to mention the efforts of other large corporations that successfully use the message that they are supportive of progressive racial politics to sell products, despite their structural role in a culture that continues to resist real racial progress. Nike's successful use of Colin Kaepernick to generate attention to its Just Do It campaign was generally read as an example of the wokeness of a new generation of Americans, making it even more unlikely that advertisers will back away from their efforts to lure millennial audiences with messages of racial harmony, notions that comfort audiences but prolong the nation's seemingly unending battle to confront the persistence of white supremacy. That is, corporate America's embrace of Kaepernick is not the same as corporate America embracing actual social justice. Given the significant sizes of the audiences that advertisers reach through traditional and social media, these messages contribute to the powerful and humane, but ultimately misleading, myth that the broad racial divisions that continue to haunt the United States don't exist. President John Kennedy (1962) once observed, "The great enemy of truth is very often not the lie—deliberate, contrived and dishonest—but the myth—persistent, persuasive and unrealistic." As long as the myth of post-racialism exists, the persistence that will be required to end racism and bring about true social justice will be diminished and delayed.

REFERENCES

Acharya, A., Blackwell, M., & Sen, M. (2016). The political legacy of American slavery. *The Journals of Politics*, (78) 3, 621–641.

Benjamin, R. (2017, March 27). *Get Out* and the death of white racial innocence. *The New Yorker*. Retrieved at: https://www.newyorker.com/culture/culture-desk/get-out-and-the-death-of-white-racial-innocence.

Bery, S. (2018, Septempber 7). Nike is funding Republican power. *Medium*. Retrieved at: https://medium.com/@SunjeevBery/nike-is-funding-republican-power-94ba7784c7cd.

Bieler, D. (2018, September 17). *Black-ish* actress says "Thank you" to Colin Kaepernick by wearing Nike to Emmys. *The Washington Post*. Retrieved from https://medium.com/@SunjeevBery/nike-is-funding-republican-power-94ba7784c7cd.

Brennan, M. (2015, April 23). With *Nightly Show* ratings down 40% from *The Colbert Report*, Remember in Late Night, Patience is a Virtue. *IndieWire*. Retrieved at: http://www.indiewire.com/2015/04/with-nightly-show-ratings-down-40-from-the-colbert-report-remember-in-late-night-patience-is-a-virtue-187900/.

Bump, P. (2018, March 21). A bright spot for Republicans among millennials: Young white men. *The Washington Post.* Retrieved at: https://www.washingtonpost.com/news/politics/wp/2018/03/21/a-bright-spot-for-republicans-among-millennials-young-white-men/?utm_te rm=.d3ac4cb16b58.

Campbell, C. P. (1995). *Race, Myth and the News.* Thousand Oaks, CA: Sage Publications.

Campbell, C. P. (2016). #IfTheyGunnedMeDown: Postmodern media criticism in a post-racial world. In R. Lind (ed.), *Race and Gender in Electronic Media: Challenges and Opportunities* (pp. 195–212), New York: Routledge.

Campbell, C. P. (2017). "Trust me. I am not a racist.": Whiteness, media and millennials. Paper presented at AEJMC Convention, Chicago.

Deggans, E. (2017, November 19). New documentary calls into question *The Simpsons'* "Apu." NPR Code Switch. Retrieved at: https://www.npr.org/2017/11/17/564936511/in-the-problem-with-apu-hari-kondabolu-discusses-south-asian-representation.

Fiske, J. (1992). British Cultural Studies and television. In R. C. Allen (ed.), *Channels of Discourse, Reassembled*, Chapel Hill, NC: University of North Carolina Press, pp. 287–326.

Gerbner, G., & Gross, L. (1976). Living with television: The violence profile. *Journal of Communication*, *26*, 173–199.

Gray, H. (1991). Television, black Americans, and the American dream. In R. K. Avery & D. Eason (Eds.), *Critical perspectives on media and society* (pp. 294–305). New York: Guilford.

Hall, S. (1980). Encoding/decoding. In S. Hall, D. Hobson, A. Lowe, & P. Wills (eds.), *Culture, Media, Language,* London: Hutchinson, pp. 128–138.

Ingraham, C. (2018, November 28). How white racism destroys black wealth. *The Washington Post.* Retrieved at: https://www.washingtonpost.com/business/2018/11/28/how-white-racism-destroys-black-wealth/?utm_term=.692b33e999d0.

Itzkoff, D. (2015, July 24). *Daily Show* writer recalls heated dispute with Jon Stewart. *The New York Times.* Retrieved at: https://www.nytimes.com/2015/07/25/arts/television/daily-show-writer-recalls-heated-dispute-with-jon-stewart.html?_r=0.

Izadi, E. (2017, April 5). "Clearly, we missed the mark": Pepsi pulls Kendall Jenner ad and apologizes. *The Washington Post.* Retrived at: https://www.washingtonpost.com/news/arts-and-entertainment/wp/2017/04/05/clearly-we-missed-the-mark-pepsi-pulls-kendall-jenner-ad-and-apologizes/?utm_term=.41d6bd2ee469.

Jan, T. (2017, September 28). White families have nearly 10- times the net worth of black families. And the gap is growing. *The Washington Post.* Retrieved at: https://www.washingtonpost.com/news/wonk/wp/2017/09/28/black-and-hispanic-families-are-making-more-money-but-they-still-lag-far-behind-whites/?utm_term=.9a3a57f9cd1a.

Jan, T. (2018, February 26). Report: No progress for African Americans on homeownership, unemployment and incarceration in 50 years. *The Washington Post.* Retrieved at: https://www.washingtonpost.com/news/wonk/wp/2018/02/26/report-no-progress-for-african-americans-on-homeownership-unemployment-and-incarceration-in-50-years/?utm_term=.c32d1 94ce71a.

Jenkins, S. (2018, September 5). Nike knows the future looks something like Colin Kaepernick. *The Washington Post.* Retrieved at: https://www.washingtonpost.com/sports/nike-knows-what-the-future-looks-like-and-its-something-like-colin-kaepernick/2018/09/04/50dbe1be-b 06b-11e8-a20b-5f4f84429666_story.html.

Jhally, S. (Producer). (1997). *Stuart Hall: Representation & the media* (video). Northampton, MA: Media Education Foundation.

Kennedy, J. F. (1962). The best commencement speeches, ever. NPR. Retrieved at: http://apps.npr.org/commencement/speech/john-f-kennedy-yale-university-1962/.

Kerner Commission. (1968). Report of the national advisory commission on civil disorders. New York: E. P. Dutton.

Kirchick, J. (2018, March 27). Gun-control advocates believe their activism will mirror the fight for gay marriage. They're wrong. *The New York Times.* Retrieved at: https://www.washingtonpost.com/news/made-by-history/wp/2018/03/27/gun-control-advocates-believe-their-activism-will-mirror-the-fight-for-gay-marriage-theyre-wrong/?utm_term=.3a2edf8 35fea.

LeDuff, K. (2016). Critical Race Theory: Everything old is new again. In C. Campbell (ed.), *The Routledge Companion to Media and Race* (pp. 65–74), New York: Routledge.

Lewis, N. (2017, August 10). Think millennials are woke? A new poll suggests some of them are sleeping on racism. *The Washington Post*. Retrieved at: https://www.washingtonpost.com/news/post-nation/wp/2017/08/10/think-all-millennials-are-woke-a-new-poll-suggests-some-are-still-sleeping-on-racism/.

Love, D. (2016). In the age of Trump white Millennials shatter ideas that young people are progressive. *Atlanta Black Star*. Retrieved at: http://atlantablackstar.com/2016/10/15/the-age-of-trump-white-supremacist-millennials-shatter-the-idea-that-young-people-are-progressive/.

Mahoney, M. (1995). Racial construction and women as differentiated actors. In R. Delgado and J. Stefancic (Eds.), Critical white studies: Looking behind the Mirror (pp. 305–309). Philadelphia; Temple University Press.

Mosendz, P. (2016, November 9). What this election taught us about millennial voters. Bloomberg News. Retrieved at: https://www.bloomberg.com/news/articles/2016-11-09/what-this-election-taught-us-about-millennial-voters.

Novy-Williams, E. (2018, September 5). Kaepernick campaign generated $43 million in buzz for Nike. Blooomberg. Retrieved at: https://www.bloomberg.com/news/articles/2018-09-04/kaepernick-campaign-created-43-million-in-buzz-for-nike-so-far?srnd=businessweek-v2.

Raggs, T. (2018, September 8). Nike enjoys 31 percent bump in online sales after debut of Colin Kaepernick campaign. *The Washington Post*. Retrieved at: https://www.washingtonpost.com/news/early-lead/wp/2018/09/08/nike-enjoys-31-percent-bump-in-online-sales-after-debut-of-colin-kaepernick-campaign/?utm_term=.919729cc50a0.

Riggs, M. (producer-director). (1991). *Color Adjustment*. California Newsreel.

Savage, L. (2014, April 1). Stephen Colbert address alleged racism on *The Colbert Report*. CBS News. Retrieved at: http://www.cbsnews.com/news/stephen-colbert-addresses-alleged-racism-twitter-controversey/.

Shoe, D., & Coscarelli, J. (2017, October 11). Eminem lashes out at Trump with freestyle rap video. *The New York Times*. Retrieved at: https://www.nytimes.com/2017/10/11/arts/music/eminem-donald-trump-bet.html.

Smith, D. S. (2015, March 26) White Millennials are products of a failed lesson in colorblindness. PBS Newshour. Retrieved at: http://www.pbs.org/newshour/updates/white-millennials-products-failed-lesson-colorblindness/.

Victor, D. (2017, April 5). Pepsi pulls ad accused of trivializing Black Lives Matter. *The New York Times*. Retrieved at: https://www.nytimes.com/2017/04/05/business/kendall-jenner-pepsi-ad.html.

Yahr, E. (2017, December 28). This latest Taylor Swift "controversy" at the end of 2017 really sums up her year. *The Washington Post*. Retrieved at: https://www.washingtonpost.com/news/arts-and-entertainment/wp/2017/12/28/this-latest-taylor-swift-controversy-at-the-end-of-2017-really-sums-up-her-year/?utm_term=.5aabaf9cdeec.

Chapter Two

Tweet *Black-ish* to Make Black Lives Matter

Race and Agenda Setting in the Age of Millennials

Natalie Hopkinson and Sharifa Simon-Roberts

The #BlackLivesMatter movement to end racial violence and inequality was a key lightning rod and flashpoint that activists catapulted to the national agenda during the 2016 presidential election. The presidential race ended with real-estate entrepreneur turned reality-TV star Donald J. Trump defeating former New York Senator and First Lady Hillary Clinton. This essay, which examines discourse on racial violence and inequality during the campaign, adds to an emerging body of research on inter-media agenda setting by analyzing multiple communication streams, including social media as well as entertainment and news media that tackled the topic during the presidential campaign. Our study adds to the growing scholarship on activism led by black youth who are disproportionately using social media and other new communication technologies to prod social change (Taylor, 2016).

The latest iteration of the movement for black equality was sparked on July 13, 2013, the day George Zimmerman was acquitted of the murder of Trayvon Martin. Zimmerman assaulted and shot to death Martin, an unarmed black suburban teenager, as the child walked home from a store. On the same day, activists Patrisse Khan-Cullors, Alicia Garza and Opal Tometi founded #BlackLivesMatter. #BlackLivesMatter was among the first of the truly millennial-led political movements, which remixed Civil Rights movement media strategies in an attempt to put racial violence and inequality on the public agenda. Nearly four years later, on February 24, 2016, ABC, one of the four major commercial television networks in the country, aired "Hope," an episode of their situational comedy *Black-ish* that amplified the issue of police brutality and paid tribute to multiple real-life victims who had become hash-tags and rallying cries of the movement. The popular TV comedy depicted an upwardly mobile black family from California joining the protest over police killings in the midst of real-life public debate over the tactics of the Black Lives Matter movement. News coverage of the conception of #BlackLives-Matter and ABC's broadcast of the "Hope" episode of *Black-ish* serve as the basis for this analysis.

FROM TRADITIONAL TO
INTER-MEDIA AGENDA SETTING

The roots of agenda-setting theory are in an era also fraught with widespread political division. In an attempt to understand who determined the key issues that drove the 1968 presidential campaign, McCombs and Shaw (1972) iden-tified the topics prioritized by the news media and compared them to the topics prioritized by the general public. The analysis that resulted from their influential study demonstrated a high correlation between the news media agenda and voters' agenda. McCombs and Shaw (1972) concluded that the news media agenda likely shaped the public agenda. This basic theoretical framework has become more nuanced over time. McCombs (2014) described three levels of agenda setting. Level one, also known as traditional agenda setting, refers to the transfer of object salience from the news agenda to the public agenda. In level two, also known as attribute agenda setting, there is a transfer of attribute salience from the news agenda to the public agenda. Finally, in level three, also known as network agenda setting, there is the transfer of "salience of relationships among a set of elements" from the news agenda to the public agenda (McCombs, 2014, p. 62).

Although agenda-setting theory has been applied to numerous studies, there has been significantly less research on inter-media agenda setting, as McCombs (2005) noted. This study represents a void as the media ecology has grown increasingly complex, and the lines between traditional news, fiction, and entertainment is ever more blurred. Today's vast media land-scape necessitates more intricate theoretical models. Holbert et al. (2003) noted that research on political communication using priming, framing and agenda setting have concentrated on news, "completely disregarding the po-tential role of diverse types of entertainment programming" (p. 429). The authors rejected the need to focus on a single media source or put up "artifi-cial barriers" between entertainment and news media. Holbrook and Hill (2005) and Soroka (2000) similarly noted that most of the research on agenda setting and priming concentrates on media that informs—news programs—rather than on media that entertains. As entertainment-oriented shows ac-count for more primetime programming than news-oriented shows on the major commercial broadcast television networks, the lack of studies on entertainment media and agenda setting in politics highlights a gap in the literature, which this study attempts to help fill.

Emerging theoretical models around inter-media agenda setting significantly advance our understanding of a combination of factors that drive public opinion beyond the original agenda-setting models. Vliegenthart and Walgrave (2008) noted that personal, individual perceptions drive traditional notions of agenda setting, whereas inter-media agenda setting looks at how organizations interact. While agenda setting focuses on "what the public thinks," in inter-media agenda setting, a primary concern is "what a medium does" (Vliegenthart & Walgrave, 2008, p. 861). Public agenda setting often occurs without the parties recognizing what is happening, whereas inter-media agenda setting is a conscious process (Vliegenthart & Walgrave, 2008).

News media often remain the focus of inter-media agenda-setting studies (Golan, 2006; Reese & Danielian, 1989; Vliegenthart & Walgrave, 2008). And the research generally centers on politics and presidential campaigns. For example, Sweetser, Golan and Wanta (2008) explored the 2004 U.S. presidential election and how advertisements and candidate blogs shaped coverage. Boyle (2001) looked at the 1996 presidential campaign and the relationships among political ads, newspapers and television network newscasts.

More recently, the rise of new communication platforms has led scholars to examine the transfer of salience from traditional media to new media and vice versa. Such research includes Ku, Kaid and Pfau (2003), who ranked the influence of candidate websites, television news and newspapers in the 2000 U.S. presidential election, and Lee, Lancendorfer and Lee (2005), who studied the inter-media impact of Web bulletin boards on news media coverage of the 2000 general election in South Korea. Messner and Garrison (2011), Wallsten (2007) and Yu and Aikat (2008) similarly tracked the salience of traditional media to new media.

Scholars have used inter-media agenda setting to determine how various media shape each other and the content produced (Reese & Danielian, 1989; McCombs, 2014; Sweetser et al., 2008). Inter-media agenda-setting effects are evident both within a particular medium—for example, the elite national newspapers tend to set the agenda for local newspapers—and they also set the agenda for television networks (Sweetser et al., 2008).

Much of the research on agenda setting is concerned with the media's influence on public opinion. However, agenda-setting methodologies can also be useful in examining the relationship among various media. For example, Soroka (2000) analyzed how the fictional film *Schindler's List* shaped the agenda of newspapers. Markovits and Hayden (1980), in assessing the impact of NBC's 1978 *Holocaust* program on audiences in West Germany and Austria, found that "long after the telecast, [*Holocaust*] remained a major subject for discussion in the West German press" (p. 74). Another study that showcases the influence of soft-news entertainment programs is Abad's (2016) study of the satirical political news program *Last Week Tonight with John Oliver*. The 25 episodes of the comedy show had "at least a moderate effect" on both Web-only and traditional news outlets (Abad, 2016, p. vi). These findings reinforce the reach of entertainment programs on not only viewers, but also other types of media.

TWITTER, SOCIAL TV AND BLACK MILLENNIALS

By the 2016 U.S. presidential campaign, social media was an increasingly pervasive force in the lives of everyday Americans as smartphones became a human appendage for many. Twitter emerged as a key place for conducting communication research for individuals, scholars and private industry. In highlighting the value of Twitter for the television industry, Redniss (2015) wrote, Twitter offers "some of the most enriched data sets available, especially on a minute-by-minute basis" (para. 4). Harrington, Highfield, and Bruns (2013) suggested that the social media platform helps to create a more active audience. According to Harrington et al. (2013),

> Twitter has become an important backchannel through which such social activity is sustained and made more widely visible. . . . Used this way, Twitter and services alike, become a kind of virtual loungeroom, connecting the active audiences of specific TV shows at an unprecedented scale and thereby amplifying audience activities even further. (p. 405)

The communities and conversation tools within Twitter, such as hashtags, are examples of how Twitter functioned as a real-time backchannel for the opinions and interior lives of users. Viewers could follow a hashtag related to the show on Twitter to gauge the reaction of others and keep abreast of the conversations taking place (Auverset & Billings, 2016; Wohn & Na, 2011).

Nielsen's (2016) *Young, Connected and Black* study reported that African Americans' use of Twitter outpaced that of the total population. As recently as 2018, the use of Twitter by black adults remained higher than any other demographic group. Similarly, people who belong to the 18–29 age group use Twitter at higher rates than people in other age brackets (Smith & Anderson, 2018). The Associated Press-NORC Center for Public Affairs Research (2017) also found that "Black teens are the most active of any group on social media and messaging applications" (p. 1). The heavy usage of Twitter by African Americans gave rise to the phenomenon of "Black Twitter." According to Brock (2012), "Black Twitter can be understood as a user-generated source of culturally relevant online content, combining social network elements and broadcast principles to share information" (p. 530). Black Twitter offered black users of Twitter the chance to network, connect and engage with "others who have similar concerns, experiences, tastes, and cultural practices" (Florini, 2014, p. 225).

It followed that issues surrounding the Black Lives Matter movement gained widespread popularity through social media, especially Twitter. Twitter served as a major platform for the Black Lives Matter movement, which was reactivated on Twitter immediately after the police killing of Ferguson teenager Michael Brown in August 2014, and again in early December 2014 when prosecutors declined to indict the Ferguson, Missouri, police officer who killed Brown and the New York police officer who killed Eric Garner. Carney (2016) noted that young people of color "employed [Twitter] to shape the national discourse about race in the wake of these high-profile tragedies" (p. 180).

ANALYZING INTER-MEDIA AGENDA SETTING

Our study was designed to examine parallel media discourses about Black Lives Matter in traditional news, a scripted entertainment show, and on Twitter. We did not aim to measure or rank effects as much as to trace thematic strains in discourses across various popular media operating simultaneously. Although agenda setting—and by extension, inter-media agenda setting—is often linked to quantitative, statistical inquiries, there is much to gain by applying a more qualitative approach to a traditionally quantitative research area (Cushion, Kilby, Thomas, Morani, & Sambrook, 2016). Similar to Lee's (2017) study, our study relied on mixed methods, as such an approach allows researchers "to examine intermedia agenda-setting influence and hence describe both similarities and differences in which the same topic is presented among the three media types to enhance the understanding of how issue salience differs among media coverage and media agendas" (p. 46).

Likewise, in this study, we sought to determine the common and divergent conceptual strains among various media on topics tied to Black Lives Matter that suggest a pattern of inter-media influence. This design aimed to take advantage of the phenomenon of "social TV," which refers to "the convergence of television and social media" (Proulx & Shepatin, 2012, p. ix). Television viewers take to Twitter "to comment on and discuss television programs in real time" (Auverset & Billings, 2016, p. 2). Several television shows, including *Black-ish*, had members of the cast and the writing staff live-tweet episodes as part of the live TV-watching experience, which was the case for this episode.

We deployed a four-step process for data collection and analysis. All media data was collected from February 21, 2016, to February 27, 2016, a week that was significant for a number of reasons. Both the GOP and Democratic U.S. presidential primaries took place in South Carolina, a state heavily dominated by black voters. The Democrats voted on February 27, 2016, and the Republican primary vote took place on February 20, 2016, in South Carolina, a key early primary. This was the final week of Black History Month, culminating a month of programming in education and media sectors. This time frame also includes the three days before, the day of, and three days after the broadcast of *Black-ish*'s episode of "Hope," whose subject matter was directly influenced by the agenda advanced by Black Lives Matter.

In step one of this process, we engaged a contractor who used Twitter's application programming interface (API) to download relevant tweets. The contractor created a spreadsheet containing tweets posted between February 21, 2016, and February 27, 2016, and included the following hashtags: #BlackLivesMatter (3,841 tweets), #Blackish (736 tweets), and #BlackishABC (29 tweets)—a total of 4,606 tweets.

Step two allowed us to examine the themes that emerged in traditional broadcast news media's reporting on Black Lives Matter. We performed a search on LexisNexis Academic for news stories that contained the term "Black Lives Matter" and aired or were published between February 21, 2016, and February 27, 2016. The news coverage data from LexisNexis Academic included all available broadcast transcripts for programs on the U.S. broadcast news outlets, as well as transcripts from major world print publications. This drew 95 scripts from broadcasts that included: ABC, BBC, CBS, CNN, CNN International, Fox Business, Fox Network News, Fox News, MSNBC, NBC and NPR. We then performed a thematic analysis of these scripts.

In step three, we conducted a content analysis of the *Black-ish* episode titled "Hope," which aired on ABC on February 24, 2016, at 9:30 p.m. EST. In addition to a close reading of the episode, we analyzed the script and reviewed published interviews with creator and showrunner Kenya Barris. To examine Twitter users' reactions to "Hope," we examined tweets created three hours before the premiere of "Hope" that used the hashtag #Blackish or #BlackishABC until February 27, 2016, at 11:59 p.m. EST. The three-day window allowed us to capture the sentiments of viewers who watched the episode live across east and west coasts feeds, as well as through time-shifted viewing. This produced 765 tweets that contained the hashtag #Blackish or #BlackishABC. Once again, the tweets were analyzed both quantitatively and qualitatively, using content analysis.

In the final step, we coded the first 600 of the #BlackLivesMatter tweets and all 765 of the tweets with #Blackish and #BlackishABC hashtags to determine the themes present. Although we coded 600 of the #BlackLivesMatter tweets, we systematically reviewed all 3,841 tweets. In coding the

600 tweets, we took Wohn and Na's (2011) lead in their study of tweets of a reality television program and a political broadcast. Wohn and Na (2011) categorized the content of tweets in the following categories—attention-seeking, information, emotion and opinion. In coding the data from Twitter for the current study, we coded the tweets using the following categories: define and defend the movement; presidential politics; black historic struggle; and conservative critique of the movement. We used these themes to code the rest of the data.

This study was guided by the following questions. What themes emerged in coverage of #BlackLivesMatter on Twitter during the study period? What themes emerged in coverage of Black Lives Matter in broadcast television news media during the study period? What themes emerged in "Hope," the episode of the ABC television show *Black-ish* and viewer reactions on Twitter during the study period? What themes, similarities, and differences can be found across news media broadcasts, Twitter, and ABC's *Black-ish* surrounding the issues related to police brutality during the study period?

TWEETING #BLACKLIVESMATTER

One of the primary goals of the Black Lives Matter movement was to increase awareness about the killing of unarmed black men by police and vigilantes who repeatedly evaded punishment. The language implied that the lack of consequences for killing black men and women suggested that the lives of black victims were unworthy of justice against perpetrators or did not matter. By 2016, the British Broadcasting Corporation (2016) estimated that the phrase "BlackLivesMatter" had been tweeted 8 million times. Black Lives Matter activists developed reputations for giving real-time updates at sites in which black men and women had been killed at the hands of law enforcement officers (Kang, 2015). One tweet in our sample recognized the role of Black Lives Matter in teaching people how to use social media tools to actively protect people and create a public record of police activities. On February 21, 2016, one user tweeted: "A thing that #blacklivesmatter taught me is that if you see the police stopping someone, you wait and stand witness to make sure they're ok."

In the week of tweets we sampled, the Black Lives Matter movement used first-level agenda setting to frame the public agenda by recording planned activists' ambushes of Democratic candidates as they campaigned for president, which were later broadcast on traditional media. By demanding that candidates acknowledge the phrase "Black Lives Matter" and attacking the candidates' past policy positions on race, the activists attempted to force the issue of police brutality and racial oppression to remain on the policy agenda of the assumed victor. The following section is a thematic review of how these issues were framed in the tweets that appeared publicly from February 21–27, 2016. We coded 600 tweets with the #BlackLivesMatter hashtag and broke them down across the following categories:

1. Define and defend Black Lives Matter movement (30 percent)
2. Presidential politics (18 percent)
3. Black people's long history of struggle (15 percent)
4. Conservative critique of Black Lives Matter (13 percent)

Approximately 24 percent of the tweets were deemed to be unrelated to the conversation of Black Lives Matter and police brutality. Users who posted these tweets added the hashtag #BlackLivesMatter in an attempt to gain attention to their own content. This in itself speaks to the power of the hashtag to attract attention.

Nearly a third of the tweets with the #BlackLivesMatter hashtag sought to define and defend the movement. One user wrote: "It's A Shame That We Still Have To Say #BlackLivesMatter In 2016 But Reality Is Reality #BLACKLIVESMATTER." Other tweets within this category were defensive, responding to a conservative critique of the movement. For instance, a user posted on February 21, 2016: "#blacklivesmatter is not #antiwhite its pro-black. you failing to realize that shows your ignorance of the situation."

The next highest number of tweets—18 percent—were related to the presidential primary contest. Senator Bernie Sanders, a liberal, self-described socialist candidate, was a key subject within these tweets. His campaign released images of Sanders as a 21-year-old activist chaining himself to someone denied housing because of their race. Twitter users shared the news when he received an endorsement from African American actor Danny Glover and generally praised Sanders as a candidate. Meanwhile, tweets that mentioned Hillary Clinton were largely negative. Many of the tweets accused her of getting funding from the prison industry; promoting policies (along with her husband, the former President Bill Clinton) that have led to mass incarceration; and in the course of her 2008 presidential bid, using subtle racism against President Obama. The GOP candidates were rarely mentioned in the tweets. Of the 3,841 tweets in the #BlackLivesMatter database, John Kasich was not mentioned, Ben Carson was mentioned once, Marco Rubio twice, Ted Cruz three times and Trump 78 times. This is a notable finding because it highlights Trump's complete domination of the discourse among the GOP candidates, even before he had secured the GOP nomination. In stark contrast, of the 3,841 tweets, there were 300 references to Clinton and 273 to Sanders.

The next largest batch of #BlackLivesMatter tweets (15 percent) spoke to the "long struggle." There were clear references to a history of police brutality in black communities and parallels to the Civil Rights movement. The fact that February was Black History Month also likely contributed to the frequency of this theme. Some examples of the "long struggle" tweets include: "We need more Malcolms and less Martins . . . the rules have clearly switched up and we missed the memo! #BlackLivesMatter." Another user tweeted a link to a *New York Times* op-ed that looked at links between two teenaged black victims of racial violence, who lived nearly a century apart: "Emmett Till and Tamir Rice, Sons of the Great Migration #BlackLivesMatter #INDIGENOUS."

The last major theme in the tweets (13 percent) came from users criticizing Black Lives Matter from a conservative point of view. The most direct answer and critique was the hashtag "#alllivesmatter," which explicitly rejects the notion that black lives are uniquely imperiled and that black people deserve special consideration (Yancy & Butler, 2015). Several of the conservative-critique tweets described both the Black Lives Matter activists and victims as "thugs." Many tweets chided activists and urged them to direct attention away from the police and back to black communities where violence takes place. As one user tweeted: "Yes, black lives do matter. It would behove [sic] the #BlackLivesMatter thugs to acknowledge black on black crime."

Similarly, another user, referring to a white suspect in multiple murders in Michigan, tweeted: "I wish black folks were as butthurt over the daily killing in Chicago black neighborhoods, as they are about #JasonDalton. #blacklivesmatter." Yet another person tweeted, "Blacks commit a disproportionate amount of crime, yet #BlackLivesMatter wonders why police disproportionately targets blacks. #CauseEffect." Although a small fraction of the total discourse, this way of framing the issue of police brutality is significant, as it is echoed in legacy media platforms—something that will be discussed in the next section.

BLACK LIVES MATTER AND THE NEWS

As a legacy medium, national network television news provides a general pulse of the imagery and narratives that drove discussions about the Black Lives Matter movement across the United States among the general population. Our review found that broadcast news coverage of Black Lives Matter was dominated by two themes, both highlighting the actions and aggression of black millennials: 1) how the movement played into presidential politics and 2) conservative backlash to Black Lives Matter.

The crucial South Carolina Democratic primary election took place on February 27, 2016, and most broadcast news coverage of Black Lives Matter was framed as part of this larger narrative of the race to the White House. (Trump won the GOP primary in South Carolina on February 20, 2016.)

Several networks carried footage of three young Black Lives Matter activists heckling Clinton in Charleston, South Carolina, that week. A panel on *CNN Newsroom* discussed the fallout when the young activists confronted Clinton on February 25, 2016, while a camera phone video recorded. The activists demanded an apology from Clinton for her husband's 1990s crime policies that fueled mass incarceration. The topic and the phrase "Black Lives Matter" continued to be raised during a Democratic candidate town hall, which CNN televised on February 23, 2016. During that event, Clinton invited mothers of the movement against police brutality (many of their sons had been murdered by police) to stand and be recognized. These black women were later featured in one of Clinton's campaign videos narrated by famed black actor Morgan Freeman, which was released online.

On a *CNN Newsroom* segment on February 25, 2016, political correspondent Jim Newell recounted the controversial tactics of the Black Lives Matter movement, praised organizers' ability to set the agenda, and declared them well received among black South Carolina primary voters. Newell, a *Slate* political correspondent, discussed the topic during a conversation with anchor Carol Costello:

> They have heckled both Hillary Clinton and Bernie Sanders. I think they have done a good job. And if you remember around this time last year when they started interrupting speeches there was a lot of talk about how maybe this was, you know, an inappropriate way to bring up their issues. But if you see now, if you listen to both Hillary Clinton and Bernie Sanders' speeches, they're talking a lot about the issues that Black Lives Matter has brought to the fore. (Costello et al., 2016)

The other major narrative on the television news broadcasts was the conservative critique of Black Lives Matter. Fox Business News and Fox News Network carried several segments that aired February 23–25, 2016, and included video surveillance footage of an incident in which a former U.S. marine and Iraq war veteran was allegedly beaten and robbed outside a drugstore in Washington, D.C. The alleged victim appeared on television and claimed the young black attackers demanded that he support Black Lives Matter and beat him when he refused. It was later revealed in different local news outlets that the veteran had been drinking alcohol, and the teens accused him of initiating the confrontation by using a racial epithet against them. Fact-checkers later rejected the marine's claim that Black Lives Matter was in any way involved (Snopes, 2016). However, the story and footage of the marine getting beaten was carried on Fox News Business channel in multiple segments during the week with no mention of the teens' version of events.

On a February 26, 2016, broadcast, Kevin Jackson, a conservative black male commentator on Fox Business News argued the roots of the attack on the marine was "Barack Obama's Justice Department," which had encouraged young people to become "free-range hoodlums." This echoed a February 23, 2016, analysis by black female conservative commentator Crystal Wright: "This goes back to President Obama, Hillary Clinton, and Democrats stoking anti-cops rhetoric and saying black lives are the only lives that matter even when the blacks are criminals, and they're wrong" (Bolton, 2016). She blamed the Democrat's leading cities such as New York and Baltimore for not holding "young black men accountable for their criminal behavior." She pointed to another incident in Columbus, Ohio, in which young black men brandished weapons and threatened violence on a social media live stream before being arrested. She also presented grossly inaccurate data on police killings and young black men:

> It's harrowing to think young black men now feel emboldened. I mean, again, this goes back to what I've talked about the last two segments, right? There is this apologetic narrative going on that young black men are never, you know, they're not criminal and the media is playing that out. Oh, no, you know, young black men are the ones being hunted down by police. And again, I go back to federal data which shows that police officers are killed 40 percent of the time by black men—young, you know, black men. And cops are killed at a rate of 2.5 times higher by young black men than blacks are killed by police officers.
>
> So, this is, you know—thanks to what has been happening over the last three years with Trayvon Martin and Michael Brown and the president helping it, you know, this is what we have, young black men thinking that they can brandish weapons and social media, and then go out and kill innocent Americans. This needs to stop. (Bolton, 2016)

Wright, the Fox commentator, got her facts wrong. In 2016, 64 police officers were killed in firearm-related incidents (Domonoske, 2016). In contrast, 1,093 Americans were killed by police in 2016, and black men were nine times as likely to be killed as any other demographic group (Swaine & McCarthy, 2017).

Two other stories that also emphasized the conservative critique of Black Lives Matter involved Facebook headquarters and the black pop music star Beyoncé. On February 26, 2016, on the program *Risk and Reward*, Fox Business News commentators criticized Facebook founder Mark Zuckerberg's memo to employees imploring them not to deface "Black Lives Matter" messages on company blackboards by replacing them with "All Lives Matter." Further, multiple cable networks carried broadcasts that continued criticism of Beyoncé's February 6, 2016, performance at the Super Bowl in which she and her dancers wore all-black paramilitary gear. This performance led police to call for a boycott of Beyoncé's performances, alleging that her costumes were racist and "anti-police." On a February 22, 2016, broadcast of *CNN Tonight with Don Lemon*, a white male "law enforcement analyst" alleged that her dancers' costumes resembled the style of an organization he claimed assassinated police officers.

Whether it was the presidential politics narrative, or the conservative critique of Black Lives Matter, both narratives on broadcast news emphasized young black bodies as aggressors and initiators of discord and havoc on the political system and on the streets of urban cities. None of the news broadcasts drew attention to what, if any, progress was made in addressing why so many young black men and women were killed by police and ways to hold law enforcement accountable for this loss of human life.

"HOPE": COMPLICATING THE NARRATIVE ON FICTIONAL TV

The forces that set the agenda for the creators of the "Hope" episode on the ABC hit comedy *Black-ish* were revealed in several interviews published the week it aired in February 2016. Creator and showrunner Kenya Barris, who often based the show's story lines on his real family life, described watching live TV news and seeing protests in Ferguson dominated by Black Lives Matter activists with his family (Fienberg, 2016). "Why these people so mad?" his five-year-old son asked him (as cited in Butler, 2016). In interviews with the trade press, Barris explicitly rejected any alliance or affiliation with the Black Lives Matter movement. Instead, he claimed the show was a reaction to the explosion of social and other media, which forced parents to have difficult conversations with young people about what was going on in the world:

> I didn't want to politicize the show. I believe [Black Lives Matter is] a politicized movement and my personal believe [sic] on that has nothing to do with what the show is and I don't think that that particular movement is what this family's conversation was about. Police brutality happened to be the thing that the family was talking about. . . . I think it's a really important conversation to have. But at the heart of what the episode's about, it's about talking to kids about things that 20 years ago you may have not had to talk to them about, because you could just turn the television off, but now with all the images and all the access to information and news that is happening on a day-to-day basis, you can't turn those images off. (Fienberg, 2016, para. 21)

Nevertheless, it is clear from Barris' comments in numerous interviews that Black Lives Matter media intervention set the agenda for the topics to be addressed on the program (Butler, 2016; Fienberg, 2016; Fretts, 2016). The resulting episode, "Hope," earned a rating of 3.9/7 for Live + Same Day Household Ratings (Cynopsis Media, 2016). In comparison to other shows on major commercial networks at the same time, "Hope" was the third most popular program, coming in behind CBS's *Criminal Minds* and NBC's *Law & Order: SVU* (Cynopsis Media, 2016). The episode is set primarily in the living room of the Johnson family home. It captures a conversation about police brutality among an upwardly mobile black family that comprises three generations—grandparents, parents, and grandchildren. The conversation takes place as the family sits around the television watching news coverage of a grand jury's decision not to indict a police officer who killed an unarmed black youth and the protests that followed. The episode ends with family members deciding to participate in a protest of a fictional police brutality case in California.

Several themes in "Hope" echoed the review of Black Lives Matter discourse on Twitter and national news coverage. Some characters, notably the oldest son Junior, *defined and defended* the movement against police brutality. Other characters, notably a monologue from the husband/father Andre, "Dre," addressed *presidential politics*, and the election of Barack Obama in particular. The grandparents addressed the historic *"long struggle"* against American injustice drawing on their personal life histories. Another character, the wife/mother Bow, voiced the *conservative critique* against protestors, noting that one victim was "no angel" and that police should be expected to protect themselves against aggression. Like the findings from the tweets, the word "thug" also appears in "Hope." However, unlike Twitter, where some users suggested that thugs were synonymous to young black men, to Pops, the police were the thugs.

The title "Hope" captures the challenge of preserving a sense of possibility for young black children who learn that police face no consequences for killing black people. Real-life incidents associated with the Black Lives Matter movement emphasize this theme. At times, the references were direct—for example, when Dre (the father) and Pops (the grandfather) specifically name young unarmed black people who were killed in police custody such as Freddie Gray and Sandra Bland. At other times, the references were subtler. For instance, the characters talk about the particulars surrounding cases of police brutality, without mentioning the names of the black men whose lives were taken. In these cases, the contextual clues make clear these references are to black men killed by police: Walter Scott, Laquan McDonald, Eric Garner and Samuel DuBose. The sheer number of names of victims of racial violence referenced during the episode underscores the vast and overwhelming scope of the issue and keeping track of the circumstances surrounding each case proves difficult for the Johnson family.

In spite of the long struggle African Americans have endured, the characters try to preserve a sense of hope and possibility for the future. The producers, writers and actors convey this message in various ways. Just before the halfway mark of the episode, there is a montage of archival footage that includes: John F. Kennedy Jr. saluting his father's casket; Senator Robert F.

Kennedy with supporters shortly before his assassination; newspaper footage reporting on the killing of Malcolm X and Mahatma Gandhi; and a headline from the *Chicago Courier* that reads, "No Criminal Charges In Tamir Rice Police Shooting." The montage ends with a portrait of the 12-year-old victim Rice, who was killed by Ohio police while playing with a toy gun, which calls attention to his age and innocence. A lengthy speech by the family patriarch Dre about the election of President Barack Obama, a symbol of hope for the black community, is spliced with video footage from President Obama's 2009 inauguration.

The episode's soundtrack also evokes notions of resistance, a long struggle tied to the electoral process. The soundtrack includes Marvin Gaye's *Inner City Blues,* Bob Marley's *Redemption Song,* and ends with John Legend's *If You're Out There,* which the singer and activist debuted at the 2008 Democratic National Convention. The lyrics, along with the supporting images of children and peaceful protests, communicate that there are reasons to remain hopeful, and justice will prevail.

In sum, the show illustrated the human dimensions of the impact of racial violence and inequality on even relatively privileged and upwardly mobile families such as the Johnsons. It highlighted the psychological terror and emotional toll each instance of unpunished police killings takes on a black family. Its stirring soundtrack and snappy dialogue created a nuanced exploration of the topic, mostly absent in news media coverage. Importantly, the Johnson family ends the episode by deciding, as a family, to join the protest. Despite the showrunners' Barris' claim to the contrary, the Johnsons, a wealthy, upwardly mobile, cisgender, "respectable" nuclear family was an effective medium for the message. Considering that the patriarch Dre works as an advertising executive, the entire episode could be read as product placement for the Black Lives Matter movement.

The episode marked an important moment in Black Twitter and social TV. According to our review of related social media, an overwhelming number of Twitter users expressed gratitude, described feeling emotionally overwhelmed, noted connections to the historical struggle, echoed their own fears about whether President Barack Obama—both a symbol of hope and target of hate—would remain safe. One tweet, which referenced both Beyoncé's Superbowl performance and the year when slaves were emancipated from slavery in the United States, was representative: "So BHM [Black History Month] almost over & after Beyoncé & Kendrick Lamar performance & now #blackish I dont [sic] think white people been this mad since 1863." Others defended those who attacked the program. Those criticisms of *Black-ish* did not use the #blackish or #blackishABC hashtags so the tweets did not appear in the researchers' dataset: "People really upset because #blackish spoke the truth??" another user tweeted. "Just caught the newest episode of #blackish and @ABCNetwork did a great job portraying the point of view of black families across the US" another tweeted.

CHARTING AGENDA SETTING AND
BLACK LIVES MATTER

The chart in Figure 2.1 traces the flow of agendas set among the communication channels described in the datasets in this study:

The chain of action begins at the top with Black Lives Matter. As previously mentioned, Black Lives Matter is a political movement and also a news media source in its own right. Members of the organization used cell phones to record and live-broadcast interactions with police at protests and in everyday life, bypassing traditional news media in many cases. Black Lives Matter also effectively served as a news aggregation network that amplified local news media reports of police killings to a national audience. Black Lives Matter thus deployed first-level agenda setting to influence what was covered in traditional national news broadcast media. They were effective in this regard in that the topic and even the phrase "Black Lives Matter" continued to stay at the top of television newscasts during the sample period.

One important branch follows the arc of Black Lives Matter's influence among the discussion among the general public on Twitter. Black Lives Matter uses both first- and second-level agenda setting to influence the public discourse on police brutality, both in social media and on traditional news media such as broadcast television and cable networks. On this first level, Black Lives Matter wants people to think about the value of black lives each time such a life is lost.

The rest of the chain of communication proceeded as follows: traditional news media deployed first-level agenda setting to influence entertainment programming. That is, those television news reports of Black Lives Matter protests reached the family of *Black-ish* creator Kenya Barris. This action places the topic of racial violence and inequality on the agenda of his comedy show. In the "Hope" episode, *Black-ish* then exemplifies second-level agenda setting by creating an alternative narrative for framing the topic of racial violence on television networks. Those narratives emphasize many of the same overarching themes as on social media. However, they also emphasize the human tolls of the mounting number of tragedies and point to a source of hope for a more peaceful way forward, which ends with the family joining a public protest. The final link in the chain of second-level agenda setting is how ABC viewers continue the discussion on Twitter. Thus, there is yet another layer of discourse on racial violence and inequality, distilled through the filter of Black Lives Matter, *Black-ish* and traditional news media.

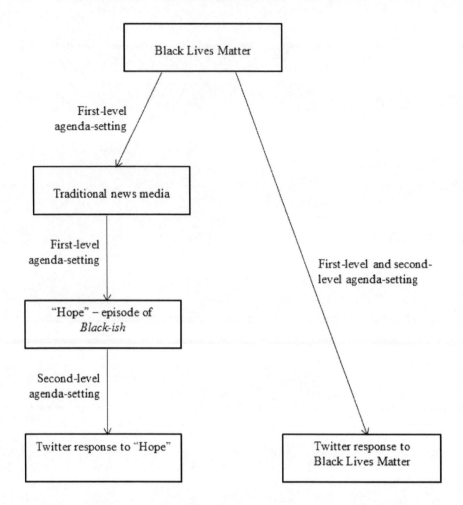

Figure 2.1. Flow of agendas in the communication channels of this study. Created by author.

Traditional news coverage of racial violence and inequality, driven by the Black Lives Matter movement, lacked the same scope of humanity and nuance as the entertainment program and on social media. Notably, the issues that Black Lives Matter brought to the fore—specific incidents of police killings raised by the movement, the loss of black life, the need for accountability for loss of life, and policies that would stop the loss of black life—are not raised directly in the traditional news media analyzed. Traditional news sources framed the topic of Black Lives Matter in terms of how it motivated and influenced voters in the political horse race to secure the Democratic nomination. Traditional media positioned Black Lives Matter as delivering a potential voting bloc in the South Carolina primary. Simultaneously, the broadcast news debated the methods adopted by supporters of Black Lives Matter and acknowledged the movement's ability to force candidates and the media to pay attention.

Perhaps most crucial to understanding public discourse among the electorate is a theme that emerged on all three media: the conservative critique. Although only 13 percent of the tweets in the sample of #BlackLivesMatter tweets during the study's time period reflected a conservative critique of the movement, it more closely reflects attitudes of a large number of voters who are not active on Twitter, who are older and less ethnically diverse than the average Twitter user. The infrequency of tweets about the candidates vying for the GOP's nomination may be partly due to the fact that Black Lives Matter activists never targeted or addressed GOP candidates and only targeted Democratic candidates for president.

As Boxell, Gentzkow and Shapiro (2018) have shown, cable television was much more influential in shaping the opinions and object salience for white voters than social media. For viewers of cable television networks, the image of young black people confronting a white blonde woman in her late 60s (Clinton) may have fed into the conservative critique framed on Twitter that the activists were "thugs." A questionable incident involving the robbing of a veteran also fed the "black thug" narrative. Ironically, despite some Twitter users ascribing the label of "thug" to black people, Pops' comments during the "Hope" episode suggest that members of the black community hold an opposing view—the police are the real thugs. "Police brutality" or "police killings" were rarely mentioned in news coverage.

AGENDA SETTING IN THE
AGE OF BLACK LIVES MATTER

#BlackLivesMatter was a political and media movement that was a highly effective tool to put the topic of racial violence and inequality on the public agenda. By trending on Twitter and Facebook and giving real-time accounts on the ground in the aftermath of incidents of police brutality and during protests, the hashtag influenced the agenda of television news, social media and entertainment programs. On this first level of agenda setting, the rhetorical framing of "Black Lives Matter" was effective in forcing the public to discuss the value of black lives each time a precious life is taken.

However, stories and images drive discourse and perceptions of reality more than facts. Once on the public agenda, the topic of racial violence ran into the headwinds of historical depictions of black men, in particular, as threats who must be neutralized by police. Thus, the confrontational tactics of the Black Lives Matter movement sent a message to some viewers that black people need to be brought to heel, which was echoed in the conservative critique of the movement on some cable networks and on Twitter. While Black Lives Matter activists argued they needed protection from the police, conservative critics argued that the general population needed police protection from black "thugs."

ABC's fictitious television program was effective in deepening the discourse and unfurling its many dimensions. It humanized the victims of racial violence and those who feared more racial violence more effectively than its nonfiction television and social media counterparts. Thus, first-level agenda setting was in effect—social media and traditional media told entertainment media what to think about. But second-level agenda setting—how to think about the issue—differed between the broadcast news agenda and agenda of scripted program. The entertainment agenda, exemplified by *Black-ish*, emphasized the human connections, fears and hopes from the perspective of the black community using universal values common to all families, regardless of race.

Our study, thus, concludes that in the case of racial violence, scripted content was more effective than either social media or news media "facts" in framing the salience of issues critical to public discourse—the need for protection and justice for black people. However, for many members of the general public, the same images of Black Lives Matter protesters also emphasized the need for protection. Conservative critics came to vastly different conclusions about who needed protection and from whom. This may have contributed to the stalled momentum of the Black Lives Matter movement and the election to the presidency of Trump, a candidate who, like Nixon before him in 1968, promised to restore "law and order" in a country reeling from unrest.

REFERENCES

Abad, A. (2016). *Exploring intermedia agenda setting effects of Last Week Tonight with John Oliver* (Master's thesis). Retrieved from http://etd.lsu.edu/.

Auverset, L. A., & Billings, A. C. (2016). Relationships between social TV and enjoyment: A content analysis of *The Walking Dead*'s Story Sync experience. *Social Media + Society*, *2*(3), 1–12.

Bolton, D. (2016). Risk and reward with Deidre Bolton. Fox Business. Retrieved from https://archive/org/details/FBC_20160223_220000_Risk_and_Reward_With_Deidre_Bolton.

Boxell, L., Gentzkow, M., & Shapiro, J. M. (2018). A note on Internet use and the 2016 U.S. presidential election outcome. *PLoS ONE*, *13*(7): e0199571. Retrieved from http://journals.plos.org/plosone/article?id=10.1371/journal.pone.0199571#abstract0.

Boyle, T. P. (2001). Intermedia agenda setting in the 1996 presidential election. *Journalism & Mass Communication Quarterly*, *78*(1), 26–44.

British Broadcasting Corporation. (2016, February 25). TVEyes. BBC2 Wales transcript. Newsnight.

Brock, A. (2012). From the blackhand side: Twitter as a cultural conversation. *Journal of Broadcasting & Electronic Media*, *56*(4), 529–549. doi: 10.108008838151.2012.732147.

Butler, B. (2016, February 25). How *Blackish* tackled police brutality while staying true to its roots. *The Washington Post*. Retrieved from https://www.washingtonpost.com/news/arts-and-entertainment/wp/2016/02/25/how-blackish-tackled-police-brutality-while-staying-true-to-its-roots/?utm_term=.f3e9c60e2a0a.

Carney, N. (2016). All lives matter, but so does race: Black lives matter and the evolving role of social media. *Humanity & Society*, *40*(2), 180–199.

Costello, C., Serfaty, S., Myers, C., & Frates, C. (2016, February 25). *CNN Newsroom* [Television broadcast]. Atlanta, GA: CNN. Retrieved from http://www.cnn.com/TRANSCRIPTS/1602/25/cnr.01.html.

Cushion, S., Kilby, A., Thomas, R., Morani, M., & Sambrook, R. (2016). Newspapers, impartiality and television news: Intermedia agenda-setting during the 2015 UK general election campaign. *Journalism Studies*, *19*(2), 162–181.

Cynopsis Media. (2016, February 26). Fox renews Bones for farewell season; Scripps acquires full ownership of Travel Channel; Madeline Stowe heading to Syfy's 12 Monkeys. Retrieved from https://www.cynopsis.com/022616-fox-renews-bones-for-farewell-season-scripps-acquires-full-ownership-of-travel-channel-madeline-stowe-heading-to-syfys-12-monkeys/.

Domonoske, C. (2016, December 30). Number of police officers killed by firearms rose in 2016, study finds. *National Public Radio*. Retrieved from: https://www.npr.org/sections/thetwo-way/2016/12/30/507536360/number-of-police-officers-killed-by-firearms-rose-in-2016-study-finds.

Fienberg, D. (2016, February 24). *Black-ish* boss on tackling police brutality: "I didn't want to politicize the show." *The Hollywood Reporter*. Retrieved from https://www.hollywoodreporter.com/fien-print/black-ish-boss-police-brutality-869397.

Florini, S. (2014). Tweets, tweeps, and signifyin': Communication and cultural performance on "Black Twitter." *Television & New Media*, *15*(3) 223–237.

Golan, G. (2006). Inter-media agenda setting and global news coverage: Assessing the influence of the *New York Times* on three network television evening news programs. *Journalism Studies*, *7*(2), 323–333.

Fretts, B. (2016, February 24). *Black-ish* show runner Kenya Barris on police brutality and *The Cosby Show*. *The New York Times*. Retrieved from https://www.nytimes.com/2016/02/25/arts/television/blackish-kenya-barris-police-brutality-episode.html.

Harrington, S., Highfield, T., & Bruns, A. (2013). More than a backchannel: Twitter and television. *Participations: Journal of Audience & Reception Studies*, *10*(1). Retrieved from http://www.participations.org.

Holbert, R. L., Pillion, O., Tschida, D. A., Armfield, G. G., Kinder, K., Cherry, K. L., & Daulton, A. R. (2003). *The West Wing* as endorsement of the U.S. presidency: Expanding the bounds of priming in political communication. *Journal of Communication*, *53*(3), 427–443.

Holbrook, R. A., & Hill, T. G. (2005). Agenda-setting and priming in prime time television: Crime dramas as political cues. *Political Communication*, *22*(3), 277–295.

Kang, J. K. (2015, May 4). "Our Demand is Simple: Stop Killing Us. How a group of black social media activists built the nation's first 21st century civil rights movement." *The New York Times*.

Ku, G., Kaid, L. L., & Pfau, M. (2003). The impact of web site campaigning on traditional news media and public opinion information processing. *Journalism & Mass Communication Quarterly*, *80*(3), 528–547.

Lee, B., Lancendorfer, K. M., & Lee, K. J. (2005). Agenda-setting and the internet: The intermedia influence of internet bulletin boards on newspaper coverage of the 2000 general election in South Korea. *Asian Journal of Communication*, *15*(1), 57–71.

Lee, M. (2017). *Exploring the intermedia agenda-setting relationships and frames in the high-choice media environment* (Master's thesis). Retrieved from http://hdl.handle.net/11299/188783.

Markovits, A. S., & Hayden, R. S. (1980). "Holocaust" before and after the event: Reactions in West Germany and Austria. *New German Critique*, *19*(1), 53–80. Retrieved from http://www.jstor.org/stable/487972.

McCombs, M. (2005). A look at agenda-setting: past, present and future. *Journalism Studies, 6*(4), 543–557.

McCombs, M. (2014). *Setting the agenda: Mass media and public opinion* (2nd ed.). Cambridge, UK: Polity Press.

McCombs, M., & Shaw, D. (1972). The agenda-sending function of mass media. *Public Opinion Quarterly, 36*(2), 176–187.

Messner, M., & Garrison, B. (2011). Study shows some blogs affect traditional news media agendas. *Newspaper Research Journal, 32*(3), 112–126.

Nielsen. (2016). *Young, connected and black.* Retrieved from http://www.nielsen.com/us/en/insights/reports/2016/young-connected-and-black.html.

Nielsen. (2017). *The Nielsen total audience report: Q2 2017.* Retrieved from http://www.nielsen.com/us/en/insights/reports/2017/the-nielsen-total-audience-q2-2017.html.

Proulx, M., & Shepatin, S. (2012). *Social TV: How marketers can reach and engage audiences by connecting television to the web, social media, and mobile.* Hoboken, NJ: John Wiley & Sons Inc.

Redniss, J. (2015, March 12). Thanks, Nielsen, for that Twitter study—but it's time we "total it up" with you. [Web log post]. Retrieved from http://www.adweek.com/lostremote/thanks-nielsen-for-that-twitter-study-but-its-time-we-total-it-up-with-you/50907.

Reese, S. D., & Danielian, L. H. (1989). Intermedia influence and the drug influence: Converging on cocaine. In P. Shoemaker (Ed.), *Communication campaigns about drugs: Government, media, and the public* (29–46). Mahwah, NJ: Lawrence Erlbaum Associates, Inc.

Smith, A., & Anderson, M. (2018). *Social media use in 2018.* Washington, DC: Pew Internet & American Life Project. Retrieved from http://www.pewinternet.org/2018/03/01/social-media-use-in-2018/.

Snopes. (2016). Marine assaulted at McDonald's by Black Lives Matter activists? Marine veteran Christopher Marquez was involved in an altercation at a Washington, D.C. McDonald's, but police said there was no indication the argument involved Black Lives Matter. Retrieved from https://www.snopes.com/fact-check/marine-attack-blm-claim/.

Soroka, S. N. (2000). Schindler's List's intermedia influence: Exploring the role of "entertainment" in media agenda-setting. *Canadian Journal of Communication, 25*(2), 211–230. Retrieved from http://www.snsoroka.com/files/2000Soroka(CJC).pdf.

Swaine, J., McCarthy, C. (2017, January 8). Young black men again faced highest rate of US police killings in 2016. *The Guardian.* Retrieved from: https://www.theguardian.com/us-news/2017/jan/08/the-counted-police-killings-2016-young-black-men.

Sweetser, K. D., Golan, G. J., & Wanta, W. (2008). Intermedia agenda setting in television, advertising, and blogs during the 2004 election. *Mass Communication & Society, 11*(2), 197–216.

Taylor, K. Y. (2016). *From #BlackLivesMatter to black liberation.* Chicago, IL: Haymarket Books.

The Associated Press-NORC Center for Public Affairs Research. (2017). *Instagram and Snapchat are most popular social networks for teens; Black teens are most active on social media,   messaging   apps.*   Retrieved   from   http://apnorc.org/PDFs/Teen%20Social%20Media%20Messaging/APNORC_Teens_SocialMedia_Messaging_2017_FINAL.pdf.

Vliegenthart, R., & Walgrave, S. (2008). The contingency of intermedia agenda setting: A longitudinal study in Belgium. *Journalism & Mass Communication Quarterly, 85*(4), 860–877.

Wallsten, K. (2007). Agenda setting and the blogosphere: An analysis of the relationship between mainstream media and political blogs. *Review of Policy Research, 24*(6), 567–587.

Wohn, D., & Na, E. (2011). Tweeting about TV: Sharing television viewing experiences via social media message streams. *First Monday, 16*(3–7).

Yancy, G., & Butler, J. (2015). What's wrong with "all lives matter"? *The New York Times.* Retrieved from https://opinionator.blogs.nytimes.com/2015/01/12/whats-wrong-with-all-lives-matter/.

Yu, J., & Aikat, D. (2008). News on the web: Agenda setting of online news in news web sites of major newspaper, television, and online news. Paper presented at the annual meeting of the International Communication Association, NYC, NY. Retrieved from http://citation. allacademic.com/meta/p_mla_apa_research_citation/0/1/5/2/2/p15225_index.html.

Chapter Three

Reading Race and Religion in Aziz Ansari's *Master of None*

Nadeen Kharputly

Comedian and actor Aziz Ansari emerged in the mid-2010s as an important figure for many young people who have not felt adequately represented on television in the United States. His Netflix show, *Master of None,* appeals to a number of communities that have traditionally been underrepresented on television, and these include immigrants of color, South Asian Americans and Muslim Americans. In particular, one episode of the show, titled "Religion," focuses on the dynamics between Muslim American millennials and their more pious parents. "Religion" offers an important exception to the ways in which Islam has typically been depicted on American television.

In this chapter I provide an analysis of the show and examine the different responses that Muslim Americans have to the portrayal of Islam on the show, focusing on the "Religion" episode in particular. The opinions that I have collected here range from select articles online by Muslim American writers to a podcast featuring a variety of Muslim American voices, *See Something, Say Something* (2016–present). These opinions serve as an important measure for the expectations placed on representations of Islam and Muslims in U.S. popular culture. The tensions between Ansari's depictions of Islam in *Master of None* and the Muslim American responses to those depictions highlight both the burden of responsibility placed on Ansari and the expectations demanded by Muslim American audiences. Younger audiences who have grown up with 9/11 as a defining moment in their lives have waited a long time for a show like *Master of None* to come along, but their responses also indicate how much more work is needed to reflect the vast range of experiences for Muslim Americans today.

AZIZ ANSARI AND THE
MILLENNIAL TAKE ON ISLAM

Born in South Carolina in 1983 to Indian-Muslim immigrants from Tamil Nadu, Aziz Ansari is an actor and comedian known for his stand-up comedy, his recurring role on the NBC sitcom *Parks and Recreation* (2009–2015), and his 2015 book *Modern Romance* (co-authored with the sociologist Eric Klinenberg). More recently, Ansari has received wide acclaim for his starring role on the Netflix series *Master of None* (2015), which he also writes and produces with his collaborator Alan Yang.

Several of Ansari's television roles are based on aspects of his life. Both Tom Haverford in *Parks and Recreation* and Dev Shah in *Master of None* are children of South Indian–Muslim parents, but they each drink alcohol, eat pork, and engage in sexual relationships, much like Ansari himself. These practices are either strictly forbidden according to religious scripture or frowned upon within more conservative Muslim families. While neither Tom Haverford nor Dev Shah would identify as Muslim, audiences would read these characters as Muslim, which would make them serve as prominent examples of Muslim Americans on television. However, Ansari has demonstrated little interest in becoming a representative for Muslim Americans. Jada Yuan writes in *Vulture*,

> Ansari is not personally religious, and he feels uncomfortable being pointed to as a model Muslim American, not, he says, because he's ashamed but because "religious people deserve a better representative than a guy who's doing a show about fucking and drinking and eating pork all the time." (Yuan, 2017)

But at the same time, Ansari appears to be conscious of the fact that no matter how he identifies, he is unable to completely rid himself of the burden of responsibility that is ascribed to anyone who is or who looks like they could be Muslim. Writing in the aftermath of the June 2016 attacks at the Pulse nightclub in Orlando, Ansari states, "I myself am not a religious person, but after these attacks, anyone that even looks like they might be Muslim understands the feelings my friend describes" (Ansari, 2016). The friend in question, who is Muslim American, had been quoted previously in Ansari's piece as saying: "I just feel really bad, like people think I have more in common with that idiot psychopath than I do the innocent people being killed. . . . I'm really sick of having to explain that I'm not a terrorist every time the shooter is brown" (Ansari, 2016).

Ansari articulates something important here when he asserts that even someone who no longer identifies as a Muslim might still feel the frustration of being associated with terrorists and then "hav[e] to explain that I'm not a terrorist" (Ansari, 2016), a responsibility that many Muslims in this country have been burdened with in the aftermath of 9/11. Understanding that even atheists who were previously raised as Muslim may not be able to escape some of the responsibilities tied to that identity in the United States, Ansari occupies a peculiar role in popular culture with the tensions between his chosen identity and his perceived identity.

VISIBLE MUSLIMS IN THE POST-9/11 AGE

Ansari and the friend he quotes in his *New York Times* piece allude to the ways in which Muslims in this country are racialized. In the years since 9/11, anyone who "looks" Muslim, regardless of their identity, is faced with suspicion due to the Islamophobic climate that criminalizes brown men with facial hair, or brown men and women with religious head coverings. Nadine Naber (2008) points to Althusser's notion of interpellation to illustrate that even non-Muslim subjects can be signified as a threat due to the War on Terror and attendant government policies and Islamophobia (Jamal & Naber, 2008, pp. 277–278). This is particularly illustrative with the death of Balbir Singh Sodhi, the first victim of Islamophobic backlash in the immediate aftermath of 9/11. Sodhi, a Sikh American, was mistaken for a Muslim because of his beard and turban and murdered in retaliation (the perpetrator had previously bragged about killing the "ragheads responsible for September 11" and screamed "I'm an American all the way! . . . Arrest me and let those terrorists run wild" upon his apprehension) (Peek, 2010, p. 28). Ansari himself has discussed an incident in which someone had called him a terrorist in public in the months after 9/11, which occurred when he was a college student living in New York City (Ansari, 2016). While the murder of Balbir Singh Sodhi illustrates how even non-Muslims can be victims of Islamophobia, the incident with Ansari points to the difficulty (if not impossibility) of distancing oneself from one's religious identity in this country, even if one does not identify as Muslim. Hence, Ansari's personal choices will not necessarily stop others from reading and treating him as Muslim. Salwa Tareen expresses this perfectly in her analysis of *Master of None*'s "Religion" episode:

> This fluctuating calibration relies upon a mix of racial and religious stereotypes to create the monster that is anti-Muslim hatred. As a result, the racialization of what is *perceived to be* Muslim casts a much larger net than those who are in fact practicing Muslims. (Tareen, 2017)

The work of Pakistani American playwright Ayad Akhtar illustrates this phenomenon of ascribing a religious identity to former Muslims in spite of their individual choices. Speaking of his own protagonist in his play *Disgraced*, which won the 2013 Pulitzer Prize for Drama, Akhtar notes that the character Amir "wouldn't see himself as a Muslim, and unfortunately in a post-9/11 world, that's not a nuance that exists. You can't say, 'I was brought up Muslim, but I'm not Muslim'" (Musiker, 2015). Here, Akhtar points to a wider phenomenon that prevents those who were raised as Muslim or those whose families are Muslim to be perceived as non-Muslim. This in turn indicates the extent to which Islam is understood as a permanent part of one's identity. The protagonist himself is also unable to achieve this detachment: At the end of the play, Amir attributes several hateful views to his religious upbringing, which he says is "tribal . . . It is in the bones. You have no idea how I was brought up. You have to work *real* hard to root that shit out" (Akhtar, 2012, p. 67). These comments are among the many that lead *Disgraced* to be considered controversial for its portrayal of Muslim American identity. What Amir says points to a wider phenomenon of assuming, incorrectly, that those who were raised as Muslim can never "root out" their religious upbringing.

The imposition of Muslim identity on nonreligious individuals is not only constituted in these negative and threatening ways. Muslims themselves may do this when they want to connect to one another on a religious and cultural basis. For instance, in the first episode of the podcast *See Something, Say Something*, the host and his guests, who are all Muslim American, semi-jokingly state that they "want to claim Aziz" as a Muslim American who is producing compelling representations of Muslims in American media, despite the fact that they know that he does not identify as Muslim and is therefore "not part of our crew" (Akbar, 2016). However, one of the guests argues in favor of including him in this category: "As a Muslim-named person, he's representing something. If people with turbans now represent Muslims, Aziz Ansari can represent Muslims . . . he recognizes his own truth and speaks about his own life with nuance" (Akbar, 2016). These comments signal the expectations that someone like Aziz Ansari, a nonreligious member of a Muslim family, has to face when he chooses to represent Muslims on television. This is all to say that the reality of Ansari's identification as an atheist may not prevent him from bearing some of the responsibilities placed on those who represent Muslims in the United States. But why is that the case?

MUSLIM AMERICAN CULTURAL PRODUCTION

Consider the ways in which Muslims have been portrayed on television in the United States. Some of the most well-known examples of Muslims on television include *24*, *Homeland*, and *Quantico*, and these often feature Muslims as terrorists or, in contrast, as FBI agents. (*Quantico* features a Muslim FBI agent wearing a hijab.) These shows, among others, were created in response to the War on Terror and prominently feature Arab and Muslim characters, but most of them are "portrayed as grave threats to U.S. national security" (Alsultany, 2012, p. 20). Even when these shows have adapted and diversified their portrayals in response to concerns about "blatant, crude stereotyping" (Alsultany, 2012, p. 20), there remains a clear attachment to the War on Terror. Alsultany shows how seven different representational strategies to feature and diversify the presence of Muslims on television demonstrate that these shows "remain wedded to a script that represents Arabs and Muslims only in the context of terrorism and therefore do not effectively challenge the stereotypical representations of Arabs and Muslims" (Alsultany, 2012, p. 27). In the years since Alsultany published these findings, representations of Muslims or Muslim Americans with little to no connection to the War on Terror continue to be rare.

As for television shows that focus on so-called "normal," everyday Muslims, the options are more limited. A reality show titled *All-American Muslim,* which showcased a Muslim American family in Dearborn, Michigan, was cancelled after one season, ostensibly due to low ratings but more realistically due to a concerted effort by a Tampa-based hate group, the Florida Family Association, to pressure corporations (such as Lowe's) to withdraw their sponsorships. There has also been a smattering of web series in recent years, such as Aasif Mandvi's *Halal in the Family*, a sitcom about a Muslim American family, the Qu'osbys (a play on the Cosbys), and Yumna Khan and Nida Chowdhry's *Unfair & Ugly*, a web series featuring a South Asian, Muslim American family in Southern California. But these shows tend to be exceptions to the norm. The idea of a Muslim inhabiting a world where the threat of terrorism does not reign does not seem to present much of an appeal for mainstream American audiences. In sum, the options for seeing Muslims on television with no connection to the War on Terror are limited, which is why the expectations are high for *Master of None*, which weaves Muslim identity fairly seamlessly into its thematic concerns.

THE APPEAL OF *MASTER OF NONE*

Master of None resembles in some ways many of the shows about young people living improbably lavish lifestyles on modest salaries in New York City—*Friends*, *Sex and the City*, *Girls*, and *Broad City* are a few of the examples of this genre. The show revolves around the life of Dev Shah, a struggling actor whose life intersects with various other thirtysomething New Yorkers, played by Eric Wareheim, Lena Waithe and Kelvin Yu, among others. The show also prominently features Dev's parents, who are played by Ansari's own parents. Each episode offers a snapshot of everyday life in the city, much like other shows set in New York City. However, *Master of None* is set apart by its diverse cast amidst American television shows that have been criticized for their lack of diversity, notably in the form of all-white casts (Adewunmi, 2015).

Master of None is not only produced by a person with a Muslim background, it also depicts Muslim Americans in ways that depart from the tactics that Alsultany discusses in her analysis of television shows after 9/11. As BuzzFeed writer Bim Adewunmi says on an episode of the *See Something, Say Something* podcast, the show "tell[s] very little stories . . . the kinds of stories [that] television has been telling for a long time, but for white people. . . . It's the same stories, except not the same stories by virtue of who is the star" (Akbar, 2017). By "little stories," Adewunmi means that the episodes focus on the quotidian aspects of the characters' lives, from the day-to-day routines of cohabiting couples ("Mornings") to conversations about whether or not the protagonist and his friends want children in the future ("Plan B"). Adewunmi's comment that these are "the same stories, except not the same stories by virtue of who is the star" speaks to the relative lack of representation of people of color on television, and how important *Master of None* stands out in that regard, especially considering its mainstream appeal. The show is not expressly about being Indian American or Muslim American—it just happens to feature characters of these backgrounds. And this is part of what makes *Master of None* relatable to millennial audiences: from the rituals (and horrors) of modern dating to the relationships that the protagonists have with their immigrant parents, the show focuses on thematic concerns that are familiar to a wide swath of younger viewers. It has been described as "a fascinating, spot-on window into the modern millennial's perspective on life and work" and praised for its portrayal of all the different ways in which young people in America come of age with "student loan debt, bad roommates, ill-suited relationships and stop-and-start self-discovery in favor of a more quiet contemplation of adulthood" (Kadakia, 2015; Henderson, 2015).

The show's relatability is integral to its subtle yet powerful depiction of Islam in this country. *Master of None* is not explicitly a television show about a Muslim, nor is it in any way a pointed attempt to illustrate how Muslims are just as "normal" as any other group of Americans. It is merely a series of snapshots into the lives of thirtysomethings in New York, and two of the characters—Dev's parents—happen to be practicing Muslims. Islam is neither the focal point of the show nor a threatening element in any way, allowing audiences to engage with the thematic issues of the show—relationships, careers and food—and see how religion occasionally intersects with those issues.

THE "RELIGION" EPISODE

These dynamics are most evident in the third episode of Season Two, titled "Religion," which revolves around Dev's relationship to Islam and to his family. Dev's aunt, uncle and cousin have come for a visit to New York, where Dev and his family live. Dev's parents (played by Ansari's own parents) spend time with the aunt and uncle, and during those occasions they ask Dev to pretend to be religious around them. At one point, Dev's father asks him to say that he is fasting for Ramadan and even boasts that his son prays five times a day, much to his son's chagrin. These dynamics illustrate the tensions between Dev and his parents, who understand that their son is not observant but nevertheless ask him to pretend otherwise in the presence of their more pious relatives. Dev, on the other hand, does not want to keep up this pretense, and the episode unfolds with his increasing reluctance to abide by his parents' wishes. This is a familiar dynamic to individuals of any religious tradition where younger generations do not necessarily connect to their practices and their faith as much as the older generations.

Meanwhile, Dev catches up with his cousin Navid (played by Ansari's cousin, Harris Gani) where they learn about each other's respective religious practices, specifically regarding their adherence to Islamic dietary practices. Dev drinks alcohol and eats pork regularly, whereas Navid has just started drinking for the first time in his life. Upon learning that Navid has never eaten pork, Dev gives him a bite of his Cubano sandwich (during Ramadan, no less: the holiest month of the year for Muslims), and Navid is enraptured. Soon after, Navid suggests that they forgo Eid prayers in favor of attending a barbecue festival titled "Hog Wild Weekend," to which Dev responds, "You want to skip Eid prayer and go to a barbecue festival? That's bad, even for me." They end up going and eat as much pork as they can manage.

Emboldened by these developments, Dev comes to a head with his parents when they go out to dinner to celebrate Eid with the extended family. Frustrated with having to hide the reality of his experiences, he orders a pork-based dish in front of his entire family. This is the first time Dev's mother has seen him eat pork in her presence, and the first time his aunt and uncle realize that his piety has been a farce all along. Stunned and embarrassed by this act, his parents ask Dev if he is serious, to which he replies, "I'm not that religious, and I eat pork. But it's okay, 'cause I'm a good person." Humiliated, his parents leave the restaurant, and the show cuts to a scene in his parents' living room, where Dev and his parents have a heated conversation about what Islam means to each of them. Several weeks then pass by where Dev's mother refuses to talk to her son.

The rest of this episode unwinds with a poignant conversation between Dev and his father, who explains that the decision to eat pork in front of his mother and other relatives is "not about the religion. It's about you ignoring us, not realizing who you are. . . . When you act like this, we feel like we failed you." This conversation illustrates that ultimately, this episode is, as producer and writer Alan Yang stated, "not even really about religion" (Harris, 2017). It is more so about navigating the cultural terrains between Americans and their immigrant parents, and how attempts to impart their values to their children are fraught with all kinds of difficulty. The tensions explored in this episode are not exclusive to Muslim American families: anyone who has clashed with their parents over a particular choice will relate to these family dynamics.

One of the most striking scenes in the episode appears at the very end, which juxtaposes Dev's parents praying at their mosque while Dev attends a happy hour with his friends. It is a harmonious scene that depicts the members of the Shah family socializing in their respective ways (although this is not to equate prayers with happy hour, nor to suggest that prayers are merely a social activity). The image of Dev's parents praying and cheerfully mingling with their friends at the mosque is accompanied by Bobby Charles' serene "I Must Be in a Good Place Now." It is incredibly rare to find images of Muslims praying on television that have not been framed in an ominous manner. Producer Alan Yang has said, "Typically when you see Muslims depicted, they're terrorists about to bomb somebody, and there's scary music playing. So that was part of it, but not reason enough to do the episode" (Izadi, 2017). Ansari himself has noted during his *Saturday Night Live* monologue that scenes featuring an Arab or Muslim character praying are often accompanied with "that scary-ass music from *Homeland*" (Deb, 2018). For Ansari to foreground the sociability of these two scenes sends a powerful message that resists typical framings of Muslim prayers as an ominous act that precedes violence or as a ritual that is alien to everyday life in the United States.

There is nothing particularly solemn in the delivery of this scene. Ansari is not embarking on a concerted effort to humanize Muslim prayers or Muslims themselves for his audience. He merely shows how various members of the same family partake in different rituals. The juxtaposition of prayer and happy hour might seem sacrilegious to observant Muslims who abstain from alcohol, but at the same time it is a representation of the realities that concern Dev and his family. The "Religion" episode, then, offers a glimpse into some of the tensions that are faced by Muslim American families and illustrates how these tensions are not so alien from some of the usual challenges faced by families of all backgrounds.

MUSLIM AMERICAN RESPONSES TO
THE "RELIGION" EPISODE

When *Master of None* first emerged on the scene, many South Asian and Muslim Americans were thrilled to welcome a show that focused on the everyday life of a protagonist who resembled them, and to see him negotiate between his different identities: as an American, a second-generation immigrant, and a former Muslim. Writer Omer Aziz claims that

> Ansari's show launched brown folks into the mainstream of American culture. He depicted us as ordinary human beings, and his portrayal of struggling to live up to the expectations of his Indian American and Muslim parents especially struck a nerve. (Aziz, 2018)

That the writer draws attention to Ansari's depiction of "brown folks" as "ordinary human beings" reiterates how exceptional these narratives are relative to the more common depictions of Muslims as terrorists or FBI agents, and how starved Muslim American audiences have been for the depiction of these kinds of everyday narratives on television. Another Muslim American writer, Amil Niazi, was particularly touched by the way Ansari "was able to deftly capture genuine hurt and frustration through a funny, realistic portrayal of our experiences in pop culture and how that informs how others see us and inevitably how we see ourselves" (Niazi, 2017). Niazi points to the awareness that Muslim Americans have not just of themselves but of how "others see" them. This awareness is reminiscent of W. E. B. DuBois's notion of double consciousness. Like black Americans, Muslim Americans are keenly aware of their existence in a world that frames the components of their identity as oppositional rather than mutually constitutive. In the aftermath of 9/11, American national identity was in many ways constructed in direct opposition to the threats that were and are perceived to be espoused by Islam and Muslims. These tensions thus inform how Muslim Americans encounter depictions of their experiences on television: They are conscious not just of their own reactions to the show but are also aware of how other Americans might interpret what they see.

Consider, for instance, Ansari's portrayal of Dev, who eats pork, drinks alcohol, and engages in casual sexual relationships. Comedian Negin Farsad contrasts these choices with the "tired terrorist tropes" that are far more familiar to television audiences (Farsad, 2017). Farsad correctly notes that the scenes depicting Dev eating bacon "gives Muslims the same sense of spectrum that Christians and Jews have long enjoyed. You can show up to church almost never and still be considered Christian, and you can eat a ham sandwich and still be considered a Jew" (Farsad, 2017). Muslims, on the other hand, do not appear to get the same flexibility that Christians and Jews seem to get in regard to conflicts between their identities and their practices. The notion of an unobservant Muslim is an unfamiliar concept confined to that of unobservant Christians and Jews. *Master of None* holds space for that concept. Farsad continues, "if you're a booze swilling, bacon-breathed Muz, as I am, there is little to no reflection of you in popular media." Ansari has certainly offered this reflection for many non-observant Muslims. And for non-Muslims, he has provided insight into the ways in which people identify—or don't identify—as Muslim. These kinds of depictions exist both for Muslims like Farsad and for non-Muslims who know very little about range of experiences belonging to different Muslims, observant and otherwise.

However, many Muslim Americans were critical of Ansari's portrayal of Muslims in the "Religion" episode. For instance, writer Riad Alarian notes that Negin Farsad's review of the episode seems at first "to be a celebration of Muslim diversity." In Alarian's view, however, Ansari instead develops "an image of the Muslim that is practically detached from anything Islamic in the theological sense, it represents an attempt to gratify liberal fears of the religiously conservative Other" (Alarian, 2017). This is an important observation of the ways in which, in this context, a positive portrayal of Muslims is one that is predicated on the absence of religious values; that is, what Alarian calls "Islam-lite," or "the visible absence of Islam in the actions and mannerisms of self-identified Muslims." One caveat in response to this point is that Dev never specifically identifies as Muslim on the show, so it is unclear to what extent it is fair to label the character as a "self-identified Muslim," as Alarian does. This ties back to my earlier point that even non-observant or former Muslims will still be perceived as Muslim despite their own preferences. However, Alarian's wariness stands: The depictions of Dev Shah "gratify liberal fears" by secularizing him and his interpretation of Islam. These portrayals, then, do not offer a diverse portrayal of Muslims— they provide a Westernized portrayal of Muslims.

Alarian situates Farsad's response to Dev's character within a wider phenomenon that he calls the "Humanizing Muslims Industry," which aligns Muslims with "mainstream liberal norms" in order to make them "palatable to Western audiences" (Alarian, 2017). This in turn marginalizes more conservative Muslims, and even suggests, as Alarian notes, that conservative Muslims and extremists are "equally contemptible." On the one hand, while liberal portrayals of Muslims are a welcome change from the terrorist tropes, they don't necessarily curb bigoted perceptions of Muslims; instead, they endorse a limited view of "good" Muslims, if we are to take Alarian's position. This leaves us with a dichotomy that pits good, liberal Muslims against bad, conservative Muslims rather than offering a range of different perspectives on what it means to be a Muslim American.

A middle-ground position is presented by another Muslim American writer, Tekkai Wallace, who appreciates both Farsad and Alarian's views—that the episode simultaneously serves as a celebration and a reduction of Muslim diversity. Wallace notes that "just as there are Muslims like Ansari who smoke, eat, and drink, there are also a great deal of Muslims who conservatively practice a faith and its rituals" (Wallace, 2017). This view is supported by the final scene in the episode, which simultaneously shows Dev's parents at the mosque and Dev at the bar. Wallace's perspective is especially valuable because it reminds us that while popular representations of Muslims continue to be fraught with tension, they are still representative of individual choices. To this effect, Wallace writes,

> The thing about Ansari's character, Dev, is that his experience is *his*. Articles like mine only exist because there is a cultural battle about what Dev's experience and life *should be*, instead of a simple acceptance of how one individual chooses to live his life. We are all looking for some sort of way to live at peace with ourselves. (Wallace, 2017)

Wallace's last remark signals an important point about the Muslim American responses to *Master of None*. They reflect deeper concerns with popular representations of Muslims in the United States, and these are that the representations offer a way of navigating one's religious and cultural identity. The reactions to Ansari's depiction of Muslim American identity on *Master of None* reflect the individual tensions of each viewer, which in turn echo the wide range of responses to the show. This point is exemplified by some of the responses from the Muslim American podcast, *See Something, Say Something*. Episode 25 of the podcast, "From Zero to Pork," involves a conversation between the host, Ahmed Ali Akbar, and two other Muslim American BuzzFeed writers, Bim Adewunmi and Abid Anwar. Their responses to the episode are mixed and complex, which is a reflection of their various experiences vis-à-vis their religious and cultural identities. Each of these speakers are Muslim to varying degrees—some of them practice occasionally, others do not. Hence, they offer a range of different responses to the portrayal of Muslims on the episode of the show because they themselves embody a range of different experiences.

Over the course of their conversation, Akbar, Adewunmi and Anwar share aspects of the show that they appreciate, and one of these is the depiction of first- and second-generation Muslims who "have various caveats on their Muslimness" (Akbar, 2017). Akbar expands on this and explains, "For most of us . . . we're not great Muslims and we want to be better and there are some complex feelings about our religion beyond 'I'm not Muslim'" (Akbar, 2017). These struggles are relatable to many Muslims in this country and all over the world; indeed, they make the conflicts between Dev and his parents relatable. For the writers featured on the podcast, moments depicting these conflicts constitute the strongest parts of *Master of None* because they are thought to be the most realistic and the most familiar to Muslims of varying levels of practice.

The speakers also discuss aspects of the episode that frustrate them—and that are also thought to be the most unrealistic and unfamiliar to their experiences. One of these is the moment where Dev's cousin Navid goes from "zero to pork"—he has his first bite of pork from Dev's sandwich, and then, the next day or shortly thereafter, suggests that he and Dev skip Eid prayers to go and eat a barbecue festival's worth of pork. Akbar and his guests argue that this turn of events is unrealistic for several reasons (Akbar, 2017). Among these reasons is that they think that it would "take more than one conversation with your cousin to start eating pork," let alone to attend a pork festival shortly after. Akbar claims that this scene "requires more thought than the show depicted" (Akbar, 2017). In her review of the episode, Salwa Tareen emphasizes the gravity of the situation by claiming that Dev and Navid's actions are

> the equivalent of skipping Christmas dinner for a BBQ festival. As a result, the scene is fun, light-hearted, but ultimately outrageous. The point here is not that Muslims, including myself, do not regularly skip out on religious gatherings or activities, but the pace at which *Master of None* depicts Navid's shift from the label of "religiously observant" to hog-wild (literally) is jarring. (Tareen, 2017)

The contrasting reactions about the most realistic and unrealistic parts of the episode serve as an important measure for how Muslim Americans navigate their identities in response to popular culture. These are deeply personal reactions—of which they are very aware, as the speakers state in the podcast—to individual choices made by Ansari.

The speakers are also aware of the fact that they are criticizing one of the very few people of color to offer these representations on television. Adewunmi states that this is "because, at the back of our minds, even though we know they're the only one, we want them to tell *all* the stories . . . and tell them all really well" (Akbar, 2017). The speakers spend a good portion of the podcast episode discussing the burden of responsibility that falls on Aziz Ansari for his depiction of Muslims. They see Ansari as someone who has willingly taken on that burden of representation, and at the same time they understand that "no one should have that responsibility" (Akbar, 2017). But they also expect more because the landscape of cultural productions is still so limited.

The conversations around Aziz Ansari and *Master of None* show how representations of Islam in popular culture have yet to achieve a wider level of satisfaction for many Muslim Americans. But on the other hand, these conversations also illuminate the richness of the experiences lived by many Muslim Americans; their appreciation of and frustration with Ansari and his show offer a more accurate reflection of their experiences than the show itself. While depictions of Islam on television still have a long way to go, the conversations that are being had by young Muslim American viewers serve as a testament to the change that is to come.

REFERENCES

Adewunmi, B. (2015, June 11). Aziz Ansari's *Master of None* nails race perfectly. *Buzzfeed.* Retrieved from https://www.buzzfeed.com/bimadewunmi/the-effortless-diversity-of-aziz-ansaris-new-netflix-show.

Akbar, A. A. (2016, October 28). Saying "nah." *See Something, Say Something. Buzzfeed.* Retrieved from https://www.stitcher.com/podcast/buzzfeed/see-something-say-something/e/48078893.

Akbar, A. A. (2017, May 18). From zero to pork: *See something, say something. Buzzfeed.* Retrieved from https://www.stitcher.com/podcast/buzzfeed/see-something-say-something/e/50201063.

Akhtar, A. (2013). *Disgraced.* New York: Little, Brown and Company.

Alarian, R. (2017, May 20). Liberal fascination with "Islam-Lite" and the humanizing Muslims Industry. *Mutfah.* Retrieved from https://muftah.org/liberal-fascination-islam-lite-humanizing-muslims-industry/#.W84iqVJOk8Y.

Alsultany, E. (2012). *Arabs and Muslims in the media: Race and representation after 9/11.* New York: NYU Press.

Ansari, A. (2016, January 20). Why Trump makes me scared for my family. *The New York Times.* Retrieved from https://www.nytimes.com/2016/06/26/opinion/sunday/aziz-ansari-why-trump-makes-me-scared-for-my-family.html.

Aziz, O. (2018, January 19). Aziz Ansari and me. *The New Republic.* Retrieved from https://newrepublic.com/article/146663/aziz-ansari.

Deb, S. (2018, January 20). Aziz Ansari's monologue on *Saturday Night Live*: Transcript. *The New York Times.* Retrieved from https://www.nytimes.com/2017/01/22/arts/aziz-ansari-monologue-transcript-snl.html.

Farsad, N. (2017, May 16). *Master of None*'s nuanced portrayal of Muslim life is a refreshing change. Retrieved from https://www.theguardian.com/tv-and-radio/2017/may/16/master-of-none-muslim-life-aziz-ansari-netflix.

Firestone, L. (2017, July 6). How Aziz Ansari explained his bacon-eating to his devout Muslim parents. *Vanity Fair.* Retrieved from https://www.vanityfair.com/hollywood/2017/06/aziz-ansari-master-of-none-moth-bacon.

Gutmann, T. (2017, June 21). The "Religion" episode: Aziz Ansari and the cultural politics of Muslim self-representation. Retrieved from http://religiondispatches.org/the-religion-episode-aziz-ansari-and-the-cultural-politics-of-muslim-self-representation/.

Harris, A. (2017, May 12). *Master of None*'s Alan Yang on how the creators resisted the urge to address Trump directly in Season 2. *Slate.* Retrieved from http://www.slate.com/blogs/browbeat/2017/05/12/master_of_none_co_creator_alan_yang_on_how_season_2_chose_not_to_address.html.

Henderson, J. M. (2015, November 19). Is Aziz Ansari's *Master of None* the show that aging millennials have been waiting for? Retrieved from https://www.forbes.com/sites/jmaureenhenderson/2015/11/19/is-aziz-ansaris-master-of-none-the-show-that-aging-millennials-have-been-waiting-for/.

Hess, A. (2016, December 6). The best new podcasts of 2016. *The New York Times.* Retrieved from https://www.nytimes.com/2016/12/06/arts/best-podcasts.html.

Ismail, A. (2017, May 22). The most radical thing about *Master of None*'s Islam episode is that it isn't about religion. *Slate.* Retrieved from http://www.slate.com/blogs/browbeat/2017/05/22/master_of_none_s_religion_episode_isn_t_about_islam.html.

Izadi, E. (2017, May 22). How *Master of None*'s religion episode proves that the show is like nothing else on TV. *The Washington Post.* Retrieved July 6, 2018, from https://www.

washingtonpost.com/news/arts-and-entertainment/wp/2017/05/22/how-master-of-nones-religion-episode-proves-that-the-show-is-like-nothing-else-on-tv/.

Jamal, A. A., & Naber, N. (Eds.). (2008). *Race and Arab Americans before and after 9/11: From invisible citizens to visible subjects.* Syracuse: Syracuse University Press.

Kadakia, C. (2015, November 18). Why watching Aziz Ansari's *Master of None* will teach you more about millennials than a thousand whitepapers. *Huffington Post.* Retrieved from https://www.huffingtonpost.com/crystal-kadakia/why-watching-azizansaris_b_8839286.html.

Malik, N. (2017, May 6). I am not your Muslim. NPR Code Switch. Retrieved from https://www.npr.org/sections/codeswitch/2017/05/06/485548424/i-am-not-your-muslim.

Musiker, C. (2015, November 21). Pulitzer Prize winning playwright on Islamophobia and religious extremism. KQED. Retrieved from https://www.kqed.org/arts/11097055/pulitzer-prize-winning-playwright-on-islamophobia-and-religious-extremism.

Niazi, A. (2017, May 18). *Master of None*'s religion episode is the most honest portrayal of modern Islam on TV. *Vice.* Retrieved from https://www.vice.com/en_ca/article/d7ae9a/master-of-nones-religion-episode-is-the-most-honest-portrayal-of-modern-islam-on-tv.

Peek, L. (2011). *Behind the backlash: Muslim Americans After 9/11.* Philadelphia: Temple University Press.

Ryzik, M. (2016, November 30). Can television be fair to Muslims? *The New York Times.* Retrieved from https://www.nytimes.com/2016/11/30/arts/television/can-television-be-fair-to-muslims.html.

Tareen, S. (2017, June 1). Bacon & (un)belief: Religion & American secularism in *Master of None. The Aerogram.* Retrieved from http://theaerogram.com/bacon-unbelief-religion-american-secularism-in-master-of-none/.

Wallace, T. (2017, May 27). *Master of None* and the Rubik's Cube of Muslim representation on TV. Retrieved from https://medium.com/oddly-specific-criticisms/master-of-none-and-the-rubik-s-cube-of-muslim-representation-on-tv-79ebaf45f99d.

Yuan, J. (2017, April 30). Aziz Ansari wanted to be the great uniter and ended up an activist. Retrieved from http://www.vulture.com/2017/04/aziz-ansari-master-of-none-season-2.html.

Chapter Four

Quaring Queer Eye

Millennials, Moral Licensing,
Cleansing and the Queer Eye *Reboot*

Robert D. Byrd, Jr.

In February of 2018, Netflix released a revival of the 2003 reality makeover show, *Queer Eye for the Straight Guy*. The new iteration, *Queer Eye*, resembles the original in many ways. Five gay men are sent on missions to makeover straight guys—wardrobe, culture, home, food and heart, and in the meantime the cast and the guest teach the audience lessons about life, love, humility, or, maybe even, politics. The *Queer Eye (QE)* reboot does have two major changes—the cast and location. The original "Fab Five" are out and replaced by: Bobby Berk, interior design; Karamo Brown, culture; Tan France, fashion; Antoni Porowski, food and wine; Jonathan Van Ness, grooming. The new cast represents a new generation of gay fashion, food and lifestyle gurus, but the new cast resembles the original in that all are cisgender gay men, three white men and two men of color. Additionally, the show made a pretty big move from New York to Atlanta for the 2018 reboot. The change in location is probably more a consequence of budgetary issues than anything else, but the dynamic of the "Fab Five" in Southern straight men's homes is interesting.

What this revival, like many others, does is allow previous fans of the show a new outlet to watch and continue their fandom, but, probably more importantly, it opens the show to a new generation of fans. The idea of a television show revival or reboot is nothing new. The mid-2010's surge in revivals, reboots, reunions and spin-offs is not new, but what is new is the change from traditional broadcasting modes to an era of "Peak TV," a term used to describe the sheer volume of television programming available to consumers through traditional network television as well as streaming ser-vices like Netflix, Hulu, and Amazon Prime (Loock, 2018a).

The current trend is so pervasive that the academic journal *Television & New Media* in 2018 dedicated a special issue to American television series revivals. Researchers in the issue examined several television revivals like: *Gilmore Girls* (The WB/The CW, 2000–2007) (Lizardi, 2018), *Full House* (ABC, 1987–1995) (Loock, 2018b) and *The X-Files* (Fox, 1993–2002) (Brinker, 2018). Loock (2018a) argued the revivals are a central feature to "Peak TV" because the name recognition cuts through the overcrowded tele-vision programming market (Loock, 2018a). Netflix seems to be leading the way in the revival market because it "promotes a nostalgic and arguably less challenging mode of viewing (in terms of form and content)" (Loock, 2018a, p. 305). What differs about the *Queer Eye* revival is that it, unlike many of the other revivals, is not a scripted comedy or drama. *QE* is a makeover reality show—a reality show with a new cast and scene. The revival was successful. Netflix released season two of the revival later in 2018 just a few months after season one dropped.

This chapter, however, is not about the success of Netflix revivals—or really about the recent trend of revivals in television. The trend is an impor-tant contextual backdrop to understanding the discourse in the television program. The purpose of this chapter is to examine the *Queer Eye* reboot through a quare theory lens to problematize the neoliberal, heterosexist and racist representations of race, racism and queer identity. The original *Queer Eye for the Straight Guy*, as you will see later in the chapter, received its fair share of academic criticism—but did show producers and creators learn from those critiques? I would argue that many of the same issues with the original iteration are still in the new show, but with possibly a few new twists. *Queer Eye*, in an effort to present all walks of life and all views, actually creates an outlet for moral licensing and cleansing for its viewers—giving its viewers the moral high ground to support and promote issues, politicians and points of view detrimental to LGBTQ people of color—specifically black LGBTQ people.

QUARE THEORY

To more closely examine the issue of race in the reboot of *Queer Eye* (*QE*), I employed a quare reading of the program. Quare theory, introduced by E. Patrick Johnson (2001), challenged queer theory for its homogenizing effects on queer identity—privileging cisgender, white gay queerness above all oth-er identities. Johnson (2001) claimed quare theory is a "theory of and for gays and lesbians of color" (p. 3). By incorporating race and class as catego-ries of sexuality, quare theory offers a tool to interrogate hegemonic whiteness in queer spaces—something Johnson argued has not traditionally been done in queer studies (2001). Quare theory then works to acknowledge the differences between groups, avoiding creation of a monolithic queer identity, which Johnson (2001) argued queer theory works to do. Johnson acknowledges that queer theory has opened new doors and possibilities in gender and sexuality research, but, at the same time, queer theory "like a pot of gumbo cooked too quickly, it has failed to live up to its full critical potential by refusing to accommodate all the queer ingredients contained inside its theoretical pot" (p. 18).

Previous media critics have employed quare theory to read queer film and television programing. Eguchi, Calafell and Files-Thompson (2014) argued that a quare reading of the film *Noah's Arc: Jumping the Broom* allowed the researchers to "further locate the racialized, gendered, and class knowledge(s) of GLBTQ members of color within the academic discourse" (p. 373). Eguchi et al. (2014) posited queer researchers must continue to question the ways in which LGBTQ people of color are discussed or positioned in queer politics and academic discourse: "By addressing these questions, hopefully, the academic discourse of GLBTQ members of color will play as praxis to go beyond academia" (Eguchi et al., 2014, p. 386). This praxis is a key piece of Johnson's (2001) argument for quare theory—as bridging of academic discourse to political praxis.

Additionally, Rodriguez (2018) used quare theory in a reading of Fox's television program *Empire*, specifically the character Jamal, a black, gay, male, wealthy, hip-hop artist. Rodriguez argued that while *Empire* offered a somewhat unheard narrative of a black gay man struggling to make it in the world of hip-hop, it did so without addressing "the lived experiences of racism, poverty, sexism, and misogyny experienced by a majority of black America" (2018, p. 238). Quare theory provided a lens to examine the ways *Empire* did and did not address the racialized and classed sexuality of the show's gay character (Rodriguez, 2018).

Another important piece of Johnson's (2001) argument for quare theory calls for queer researchers to own up to the privilege from which they critique. In way of full reflexivity, I want to own my privilege as a cisgender, white, gay man whose quare reading of *Queer Eye* is obviously influenced by my own lived experiences and racialized and class identities. With that being said, my goal here in this chapter is to examine and interrogate whiteness and privilege in *Queer Eye*, especially in its presentation of LGBTQ people of color and issues of race and racism.

QE BACKGROUND: A HISTORY OF THE FAB FIVE

The year 2003 was labeled by media outlets as the "Year of the Queer" because of the U.S. Supreme Court decision in Lawrence v. Texas, which declared sodomy laws unconstitutional, and because of the popularity of shows like *Will & Grace* and the newly launched *Queer Eye for the Straight Guy*. Bravo TV went from a largely unknown arts and culture network on the outskirts of cable television to the top of the ratings charts with a new reality makeover show, *Queer Eye for the Straight Guy*. Bravo, affiliated with NBC under the larger umbrella of Universal, landed a moneymaker in *Queer Eye for the Straight Guy*, and critics and viewers, along with advertisers, fawned over the show. Although the show provided a mainstream television outlet for a nearly invisible group, gay men, it often did so by ignoring the overarching heteronormative hegemony at play in society (Papacharissi & Fernback, 2008; Westerfelhaus & Lacroix, 2006; Clarkson, 2005).

Westerfelhaus and Lacroix (2006) critically examined the first two seasons of *Queer Eye for the Straight Guy* to shed light on what they termed a "strategic rhetoric of heteronormativity," which speaks to the natural or normal status given to heterosexuals and heterosexuality in culture, law, politics, religion and "social understandings of human sexuality" (p. 428). They argue that the typical episode of *Queer Eye for the Straight Guy* "functions as a ritual that supports the sociosexual order while seeming to challenge the order's heterosexist attitudes and values." In other words, the show intends to challenge the dominant view of queer individuals and problematize heteronormativity through visibility. In actuality, the content further perpetuates the dominant social order, which privileges the heterosexual as natural and normal and relegates queer sex to dirty, criminal and unnatural. The five protagonists of *Queer Eye for the Straight Guy*, the researchers argued, are given a brief pass within the heterosexual hegemony to violate some boundaries with the understanding that they will not go too far and that they will eventually return to status quo. They contend, "Rather than threatening the dominant order, such rituals actually promote social stability, even as they seem to challenge it. They do so by reaffirming the values and reasserting the social structure of the dominant order" (p. 430).

Therefore, they argue the Fab Five contested the hierarchy with homoerotic innuendo, touching and teasing, but failed to actually upset the hierarchy by stopping short of challenging the sociosexual hegemony (Westerfelhaus & Lacroix, 2006). Similarly, Papacharissi and Fernback (2008) claim that *Queer Eye*'s departure from the heteronormative—it reversed the typical role of the gay man in society where the gay characters had a dominant role over the straight men—was a rouse. The presence of dominant gay characters appeared to transgress the dominant heteronormative status quo and hail the homonormative alternative but fell short.

Papacharissi and Fernback (2008) also argued that although there appear to be homonormative discourses present in the show, the dominant hetero-normative power structures are "ultimately reinforced." They claim the role reversal present in *Queer Eye* "advertises a veneer of homonormativity," but the text ultimately marginalizes the queer characters into traditional hetero-sexist categories that negatively portray gay men or stereotype them as more feminine. The gay men in the show are experts at grooming, housekeeping, decorating, cooking and culture, which paints them into the realm of the feminine and does nothing to subordinate the dominant heterosexist vision of homosexuality.

According to Papacharissi and Fernback (2008), the show also complicat-ed the relationship between the gay characters and the straight men they are making over. The show presented the relationships as positive, but transient. There is no inclination that the relationships have lasting power, rather they are only the product of an unusual or extraordinary situation—they are not normal in the heterosexual sense. Ultimately, Papacharissi and Fernback (2008) argued the reality show was designed and aired to appeal to a wide variety of viewers. The researchers refer to the "polysemic structure" of the show as a source of its attraction to a wide mainstream audience. In other words, because so many different meanings could be attached to the show from different people, it appealed to both straight and queer audiences, which, in turn, appealed to advertisers.

Clarkson (2005) argued that the financial success of the original *Queer Eye* created a new masculinity—a consumer-driven masculinity that rein-forces high levels of consumption. *QE* appeared, according to Clarkson, to contest heteronormative masculinity, but does so by idealizing "American manhood as one that is predicated on effete style and taste and mandates a visually upper-class identity as a key component of hegemonic masculinity" (p. 252). This new image of American masculinity works to reify white, urban, heterosexual masculinity as the norm.

This "new" masculinity also found foes within the gay male commu-nity—those who claimed the show excluded the traditionally masculine gay viewpoint or identity. These gay men do not see *Queer Eye* as the bright, shining example of gay representation that others may have trumpeted in 2003. They also reject the show based on patriarchal, heteromasculine norms that have been used against queer people for decades (Clarkson, 2005). Clarkson argued that the *Queer Eye for the Straight Guy* masculinity created competing masculinities, but did not actually transgress hegemonic mascu-linity to the point of a complete reimagining or more inclusive masculinity. Instead it bolstered some form of the hegemony by privileging either hetero-masculine norms or by privileging consumption and class-based exclusion from the norm (Clarkson, 2005). Much of the previous research on the first iteration of *Queer Eye for the Straight Guy* focuses on issues of class, masculinity and sexuality with no significant amount of attention paid to the inter-section of race with sexuality, class and gender presentation (Booth, 2011; Lewis, 2007; Pearson & Lozano-Reich, 2009; Sender, 2006; Weiss, 2005). Since the early 2000s, more researchers have begun to pay attention to the intersectionality of LGBTQ representations on television programming. The next section reviews some of that literature.

BLACK AND QUEER ON TELEVISION

The history of black queer characters on television is short. In the history of LGBTQ representations in the media, but especially in television, queer peo-ple of color have been largely excluded. While overall representation of queer people of color in broadcast television has improved, that trend is fairly new. GLAAD in its 2018–2019 "Where We are on TV" report found that 44 percent of LGBTQ recurring characters in broadcast television are people of color—22 percent black (GLAAD, 2018). This is the most since the organ-ization began tracking representations in 2005. In 2008, GLAAD reported that 22 percent of LGBTQ characters on television were persons of color, 11 percent of which were black. These data include all regularly occurring char-acters on television—not main characters of the shows. The data also does not account for the quality of representation presented to viewers.

Previous research on media representations of black gay men, for exam-ple, often find similar tropes in representation. Riggs (1991) argued that many of the representations dilute black gay characters to jokes, festishized bodies, cartoon caricatures, or "disco diva(s) adored from a distance" (p. 252). Riggs' critique of media representations in the 1970s and 1980s held true through the early 2000s as well. Yep and Elia (2012) argued that *Noah's Arc*, one of the few if not only shows built around black gay characters, worked to reify white supremacy through sanitized representations of race, gender and class to make the show and characters more palatable for white audiences. The show relied on the trope of black hypermasculine bodies with "mythically proportioned manhood" (Perez, 2005, p. 185). In the end, re-searchers concluded that *Noah's Arc* provided a heterosexist view of race and masculinity and relied on tropes that made white, middle-class viewers com-fortable and made the show relatable to their preconceived notions of race and sexuality (Yep & Elia, 2012; Eguchi, Calafell & Files-Thompson, 2014).

More recent representations of black queer characters on television have found much of the same. Rodriguez (2018) argued that queer representations in *Empire* worked to reify a "black masculinity that is homophobic and effemiphobic" (p. 237). *Empire,* while presenting a black gay man trying to make it in the hip-hop industry, fails to grapple the issues of racism, poverty, homophobia, misogyny and sexism faced by the black community—and in the end bolstered the heteronormative status quo (Rodriguez, 2018).

The history of black queer characters on television is brief but important in understanding millennial-era representations in programming. What makes this analysis interesting is the reboot of a television program that offered very little in the way of diverse representations of the LGBTQ people—as seen by the previous research critiquing the early 2000s version of *Queer Eye*. So, what has changed with a reboot aimed at a new generation of viewers? It is probably important to first understand what the new generation of viewers thinks about race.

MILLENNIALS AND RACE

As a generation, millennials seem to pose a problem or at least questions for advertisers, politicians, and generally anyone tracking trends among various age groups in American society. One of the trends often referred to by both journalists and researchers when dissecting the millennial worldview is their level of racial resentment or comfort with diversity (Taylor & Keeter, 2010; Appolon, 2011; Maxwell & Schulte, 2018). Millennials as a group have often been dubbed the "post-racial" generation because of their role in electing Barack Obama in 2008 and 2012, but also because of their self-reported acceptance and embrace of diversity, equity and multi-racial identities (Appolon, 2011). This view offers a somewhat superficial view of the millennial outlook on race and racial resentment. Maxwell and Shulte (2018) argued that while millennials do report a substantial amount of racial resentment—their levels are significantly lower than those of their parents. The researchers add that increased levels of education among millennials could account for some of this change, but "the racial attitudes of their parents are still a very strong influence on their own racial attitudes" (Maxwell & Shulte, 2018, p. 196).

Taylor and Keeter (2010) suggested that this change in racial attitudes may only reflect millennials' feelings toward overt forms of racism—an attitude that may be more in line with what is socially acceptable. However, there is no evidence to suggest there is a reduction in more covert or subtle forms of racism (Taylor & Keeter, 2010). It's not difficult to imagine that while millennials would reject overt racism because those forms are less socially acceptable, an adherence or tolerance for covert racism would be just as prevalent as previous generations given the influence of familial attitudes. In other words, millennials could have an outward appearance of being "woke" while still harboring some of the same attitudes as their parents and grandparents. Most Americans generally try to avoid feeling or appearing prejudiced, but they can be tempted to express those views or actions in regard to certain situations (Crandall & Eshleman, 2003). This apparent desire to appear unprejudiced while simultaneously displaying behavior that suggests otherwise seems counterintuitive but may be better explained by social psychology theory.

MORAL LICENSING

Social psychologists have recently begun examining the phenomenon of moral licensing, which "refers to the effect that when people initially behave in a moral way, they are later more likely to display behaviors that are immoral, unethical, or otherwise problematic" (Blanken, van de Ven & Zeelenberg, 2015, p. 540). Moral licensing, Merritt, Effron, and Monin (2010) argued, allows people to derive confidence in their morality from previous good deeds—even when their current actions may come under fire. Also, moral licensing works in the reverse as well "when one appears immoral to others, subsequent positive actions are needed to restore the moral image (leading to compensation or cleansing)" (Blanken, van de Ven & Zeelenberg, 2015, p. 541). By creating a moral bank account of sorts, one can move in and out of dubious behavior without feeling the stress involved in making prejudiced decisions (Cascio & Plan, 2015). People are less likely to behave morally after they've made a moral decision, but also are more likely to behave morally if they know they may need to behave in a dubious manner in the near future (Merrit, Effron & Monin, 2010). What happens here is a sort of mental gymnastics that does not really make the person feel as though they've been forgiven for transgressions, but that they've not actually committed a transgression at all (Merrit, Effron & Monin, 2010).

Previous research regarding moral licensing has examined everything from likelihood to donate to charitable organizations to racial prejudice (Merritt, Effron & Monin, 2010; Blanken, van de Ven & Zeelenberg, 2015; Effron, Cameron & Monin, 2009). In their initial study, Effron, Cameron and Monin (2009) argued that people who voted for Barack Obama in the 2008 presidential election generally felt more comfortable sharing or expressing prejudiced views after the election. By showing that they were willing to support a black political candidate, which psychologically established them as unprejudiced, white supporters were more willing to transgress in the future. Their vote for Obama gave them a moral license to behave in an immoral way later because of the moral action they performed in the past (Effron, Cameron & Monin, 2009).

In addition to self-licensing, Kouchaki (2011) argued that people often feel licensed by others' good deeds. Kouchaki (2011) found that others' past moral behavior influences an individual's future behavior. This vicarious moral licensing applies to other in-group participants. So, if a person feels that someone in their group has performed a moral behavior, they may be more likely to display prejudiced or unethical behaviors in the future. As Kouchaki observed, "This indicates that past behavior is not the only means by which a person's moral credentials are established. People can acquire moral credentials through their group membership" (p. 713). This may be a way to understand how someone maybe licenses through a show like *Queer Eye*. The program's good deeds are used as a way to license and cleanse for one's own future or past transgressions, which begs the question: Can TV and media provide a way to bank vicarious moral actions through parasocial interactions with in-group actors/presenters? Moral licensing theory has not been used in a media critique, but it could be a vehicle to examine the consumption of racial and sexual representations in a different way.

EPISODE 3, SEASON 1: "DEGA DON'T"

This analysis specifically focuses on Episode 3 of Season 1 of the *QE* reboot. I want to take some space here to give a synopsis of the episode, which I will follow with an analysis in later sections of the chapter. The episode, titled "Dega Don't," focused on "hero" Cory Waldrop, a cisgender, white, straight cop and military veteran. This specific episode is filmed, in part, in Cory's hometown of Winder, Georgia—a town of about 15,000 people located nearly 50 miles northeast of Atlanta. "Hero" is what the show calls the men receiving the makeovers. Each episode features a new hero. Each hero has his own story, which is generally used to teach some sort of lesson or to provide some sort of new experience for not only the hero himself but also the five show hosts. In episode three, the Fab Five are set to makeover Cory, who is presented as a Donald Trump–supporting cop with an affinity for NASCAR. Actually, he is a NASCAR super fan hence the name of the episode, which is a reference to the NASCAR track in Talladega, Alabama. The five hosts are tasked with breaking Cory out of his "comfort zone" of "gym shorts, T-shirts, and flip flops" and his Talladega- and NASCAR-inspired costumes (O'Rourke, Woodbeck & Ortiz, 2018).

The Woke Joke

"Dega Don't" begins like nearly all of the *QE* episodes with the hosts driving along in the signature SUV discussing the current "hero" and watching video footage of the contestant talk about their fashion choices and their lifestyle. In this particular episode, Karamo Brown, the only black cast member, drives while the group discusses and cracks jokes about the hero. Suddenly, blue lights appear with the sound of an accompanying siren. Someone in the truck announces to the audience: "Oh my god no. We're getting pulled over. The question is why were we pulled over?" A white cop approaches the vehicle window asking for a driver's license from Karamo, who does not have it on him because he's in the middle of filming the show. The cop, who introduces himself as Officer Ford, returns to the vehicle and asks Karamo to exit despite objections from Karamo and other cast members. There's notable distress on the face of Karamo, who stands next to the vehicle as Ford announces that he nominated Cory for the show and the entire traffic stop is a stunt or prank for the show. The cast breaks into laughter as they pile out of the vehicle to greet Ford.

Since season one's release, several opinion pieces have been written lauding this particular episode for sparking a tough conversation about race and policing. Stories began circulating regarding the behind-the-scenes of the opening of the episode, with cast members recalling what was going through their minds as Karamo was asked to exit the vehicle without reason. Apparently, the contrived traffic stop was not received well by the cast members, who at first, according to reports, refused to finish recording the episode (Ernsberger, 2018). But even still, the "joke" was seen by white producers as a necessary evil for the greater good of a perceived deeper conversation and experience. Karamo Brown told a reporter, "It turned into something great" (Thompson, 2018).

The "joke," contrived by white show producers with help from a white cop and a white cast member, was made at the expense of a black man with no regard for the real trauma a situation like this could trigger. Buzzfeed reported in February 2018 that Southern white cast member Bobby Berk, the interior design expert, had been informed of the "joke" by producers before the cast set out on the drive (Flaherty, 2018). What's even more problematic is that there is admission in this joke—an admission of the racism in policing in the United States and that a black man would and should be fearful of being pulled over by a white cop and asked to exit a vehicle without a stated reason. Even after acknowledging the potential trauma of the situation, producers still followed through with a contrived scenario that makes light of the disregard for black bodies by police. So, what was the purpose of the joke? Was it really to start a conversation about race and policing? If so, couldn't this be achieved in a manner that does not manipulate a black man's fear and emotions?

I would argue that the producers did not see the "joke" as a problem because they have somehow managed to separate themselves from institutions that disregard black bodies—institutions like law enforcement. The producers probably see themselves as "woke" individuals—the kind of "wokeness" that would accompany producing a show about five gay men making over straight guys in the South. By separating themselves from the racist structures at play in society, they claim an absolution from the problem—they individually are not racist, so they are not part of the problem.

Producers have performed the mental gymnastics to morally license themselves to contrive a traumatic situation, laugh at that situation without addressing how problematic it is, and then use it to further license and cleanse themselves and viewers from the racism that they have just washed over. There's an undercurrent to this "joke" which implies that "a racist person wouldn't laugh at this joke; a racist would deny that this happens at all." The show's opening, however, does not work alone in this episode. The remainder of the episode continues this thread of individual racial views versus systematic racism and moral licensing/cleansing of those on the show and, through vicarious means, the show's audience as well.

"But I Listen to Wu-Tang"

The contrived traffic stop is used as a launch point for a conversation about police brutality against people of color and specifically black men. Throughout the episode, Karamo and Cory's (the police officer) conversations are seemingly designed for the two to find common ground—from Karamo's near enlistment in the military to Cory's love of Bone Thugs-n-Harmony and The Wu-Tang Clan. In one conversation, Karamo declared that the two would have been friends in high school, which leads to the following exchange:

Karamo: The perception right now especially between black people and cops, it's tension. When, uh, Henry pulled us over.

Cory: Yeah.

Karamo: I immediately I started freaking out. I really thought this is gonna be that incident where I was gonna get dragged out.

(*Cut to shot of Karamo talking to Cory listening, and back to Karamo.*)

Karamo: My kid did not wanna get his license. He was scared he was gonna get pulled over and get shot by a cop. (Queer Eye Episode Script, 2018)

Karamo and Cory continued the conversation with Cory acknowledging that some cops are excessive in their force, but that not all cops are like that.

Cory: And all police officers don't wanna be lumped into being the bad guy. I get stereotyped because of that 10 percent . . . that gets shown on the media of, you know, being excessive or killing, you know, a black guy that didn't need to have deadly force used upon him. (Queer Eye Episode Script, 2018)

Cory likened the pain cops experience from the "stereotyping" to the pain black people feel at the loss of life and civil freedoms.

> Cory: It does go both ways. And I'm glad you feel that way. Black lives mattered. They weren't able to be heard. And the police weren't heard. If we could have a conversation like me and you just did, things would be a lot better, you know, in society. (Queer Eye Episode Script, 2018)

The exchange ended with Karamo's confessional-style interview—just him on camera reflecting on the experience:

> Karamo: The beauty of what is happening is that I'm open, and I'm going to stay open, because I need him to learn from me, I need to learn from him. Because right now, our country, it just seems like it's getting worse and worse and worse. And it has to start somewhere. I'm not saying a conversation with one police officer and one gay guy will solve the problems, but maybe it can open up eyes to something more. (Queer Eye Episode Script, 2018)

The conversation between the two during a drive from Atlanta, where they had been shopping for clothes, became a talking point throughout the remainder of the episode—one of the moments of epiphany for both Cory, the hero, and Karamo, the black gay cast member.

The centerpiece of the racial reconciliation set up in this episode happens during this drive from Atlanta to Winder. Cory is given the platform to make equivalencies that paint police as victims of excessive force, the media fallout of wrongful death cases, and the "stereotypes" of overzealous policing. Again, the conversation worked to separate individuals from racist societal systems. In other words, Cory constructs bad policing as a few bad apples who tarnish the name of good police, who he argued accounts for 90 percent of police. His evidence for this equivalency and assertion—he listened to Bone Thugs-n-Harmony and Wu-Tang Clan when he was in high school. What his defense of policing and cops doesn't account for are the numbers and the history. In 2012, black people accounted for 31 percent of people killed by police even though only 13 percent of the population is black (Lopez, 2018). The disparity is even higher when looking at the percentage of unarmed people killed by police. People of color account for nearly 70 percent of unarmed people killed by police (Lopez, 2018).

What is even more alarming in the episode is that Cory's defense is presented and received as legitimate. What his false equivalency doesn't account for is power and that racism goes beyond the individual to structures of power. Be equating individual cops, or individual white people to individual black people without mentioning the societal systems at play, the conversation eliminates years of oppression, sanctioned racism, structural racism, inequalities and inequities, and it puts the onus on individuals. Cory's logic goes like this: he's not racist because he likes black music, he's a cop that doesn't like when other cops do bad things, most cops he knows are like him, he is not racist so cops are not racists, and the issue of excessive policing is the problem of a few not a problem with the system or with white society at large. The misconstruction of racism presents excessive policing as a problem of the black community, something black people have to figure out, and not a problem of the white community or at least "woke" white folk. The privilege of dissociating himself from the majority or from a pervasive system goes unquestioned. Again, this conversation is an example of moral licensing. Showing some former association with black culture or what he sees as non-racist behavior allows Cory to deny racism in law enforcement and to equivocate his perceived struggles with the real struggles of people of color. He also provides for the audience a vicarious license, a way to take the moral high ground through another's actions. Cory is most likely someone many in the audience can relate to in one way or the other whether gay or straight. Therefore, he provides the ideal vehicle for vicarious licensing.

The Big Reveal

The final chapter of the episode, just like all episodes of *Queer Eye*, includes the big reveal. The cast members meet up at the Fab Five loft to watch via closed-circuit television as the hero shows off his new skills. This time the cast members are joined by several of Cory's cop and NASCAR friends. The cast members and friends watch as Cory shows his wife and daughters the new clothes and the home makeover, and they listen as Cory recounts his conversation with Karamo.

> Cory: For some reason, I think Karamo and I hit it off really well. I think that ride from Atlanta to Winder kind of did it.
>
> Karamo: [Cut from Cory and his wife talking to the Fab Five lounge where the five hosts are with several of Cory's cop and NASCAR friends.] That ride changed my life and my heart. I kind of hated you cops before. It kind of warmed me up to you all.
>
> Ford (cop from the beginning of the episode): It's understandable. (Queer Eye Episode Script, 2018)

As the episode comes to an end, Karamo offers a moment of reflection about the episode to the audience. Again in a confessional-style interview, Karamo explains that he learned a lot from the episode.

Karamo: When I initially met Cory, I was very closed off to him. I was like, "Cory, me? Nah, not happening." Luckily, we were in this environment where I gave him a shot. I would've missed out on a really amazing guy because of these labels that we've put up on each other that, you know, we really should be breaking down. (Queer Eye Episode Script, 2018)

The show's producers have created a story line that presents a utopian model for race relations in the United States—a conversation void of a discussion about racism and homophobia in policing, the dangers black bodies face in the United States, and the actual solutions to these issues. The story shifts responsibility of the problem from police and white Americans to the black and POC (people of color) communities. By shirking the responsibility for the problem and the responsibility for solving the problem, white viewers can absolve and cleanse themselves from any culpability in racist institutions responsible for the destruction of black bodies. This shift in responsibility can be seen in both Cory and Karamo's recap of the episode. Cory said "for some reason" he and Karamo hit it off, but Karamo described the experiences as life changing. The incongruity spoke further to the show's assertion that excessive policing is an issue of the black community and not an issue of white society and racist policing tactics. Cory just had a good time and made a black friend while Karamo had a life-changing incident and experience— something that caused him to look at the world through a different lens. Cory acknowledged that he was friends with one black man based on some perceived commonalities and a couple of conversations. Karamo excused a group a people from culpability in a murderous system because he met one white cop who listened and admitted that some police are bad. The burden of understanding and reconciliation was placed on Karamo. He had to change. He had to "see the light." By creating this incongruity in responsibility, the show provides a moral-cleansing moment for Cory and the white audience viewing the episode. In effect, it tells viewers that white people only need to be open to a conversation, but black people and other people of color need to be willing and able to change.

This cleansing comes predominantly from Karamo's seal of approval. He officially signs off on the logic, argument and equivalencies presented by Cory throughout the episode. His endorsement even goes so far to suggest that the process should be repeated by other black men and cops in other places and situations. Karamo's endorsement licenses white transgressions against people of color. They can go on feeling "woke" not only because they see themselves as some anomaly in a racist system, but now a black man has told them that they're not racist or problematic. They've been absolved from responsibility, they've been allowed to relate to the oppression felt by people of color, and now they've received an official endorsement.

REIFYING THE STATUS QUO

The aim of this study was to examine the moral licensing and cleansing present in the *Queer Eye* reboot, in particular the specific episode "Dega Don't." The episode, though heralded as a statement on race relations in the United States, worked to license white America to shirk responsibility for racist policing tactics and structures that work to further oppress and destroy black bodies. The episode worked first to minimize the danger and trauma of excessive policing by making a "joke" of the problematic police tactics, then worked to equivocate the struggles of black Americans with the perceived or claimed struggles of police, and finally presented excessive policing as a problem of the black community.

Much like previous shows featuring black queer characters, *QE* works to reify and bolster the heteronormative status quo—privileging white, cisgender, straight men in power and structures and systems of power dominated by those same white, cisgender, straight men. Perhaps even more problematic is this particular show's positioning as a conduit for queer representations and a vehicle to challenge heteronormative racial, gender and sexual assumptions. However, like in the original *Queer Eye for the Straight Guy*, *Queer Eye* is aimed more at comforting the white, cisgender straight audience, and providing for that audience a moral license to maintain current racists, classist and homophobic structures that work to maintain heteronormative dominance. As a reboot, *Queer Eye* offers a new generation exposure to a previously successful program (Loock, 2018a). Interestingly, this reboot seems to also be specifically geared to its new millennial viewers. By examining racism as an overt individual issue rather than the more covert, systematic oppression of people of color, millennial viewers are allowed to continue to view themselves as less prejudiced than their parents or grandparents despite their racial resentment and inaction on changing the systems of inequity and inequality.

REFERENCES

Appolon, D. (2011). Don't call them "post-racial": Millennials say race matters to them. Color-lines. Retrieved from https://www.colorlines.com/articles/dont-call-them-post-racial-millen-nials-say-race-matters-them.

Blanken, I., van de Ven, N., & Zeelenberg, M. (2015). A Meta-Analytic review of moral licensing. *Personality & Social Psychology Bulletin, 41*(4), 540–558.

Booth, E. T. (2011). Queering *Queer Eye*: The stability of gay identity confronts the liminality of trans embodiment. *Western Journal of Communication, 75*(2), 185–204.

Brinker, F. (2018). Conspiracy, procedure, continuity: Reopening *The X-Files. Television & New Media, 19*(4), 328–344.

Cascio, J., & Plant, E. P. (2015). Prospective moral licensing: Does anticipating doing good later allow you to be bad now? *Journal of Experimental Social Psychology, 56*, 110–116.

Clarkson, J. (2005). Contesting masculinity's makeover: *Queer Eye*, consumer masculinity, and "straight-acting" gays. *Journal of Communication Inquiry, 29*(3), 235–255. doi:10.1177/0196859905275234.

Crandall, C.S. & Escheman, A. (2003). A Justification–Suppression Model of the Expression and Experience of Prejudice. *Psychological Bulletin*, 129(3), 414-446.

Effron, D. A., Cameron, J. S., & Monin, B. (2009). Endorsing Obama licenses favoring whites. *Journal of Experimental Social Psychology*, *45*(3), 590–593. doi:10.1016/j.jesp.2009 .02.001.

Eguchi, S., Calafell, B. M., & Files-Thompson, T. N. (2014). Intersectionality and Quare Theory: Fantasizing African American male same-sex relationships in *Noah's Arc: Jumping the Broom*. *Communication, Culture & Critique, 7*(3), 371–389.

Ernsberger, P. (May 9, 2018). Tan France almost quit *Queer Eye* and you actually watched the moment play out without knowing it. Bustle.com. Retrieved from https://www.bustle.com/ p/tan-france-almost-quit-queer-eye-you-actually-watched-the-moment-play-out-without-knowing-it-9034664.

Flaherty, K. (February 12, 2018). Here's how they filmed the most intense episode of *Queer Eye*. BuzzFeed.com. Retrieved from https://www.buzzfeed.com/keelyflaherty/yes-that-tense-police-officer-scene-in-queer-eye-was-real.

GLAAD (2018). *2018–2019 Where we are on TV*. New York: GLAAD.

Johnson, E. P. (2001). "Quare" studies, or (almost) everything I know about Queer Studies I learned from my grandmother. *Text & Performance Quarterly, 21*(1), 1–25.

Kouchaki, M. (2011). Vicarious moral licensing: The influence of others' past moral actions on moral behavior. *Journal of Personality & Social Psychology*, *101*(4), 702–715. doi:10.1037/ a0024552.

Lewis, T. (2007). "He needs to face his fears with these five queers!" *Television & New Media, 8*(4), 285–311.

Lizardi, R. (2018). Mourning and melancholia: Conflicting approaches to reviving *Gilmore Girls* one season at a time. *Television & New Media, 19*(4), 379–395.

Loock (a), K. (2018). American TV Series Revivals: Introduction. *Television & New Media, 19*(4), 299–309.

Loock, K. (2018). "Whatever happened to predictability?": *Fuller House*, (post)feminism, and the revival of family-friendly viewing. *Television & New Media, 19*(4), 361–378.

Lopez, G. (November 14, 2018). There are huge racial disparities in how US police use force. Vox.com. Retrieved from https://www.vox.com/identities/2016/8/13/17938186/police-shootings-killings-racism-racial-disparities.

Maxwell, A., & Schulte, S. R. (2018). Racial resentment attitudes among white millennial youth: The influence of parents and media. *Social Science Quarterly, 99*: 1183–1199. doi:10.1111/ssqu.12488.

Merritt, A., Effron, D. & Monin, B. (2010). Moral self-licensing: When being good frees us to be bad. *Social and Personality Psychology Compass* [serial online] *4*(5): 344–357.

Papacharissi, Z., & Fernback, J. (2008). The aesthetic power of the Fab 5. *Journal of Communication Inquiry*, *32*(4), 348–367.

Pearson, K., & Lozano-Reich, N. M. (2009). Cultivating queer publics with an uncivil tongue: *Queer Eye*'s critical performances of desire. *Text & Performance Quarterly, 29*(4), 383–402.

Perez, H. (2005). You can have my brown body and eat it, too. In D. Eng, J. Halberstam & J. E. Muñoz (Eds.), *What's queer about queer studies now?* (pp. 171–192). Durham, NC: Duke University Press.

Queer Eye Episode Script. (2018). "Dega Don't." Retrieved at https://www. springfieldspringfield.co.uk/view_episode_scripts.php?tv-show=queer-eye-2018&episode= s01e03.

Riggs, M. (1991). Tongues untied. In *Brother to brother: New writings by Black gay men* (pp. 249 255). Boston: Alyson Publications, Inc.

Rodriguez, N. S. (2018). Hip-Hop's authentic masculinity: A Quare reading of Fox's *Empire*. *Television & New Media, 19*(3), 225–240.

Sender, K. (2006). Queens for a day: *Queer Eye for the Straight Guy* and the neoliberal project. *Critical Studies in Media Communication, 23*(2), 131–151.

Taylor, P. & Keeter S. (2010). *Millennials: A Portrait of Generation Next*. Washington, DC: Pew Center Research. Retrieved from: https://www.pewresearch.org/2009/12/10/the-millennials/.

Thompson, C. (2018). The story behind the most tense episode of *Queer Eye*. Whimn.com.au. Retrieved from: https://www.whimn.com.au/play/unwind/the-story-behind-the-most-tense-episode-of-queer-eye/news-story/a077ec3e2688cae4428fde423db0b7d5.

Weiss, D. (2005). Constructing the queer "I": Performativity, citationality, and desire in *Queer Eye for the Straight Guy*. *Popular Communication, 3*(2), 73–95.

Westerfelhaus, R., & Lacroix, C. (2006). Seeing "straight" through *Queer Eye*: Exposing the strategic rhetoric of heteronormativity in a mediated ritual of gay rebellion. *Critical Studies in Media Communication, 23*(5), 426–444.

Yep, G. A., & Elia, J. P. (2012). Racialized masculinities and the new homonormativity in LOGO'S *Noah's Arc*. *Journal of Homosexuality*, 59(7), 890-911.

Chapter Five

#BaltimoreUprising

*Race, Representation and Millennial
Engagement in Digital Media*

Cheryl Jenkins

A 2017 survey of media diversity and inclusion in traditional American newsrooms shows a continued lag in the representation of African American news producers. The numbers are discouraging and show that although non-whites make up about 40 percent of the population in the United States, journalists of color make up about 16.55 percent of newsroom staffs (ASNE, 2017). Efforts by the American mainstream media to recruit and hire more minority journalists have traditionally garnered minimal results. Although data show a slight increase in hiring numbers over the years, the fact is most newsrooms across the country do not reflect the demographic makeup of the communities they cover (Wilson, Gutierrez & Chao, 2003; Porter, 2004; Fleming-Rife & Proffitt, 2004; Dedman & Doig, 2005).

Because of the consistent lack of African American representation in traditional mainstream media, this group of media producers has historically found alternative ways to have their voices heard, most recently through digital formats (Jenkins, 2017). And, although the reports remain dismal for traditional newsroom representation, the 2017 Newsroom Employment Diversity Survey stated that digital news organizations have fared much better in their minority hiring efforts, which is a benefit for this group to reach the growing millennial population who are more likely to consume news through digital sources.

Research from the American Press Institute (API) found that across all groups millennials are far more interested in news and information than previously thought. Earlier findings suggested that millennials might be less curious or engaged in the world around them because they were less inclined to visit traditional news sources online or to consume traditional media in other platforms. The assumption was that they spent more time on social networks like Facebook. However, the API report titled "Race, Ethnicity and the Use of Social Media for News" (2015) stated that while social networks play a preeminent role in the digital lives of millennials, these networks are now far more than social: "Millennials are not only consuming news on these social networks; they are consuming more than they intended to when they go on the networks, they are engaging with the news, and they are being exposed to a wider range of topics and opinions than many suspect."

With a growing dependency on digital media, specifically among millennials, the historical leaning of African Americans and other minority groups in this country to use alternative modes of message dissemination when telling their stories may eventually help lessen the challenges of true media diversity in the United States. Additionally, as millennials become more engaged in news consumption, the significance of more inclusive media messaging becomes essential as this group is considered to be the most diverse and multicultural in the country (Hispanic Millennial Project, 2015). As such, this chapter examines how minority news producers have capitalized on alternative and digital media formats as a result of mainstream media's failure to incorporate more diversity in their newsrooms; it specifically examines coverage of protests in Baltimore after the the death of Freddie Gray in 2015. This essay addresses the growing influence of digital media, specifically social media, on the millennial population and how African American millennials in particular have been able to use the platform to add more diverse perspectives to news stories that tackle complex and sensitive subject matter like police brutality and racism.

CALL FOR DIVERSITY

Minority groups have historically found alternative ways to have their voices heard when faced with little to no inclusion in mainstream media outlets. The problematic trend in mainstream media is that it is less inclusive of voices outside of dominant power structures in society. As I once observed,

> With over 30,000 journalists covering the news in American mainstream media, the industry continues to fail in its efforts to diversify its newsrooms with fewer minorities getting the opportunity to work in news, and news organizations suffering in their ability to report on minority populations in their community. (Jenkins, 2017, p. 135)

Further, because mainstream media have traditionally not served communities of color, more journalists from that community have created alternative modes of disseminating news deemed significant to them. One example is the creation of the Black Press. This press has been traditionally known to take a more interpretive and sometimes subjective approach when reporting on events that affect African Americans; subsequently, the nuance that has been achieved from this type of journalism seems to transition well into the digital age in which the media now exist. Black websites and bloggers help bring attention to stories that almost never see the front pages of the American mainstream news media.

According to Love (2017), in the absence of an inclusive environment, the quality of journalism suffers:

> Certain stories are simply not reported, or are told without the nuance or perspective the circumstances require. The black press has filled that void for generations. And with the advent of digital platforms, a baton has been passed to black millennial writers to continue presenting narratives, with underrepresented points of views, that would otherwise go missing—and do not necessarily reflect the white men who dominate the industry.

The Kerner Commission actually challenged the mainstream news media to "diversify their workforces, news agendas, and reporting" over 40 years ago. Released in March 1968, the commission's report, officially titled the *Report of the National Advisory Commission on Civil Disorders*, addressed the role of mass media in the violence that erupted during more than 150 riots in dozens of U.S. cities the previous year. The commission recommended in its extensive report that the news media should "take a leadership role" in helping to reverse the lack of understanding in the general public about the plight of black America during the late 1960s. This, according to the commission, could be accomplished by "news organizations engaging in voluntary self-studies of their own news content, developing sources within the black community, and by assigning regular beat reporting within African American neighborhoods" (Byerly & Wilson, 2009, p. 212).

Creating a more inclusive media workforce continues to be a problem in the industry even though the addition of more people of color in mainstream newsrooms may aid in the conception of stories that deal with complex subject matter, like issues of race. Minority journalists bring unique perspectives to topics that personally affect their lives or the lives of people who look like them. And, although white journalists may have the intellectual capacity to tell these stories, Alexander (2011) argues that there is an unspoken question in many newsrooms of whether non-minority journalists can accurately portray the full reality of what minorities experience without exploiting—or being perceived as exploiting—those they seek to cover. Additionally problematic are the long-standing story assignment issues that crop up when it comes to assigning journalists of color stories about race. As Alexander writes, "While editors demand that journalists of color justify their reasons for wanting to cover stories about ethnic minorities or the underclass, in some instances the motives of white journalists seeking to report on those same topics go unquestioned" (p. 36).

Further, the individuals producing news stories have significant influence on how complex issues are corresponded in those stories. Although most journalists adhere to specific tenants of the craft (e.g., objectivity), the way they frame a story is ultimately how consumers of that information will understand the topic. Research suggests that mass media can contribute to sustaining and even strengthening prejudicial attitudes through different forms of bias, stereotypes and frames (Jenkins & Cole, 2011). Cultural influence and differences affect interpretations of media frames in a way that media scholars have highlighted in varying degrees. In particular, the treatment of race and issues of racism when covered by the media reveal intrinsic attitudes of media professionals that may be inherent in societal ideologies. Journalists all have their own personal identities, and those identities can become a part of how or what they write. This can be troubling as research suggests that a person's own ideology and previously held beliefs can be the strongest factor for negative racial attitudes (Gans, 1979). Those attitudes may eventually affect the context of the stories reporters produce.

The continued effort by the news industry to become a more inclusive environment has garnered some positive results over the years. The 2016 Radio Television Digital News Association/Hofstra University annual survey found that the minority workforce in television news rose to 23.1 percent. That was up almost a full point from the preceding year and is the second highest level ever in television news. The minority workforce at non-Hispanic television stations also went up to the second highest level ever. The only downturn was in radio.

As this news sounds promising for the industry's hiring efforts, still, as far as minorities are concerned, the bigger picture remains unchanged. For instance, as the Radio Television Digital News Association (RTDNA) reported in 2016, "In the last 26 years, the minority population in the U.S. has risen 11.8 points; but the minority workforce in TV news is up less than half that (5.3). And the minority workforce in radio is actually down by nearly a point and a half." Hiring efforts in media management positions were also dismal. The RTDNA repored that although slightly more minority general managers were hired, only half of that small increase came among the affiliated stations of the big four television networks, ABC, CBS, Fox and NBC.

With continued concerns related to minority hiring in the media industry, many journalists of color and news agencies that focus specifically on minority communities have chosen to once again find alternative ways to disseminate their messages. The use of digital platforms such as blogs, social media and podcasts has become a beneficial tool for minority journalists to remain a vital part of the media landscape. Pavlik (2000) argued that the use of newer technologies has challenged long-standing journalism norms, particularly with regards to journalists' workflow, news content, newsroom structure, and the relationship between journalists and "their many publics" (p. 229) as online and digital platforms provide the opportunity for a more balanced back-and-forth dialogue. Adding yet another layer to this argument is the notion of traditional ethical guidelines of journalism clashing with digital spheres where even the definition of a "journalist" is debatable.

This digital wave has proven to be beneficial for journalists, particularly when they are covering topics that may need more interpretative reporting than is allowed in traditional mainstream media. The preference of the digital format also aligns minority journalists with a large demographic of the population who are more prone to obtain their news and information from online or digital sources. According to Julie (2015), 61 percent of millennials (respondents aged 18 to 34) get at least some political news from Facebook, but only 37 percent watch political news on local television. The percentages are the opposite for Baby Boomers (aged 51 to 69), with 60 percent watching local television, and 39 percent using social media for political news. Additionally, 85 percent of millennials surveyed by API in the same year said, "Keeping up with the news was important to them, but most don't go to traditional news providers to get it. Rather, they get their news through social media, often on mobile formats, where they say they can engage with the content" (Julie, 2015, p. A04).

As such, minority journalists who forgo traditional modes of message dissemination are going to platforms and channels that target a large segment of the population and are able to engage them in ways that are often not possible in more conventional media. The growth of the digital media platform also allows minority journalists to foster a more balanced means of competition with large established traditional media platforms. The financial barriers that have historically plagued minority-focused publications are limited because of internet access and the wide use of mobile devices, specifically among the millennial generation.

DIGITAL MEDIA AND MILLENNIAL NEWS HABITS

Schwalbe (2009) found that although there is no commonly accepted range of birth years, millennials are identified as those born between 1982 and 2002. They have been called the Millennial Generation, Me Generation, Generation Y (those born right after Generation X), Net Generation, Internet Generation and Digital Generation. This group has also been referred to as "digital natives" because they have grown up with digital tools and toys, as opposed to older "digital immigrants," who have had to learn digital languages. Although individual differences exist among generations that span decades, media use during childhood influences how young people learn. For example, Baby Boomers (1946–1964) have been described as passive observers shaped by television, while millennials are viewed as active learners who synthesize information from a variety of online sources.

According to the Hispanic Millennial Project (2015), a report by the online marketing research firm ThinkNow, younger Americans are likely to be multiculturally focused and fairly homogenous in their choices of digital platforms like social media, and millennials are more engaged in consuming news on these platforms than earlier studies had found. This news orientation and level of conscious navigation holds true across different ethnic groups. The American Press Institute Race, Ethnicity and Social Media Report (2015), however, found that there are some differences in the social networks that the various racial and ethnic groups use. Of the seven social networking sites the survey asked about, millennials most often name Facebook as the site they visit at least once a day to get news and information.

Moreover, according to the API report, once they are logged in, millennials across racial and ethnic groups tend to behave in similar ways on Facebook in terms of engagement with the news. A majority of millennials say they read or watch news stories posted by others on Facebook and "like" a news story they see posted to Facebook. Fewer say they personally post or share news stories to Facebook or comment on a news story posted to the social media site.

The data reveal just one significant difference between racial and ethnic groups in news engagement activities on Facebook: African Americans are more likely than whites and Hispanics to say they comment on news stories posted to Facebook. Additionally, other social media platforms are more popular for getting news and information amongst racial and ethnic minorities:

> Both African Americans and Hispanic are more likely than whites to get news and information at least once a day from YouTube (33 percent vs. 38 percent vs. 20 percent). African American and Hispanic millennials are also significantly more likely to get news from Instagram (45 percent vs. 30 percent vs. 19 percent for whites). (American Press Institute, 2015)

As the report suggested, millennials are connecting to digital platforms to obtain their news information and to stay in touch with the world. But, the authors do note that rather than news consumption occurring at certain times of the day as a defined activity—in "news sessions"—keeping up with the world is part of being connected and becoming aware more generally, and it often but not always occurs online. In many cases, news comes as part of social flow, something that may happen unexpectedly as people check to see what's new with their network or community of friends. At other times news is something they seek out on their own. Most see news as an enjoyable or entertaining experience. So, millennials are not constantly connected, but when they are online, news (keeping up with what's going on in the world) ranks relatively high among the list of activities in which they engage every day. The chart below indicates the online activities of millennials and the percentage of their engagement.

According to Julie (2015), the changing news preferences of millennials has not been lost on traditional media, with newspapers and broadcasters moving more news to digital and mobile formats. Julie found that *The New York Times* outlined its strategy for expanding its subscriber base. Its plans include trying out new features, like mobile alerts connected to readers' interests, and other technologies designed to create personalized experiences.

Moreover, traditional news media have lost most of their flair when it comes to millennial audiences, with many unable to or not concerned with identifying major network news personalities. Julie wrote,

> At least 70 percent said they had never seen the evening news and didn't know the names of the newscasters. . . . In terms of getting coverage, this group knows they have many options. There are so many opportunities—Instagram, Snapchat, Tumblr, etc. Traditional media is just one (p. A04).

According to Hendrickson (2013) millennials expect some level of engagement in their digital and or social media use. The novelty of such a

Table 5.1.   Millennial Media Engagement

Activity	Percentage of Millennials
Checking/Sending e-mail	72%
Keeping up with what friends are doing	71%
Streaming music, TV, or movies	68%
Researching topics interested in or pursuing hobbies	65%
Keeping up with what's going on in the world	**64%**
Checking weather, traffic or public transportation	57%
Shopping or researching products	56%
Finding information about events, movies, restaurants, etc.	56%
Playing games	45%

Source: American Pres Institute Media Insight Project, https://www.americanpress institute.org/publications/reports/survey-research/millennials-not-newsless/.

social system is that it allows a user to create networks that are both self selected and self managed. In addition, "given the prevalent use of non-hierarchical social networks such as Twitter, where a user can follow anyone who does not have protected tweets, there is massive opportunity for digital non-place-based interpersonal communication. It is within this digital space that computer-mediated communication and non-hierarchical social media diminish conventional communication boundaries such as location and access" (p. 3).

Although many traditional media outlets now recognize the significance of utilizing digital platforms to publish their messages in order to satisfy the changing preferences of younger audiences, many of those outlets continue to fall short at creating content for those platforms that is inclusive, thematic and nuanced. Even with new digital options in newsrooms, journalists of color make up a very small percentage of message producers in mainstream media. This is the case even as data suggests that African American millennials, the group most attracted to new digital platforms, are using technology and social media at very high rates to receive news and information.

According to Nielsen's 2016 "Young, Connected and Black" report, with continued population growth, higher education attainment and expanded access to mobile technology, African Americans' digital footprint and influence is being driven by younger influencers—black millennials, aged 18–34:

> There are more than 83 million millennials in the U.S., according to the U.S. Census Bureau, of which African Americans comprise 14 percent (about 11.5 million). African American millennials are using technology and social media to amplify their voices about how they consume information, entertainment and products. (Nielsen, 2016)

Additionally, the usage of mobile devices among African American millennials has helped to bring a heighted awareness to social issues via social media. As Nielsen reported,

> Fifty-five percent of black millennials say they spend an hour or more daily on social networking sites, which is 11 percent higher than the total millennial population. Additionally, 29 percent of black millennials say they spend three or more hours daily on social networking sites, an amount that is 44 percent higher than that of the total millennial population. (Nielsen, 2016)

Young African Americans are using social media to raise awareness about issues that affect the black community and that awareness has spilled over into the stories that are being covered by the media, both mainstream and alternative. These issues, which normally are complex and sensitive in nature, require the same interpretative approach whether disseminated in print, on television or digitally. As a result, similar concerns about the lack of minority journalists covering complex stories for mainstream media has not changed just because the channel of information has. Additional research notes that millennials who are exposed to intricate social issues either through social media or traditional media think about how those issues affect or will affect their lives. The 2017 GenForward survey found that millennials of all racial backgrounds list racism as one of the three most important problems in America. The findings are a result of a nationally representative survey of over 1,750 young adults aged 18–34 conducted bimonthly that pays special attention to how race and ethnicity influence how young adults or millennials experience and think about the world.

Findings from the survey, which provides an extensive look at how millennials think about race, the racial order, and racism in society in the age of Trump included:

- **The Racism Problem**. Millennials of all racial backgrounds list racism as one of the three most important problems in America.
- **President Trump a Racist**. Majorities of millennials of color believe the president is a racist, but white millennials are split on the issue.
- **President of Rich and White**. There is widespread agreement among millennials across race and ethnicity that Donald Trump is most sympathetic to rich people and white people.
- **Racial Order**. Millennials believe African Americans experience the most racial discrimination in American society but also have the second-most political power behind whites. Whites are cited as having the most economic and political power overall.
- **Racial Coalitions**. Overwhelming majorities of millennials across racial groups believe people of color face common challenges and could be political allies. While 84 percent of whites believe that whites and people of color could be political allies, barely a majority of Latinxs and less than a majority of African Americans and Asian Americans agree with the possibility of political alliances between whites and people of color.
- **Discrimination against Whites a big problem**. Nearly half (48 percent) of white millennials believe that discrimination against whites has become as big a problem as discrimination against blacks and other minorities, while only about a quarter of African Americans, Asian Americans and Latinxs share this view.

- **Black Lives Matter**. A majority of African Americans (56 percent) and plurality of Asian Americans (43 percent) have a favorable opinion of Black Lives Matter, but only 27 percent of Latinxs and 19 percent of whites share this view.
- **Confederate Symbols**. A majority of millennials of color believe the Confederate flag is a symbol of racism and support removing Confederate statues and symbols from public places.
- **Racial Progress**. Millennials of color cite organizing in communities as the most effective way to create racial change. White millennials cite community service and volunteering as the most effective strategy.

Source: GenForward Survey, https://genforwardsurvey.com/assets/uploads/2017/10/GenForward-Oct-2017-Final-Report.pdf.

These concerns are elevated when it comes to African American millennials, specifically, and are frequently expressed through their social media platforms. Love (2017) observed that far beyond using social media for entertainment, shopping or communication, African American millennials have elevated Twitter, Facebook, YouTube and other platforms to raise public consciousness about the issues impacting black people. The hashtags #BlackLivesMatter and #OscarsSoWhite are prime examples of this phenomenon. Love wrote,

> While black millennials fall below their counterparts in the percentage of leisure time spent on social media, they exceed the general millennial population in their overall presence on Twitter, Tumblr, Google+ and Whatsapp. That online presence has translated into the creation of a network of black news outlets specifically creating content that will meet readers and viewers where they are.

The tendency for African American millennials to use social media as a channel for social justice is not lost on news outlets covering controversial topics that often play out online. Journalists have begun quoting social media posts in stories and are often able to find reliable sources for their stories by using the platform. This puts traditional media more in line with alternative news outlets when it comes to reliance on official sources. Mainstream media have been criticized for relying too heavily on official sources for information, particularly when those sources may hold some bias in relation to the details of the story. Blackstone et al. (2017) found that the traditional approach values government sources, such as police departments or those in political office, under the assumption that these entities are more credible.

Also scrutinized is mainstream media's system of attribution, which is used for the purpose of transparency and accountability.

Journalists abiding by traditional ethical norms are expected to reveal the people or organizations responsible for supplying information used in their reports. The attribution norm is designed to encourage truthfulness from sources by publicly connecting them to the information provided, but also to protect the journalist from accusations of deliberate misinformation by revealing who or what entity relayed the information and why this person or organization was deemed credible. Bullock (2008) argued that victim perspectives may hold more credibility than official sources. Generally, when mainstream media cover sensitive or controversial issues, official sources dominate coverage even though it is the victim who has firsthand knowledge of events. While officials may offer a variety of perspectives uncovered in an investigation or legal situation, the information remains secondhand unless that official witnessed an infraction directly. Such coverage could conceivably mislead the public and is often deemed "victim-blaming."

Social media has provided a platform for audiences to see and hear firsthand victim accounts and has significantly changed how media organizations handle news framing in relation to sourcing and attribution. Social justice activists have used the platforms to help change the narrative of stories that would previously focus heavily on a victim's past or shortcomings, particularly if that victim is African American. This shift may help explain why minorities, who are often troubled by negative portrayals of people of color in mainstream news, are using social media more often for their news consumption.

Black journalists have certainly benefited from this shift to more nontraditional means of receiving news information. Those who work specifically for the contemporary Black Press and those who find their voices limited as contributors in mainstream media have utilized the platform in more effective ways than they were able to do through traditional channels. Digital platforms in general provide a less restrictive way of sharing news information and they reach a wider audience.

Moreover, the appeal of the digital platform to media consumers has been positive for minority journalists, particularly African Americans, as this platform has become this group's contemporary alternative for message dissemination. The American newsroom workforce continues to lack diversity, and journalists of color continue to find unconventional ways to tell stories that are important to their communities and add perspective often missing in mainstream reporting.

#BALTIMOREUPRISING VS. #BALTIMORERIOTS

This unconventional message dissemination is aligned with the idea of black media "witnessing" and the use of social media as "an unapologetic form of advocacy journalism" (Richardson, 2017) historically found in alternative media like the Black Press. The media coverage of the death of 25-year-old Baltimore, Maryland, resident Freddie Gray in 2015 and subsequent protests is a case in which mainstream coverage contrasted with the messages on alternative platforms, specifically social media where young African Americans were most vocal in their concerns about police brutality. Gray was arrested in April 2015 and charged with illegal possession of a switch-blade after running from police officers. Following his arrest, he rode in a police van—shackled but unsecured by a seat belt as required by police department regulations—and was found unresponsive. He died the following week (Ruiz, 2017).

What followed Gray's death was a public reaction similar to the response to the 2014 shooting death of 18-year-old Michael Brown in Ferguson, Missouri, and other instances of police violence against African Americans. Nationwide demonstrations were held in solidarity with the Baltimore protestors, and hundreds of people participated in protests outside of the Baltimore Police Department. As the number of protestors in the city grew, so did the agitation between them and the police. Eventually, destruction and violence ensued, while millions looked on via traditional news reports and social media.

The difference between the traditional media messaging about the protests and subsequent uprisings following the death of Gray on social media, specifically Twitter, and what was reported by "citizen journalists" and others on that platform was glaring. As many news channels used Baltimore-related hashtags on Twitter to publicize their coverage and Twitter users used the platform to point out the problems with the news coverage of the demonstrations, the digital space became a useful option for broadening the story. Hashtags on Twitter are generally used to help compartmentalize the vast amount of information that is regularly streaming online and are also used by news outlets to get their coverage into the mix of posts about a topic. In the case of the unrest in Baltimore, two main hashtags emerged and were most frequently used: #BaltimoreRiots and #BaltimoreUprising.

According to Ferguson (2015), the incident demonstrates how just using a keyword to search for topics on Twitter is not as significant as using the hashtag: "The addition of the hashtag gives a word or phrase a whole new meaning. #Baltimore has a heavier meaning than (the search term) Baltimore—#Baltimore is a social phenomenon." Of the two hashtags that dominated the social media site during the heaviest period of news coverage in Baltimore, #BaltimoreRiots sparked the most outrage, especially from the people who did not characterize the events in the city as "riots." The negative connotation of the word and the highly racialized context of the unrest further divided factions affected by the events that had occurred in the city.

An examination of tweets using the hashtag #BaltimoreRiots or that used words or images that referenced or alluded to "riots" in their description of the unrest shows that most were from traditional news sources like *The Guardian* (April 28, 2015, "Baltimore protests turn into riots as mayor declares state of emergency."); *The Baltimore Sun* (April 27, 2015, "Mayor Stephanie Rawlings-Blake . . . drew a distinction between peaceful protesters and 'thugs' she said engaged in rioting Monday intent on 'destroying our city."); or Fox News (April 29, 2015, "DanaPerino on #BaltimoreRiots: 'It wasn't a spontaneous eruption. . . . There was time to prepare.'"). These tweets were posted within days of Gray's reported death.

In most instances, tweets with the hashtag #BaltimoreRiots characterized those who filled the streets of Baltimore in a negative way. They were not afforded the gravity of the word "protester" as many had actually described themselves. Even African American comedian Chris Rock (April 29, 2015) tweeted, "I wish we could bring Martin Luther King back to life so we can show these young kids how to protest the correct way." The word protestor is often associated with Martin Luther King Jr. when used to describe an effective nonviolent direct action used to overturn systemic segregation and racism in the United States. The #BatimoreRiots tweets limited the discussion about the unrest to that of looters set on destroying the city. Very few reports with that hashtag, including those attached to mainstream news sources, connected the visible havoc and destruction to legitimate resistance against the systemic racism that is at the root of police violence against African Americans.

That changed on April 27, 2015, when Twitter handle @dogluvr38 tweeted, "Would be nice if we could get #BaltimoreUprising trending instead of 'riots'." Following this tweet, almost in line with the general calming of the protests in the city on the day it was written, the use of the hashtag #BaltimoreRiots began to compete with the more nuanced #BaltimoreUprising. According to Moyer (2015) the hashtag change added political meaning to what was happening and the connotation of "uprising" attached that meaning to the protest. Naming in itself is a political act. Many of the tweets that used the more favorable "uprising" hashtag were accompanied by photos that depicted images of more peaceful actions by protestors, many standing in silence facing police officers who were dressed in riot gear. The language and imagery had shifted dramatically from the more tumultuous posts and reports from the days before. #BaltimoreUprising was also more commonly used among young activists who saw the media's depictions of their efforts in Baltimore as imprecise and often one-sided.

Tweets using the "uprising" reference included comments like, "This is not a riot . . . it's an uprising. #BaltimoreUprising" (@Bipartisanism, April 29, 2015), as well as a debate over mainstream news coverage. For instance, one thread challenged Austin (Texas) American journalist Phil Jankowski regarding the stark difference in how his newspaper had covered the Baltimore incident compared to its coverage of a far more violent biker rally in Waco: "@PhilJankowski even look at your paper's coverage of #BaltimoreUprising. Stark language/tone difference" (@deray, May 18, 2015); "No one was killed in #BaltimoreUprising. Nine dead in #Waco. Look at the different treatment" (@BeattyLaw, May 17, 2015). Other tweets: "During the #BaltimoreUprising there was SOME isolated 'rioting,' however labeling the whole thing as such is patently dishonest" (@BaltoSpectator, May 7, 2015); and "THIS IS NOT HOW AMERICAN CITIZENS SHOULD BE TREATED! #BaltimoreUprising" (@amandaseales, May 3, 2015).

The "uprising"-themed tweets were posted by a mixture of well-known young social justice activists like DeRay McKesson (@deray), celebrity activists like Amanda Seales, and alternative news sources like Bipartisan Report (@Bipartisanism). Their responses added to the digital curation of counter narratives to social media posts labeling the unrest in Baltimore as "riots" in very generalizable ways. It was an extension of citizen journalism and advocacy frequently found on digital and social media platforms and is part of the growing practice of effective online activism. What happened following the transition from #BaltimoreRiots to #BaltimoreUprising was more tempered language by mainstream media and officials describing the unrest in the city. For example, the *Baltimore Sun* published an editorial titled, "Why we should call recent Baltimore events an 'uprising'" on September 24, 2015, which criticized the unfair characterizations of what happened in Baltimore seen online and on other media platforms.

Further, the twenty-first-century sites of black rhetorical resistance are found in digital spaces like Twitter and mobile videos posted to other social media sites. Black Twitter, which has become a significant part of the black public sphere (Richardson, 2017), has shown the potential to contribute substantial content to modern-day protest journalism. There is an evolving relationship between African American millennials and social media. According to Bailey (2017), millennials from this group have the opportunity to serve as contemporary socio-political agents who can express their political views and the changes they would like to see:

> Dialogue surrounding social change provides this generation the opportunity to disrupt American cycles of systemic oppression that often disenfranchise African American people. Posts, tweets and hashtags are used to create sociopolitical discussion that may provide black America with the information and

transparency they need in order to be engaged in productive political conversations (p. 2).

HOPE FOR THE FUTURE?

The mainstream news media continue to fall short in their efforts to have a diverse workforce that reflects the makeup of the public it covers. As such, alternative forms of media storytelling have once again transcended the traditional channels of dissemination and enabled both minority and citizen journalists to have ways to tell stories that directly affect them and their communities. Historically, those alternative options have provided space to tell stories often ignored or poorly reported on in traditional news sources. Most recently, minority journalists as well as citizen journalists have found that the use of online and digital platforms allow them not only a chance to tell their stories, but the opportunity to often do so without the limitations of traditional journalistic tenants. These digital news organizations and social media platforms not only allow for more inclusive media messaging, but also attract the large millennial population in this country who are less likely to receive their news information from traditional news outlets. Demographically, this group tends to be more multicultural and has been found to be just as concerned about complex issues in our society as are older generations.

Additionally, because of their affinity for social media engagement, millennials are also more personally invested in news stories that address problematic social issues in society. When minority journalists use the digital platform to disseminate messages unique to their communities, the messaging is no longer linear in scope. Social media hashtags, "likes," and news-sharing create the opportunity for instant reaction and sometimes full-on resistance to systemic oppression in this country and around the world. Social media specifically has been used to mobilize members of the black community and other marginalized groups during instances of social injustice inflicted upon members of those particular communities.

While the internet has helped to widen the reach of African American and minority journalists and allowed them to connect with the large millennial population in ways that are beneficial to their unique storytelling, there are still challenges that interfere with those efforts.

According to Love (2017), mainstream newsrooms have made some progress, but are not where they should or need to be. Love argued that options now available on digital platforms are key to enhancing the media landscape and giving minority journalists the space to tell their stories and affect social change:

> By empowering themselves and their followers—without gatekeepers and intermediaries in the traditional media sense—young, black journalists have

reached a broad audience. They can educate and mobilize others to act on a given issue, and connect with local, national and global social justice movements. A videographer or documentarian can broadcast a crime in progress—such as a police beating of an unarmed motorist—live and in real time, before an audience of thousands if not millions. In that regard, technology is the great equalizer, a check on the abuse of official power and a call to reform harmful patterns and discriminatory practices.

A key issue is that although minorities are a large part of the new media and digital environment, they still lag behind in ownership of those platforms. Additionally, those news outlets that are part of the traditional Black Press have been slow to convert from print to digital. Outside of well-known systemic barriers, there are two main issues that have been blamed for the lag: money and training.

According to Burkins (2017) the dearth of black publishers is more pronounced in the nonprofit sector, where digital operations such as Voice of San Diego and The Texas Tribune have made names for themselves as community watchdogs. For-profit options are limited. Additionally, as Burkins observed, is that a lack of training in entrepreneurship may help explain why more African American journalists have not taken the ownership route in the profit sector.

African Americans are also poorly represented in the corporate tech world, where platforms they use to spread their unique messages are created and managed. According to Grant (2018), tech companies know that they have a race problem, but their efforts to address it have yielded little:

> Facebook Inc. says that three percent of its U.S. workforce is black, up from two percent in 2014, while black workers in technical roles stagnated at one percent. Only two percent of Google's workers are black, a figure that has remained static for the past three years. The latest data from the U.S. government, released in 2016, reinforces the point: Blacks made up seven percent of U.S. high-tech workforce, and just 3 percent of the total Silicon Valley workforce.

Because minority representation in media content and message creation is positively influenced by the growth and popularity of digital media, perhaps there is hope for the future. However, systemic issues that have long plagued traditional journalism also plague the technology industry and may well limit its ability to provide the kind of useful and complex insight necessary to combat racism in the age of millennials.

REFERENCES

Alexander, A. (2011). What often goes unsaid. *Nieman Reports*, *65*(3), 36.

American Press Institute. (2015). *Race, ethnicity and the use of social media for news*. Retrieved at: https://www.americanpressinstitute.org/publications/reports/survey-research/race-ethnicity-social-media-news/.

Anderson, M., Skye, T., Rainie, L., & Smith, A. (2018). *Activism in the social media age*. Pew Research Center. Retrieved at: http://www.pewinternet.org/2018/07/11/activism-in-the-social-media-age/.

ASNE. (2017). *Newsroom diversity survey*. American Society of News Editors. Retrieved at: https://www.asne.org/content.asp?contentid=515.

Bailey, J. R. (2017). *An examination of the relationship between black millennial social media use and political activism* (Master's thesis). Retrieved from https://scholarworks.gsu.edu/aas_theses/42.

Bialik, K., & Matsa, K. E. (2017). *Key trends in social and digital news media*. Pew Research Center. Retrieved at: http://www.pewresearch.org/fact-tank/2017/10/04/key-trends-in-social-and-digital-news-media/.

Blackstone, G. E., Cowart, H. S., & Saunders, L. M. (2017). TweetStorm in #ferguson: How news organizations framed dominant authority, anti-authority, and political figures in a restive community. *Journal of Broadcasting & Electronic Media, 61*(3), 597–614.

Bullock, C. (2008). Official sources dominate domestic violence reporting. *Newspaper Research Journal, 29,* 6–22.

Burkins, G. (Spring 2017). Where have all the black digital publishers gone? *Columbia Journalism Review*. Retrieved at: https://www.cjr.org/local_news/where-have-all-the-black-digital-publishers-gone.php.

Byerly, C., & Wilson, C. (2009). Journalism as Kerner turns 40: Its multicultural problems and possibilities. *Howard Journal of Communications, 20,* 209–221.

Cohen, C. J., Fowler, M., Medenica, V. E., & Rogowski, J. C. (2017). *The "Woke" generation? Millennial attitudes on race in the US*. GenForward. Retrieved at: https://genforwardsurvey.com/assets/uploads/2017/10/GenForward-Oct-2017-Final-Report.pdf.

Dedman, B., & Doig, S. K. (2005, June 1). Newsroom diversity has passed its peak at most newspapers, 1990–2005 Study shows. Powerreporting.co. Retrieved from: http://www.powerreporting.com/knight/.

Ferguson, Z. (2015, April 29). Twitter hashtags for the Baltimore riots each have distinctive meanings on the social media site. *Bustle*. Retrieved from: https://www.bustle.com/articles/79919-twitter-hashtags-for-the-baltimore-riots-each-have-distinctive-meanings-on-the-social-media-site.

Fleming-Rife, A., & Proffitt, J. M. (2004). The more public school reform changes, the more it stays the same: A framing analysis of newspaper coverage of Brown v. Board of Education at 50. *The Journal of Negro Education, 73*(3), 239–254.

Gans, H. (1979). *Deciding what's news: A study of CBS Evening News, NBC Nightly News, Newsweek and Time*. New York: Random House.

Grant, N. (2018). "Very lonely." The unsettling hum of Silicon Valley's failure to hire more black workers. *Bloomberg*. Retrieved at: https://www.bloomberg.com/news/articles/2018-06-08/tech-companies-still-aren-t-hiring-black-workers.

Hendrickson, E. (2013). Learning to share: Magazines, millennials, and mobile. *Journal of Magazine & New Media Research, 14*(2), 1–7.

Hispanic Millennial Project (2015). African American millennials media and technology and habits report. Retrieved at: https://www.slideshare.net/ThinkNow_Research/african-american-millennials-media-and-technology-habits-report.

Jenkins, C. (2011). Newspapers and representations of race, In C. Campbell, K. LeDuff, C. Jenkins & R. Brown (Eds.), *Race and News: Critical Perspectives* (pp. 22–42). New York/Abington: Routledge/Taylor and Francis Group.

Jenkins, C., & Cole, H. (2011). Nappy-headed hos: Media framing, blame shifting and the controversy of Don Imus' pejorative language. In C. Campbell, K. LeDuff, C. Jenkins, & R. Brown (Eds.), *Race and News: Critical Perspectives* (pp. 177–198). New York/Abington: Routledge/Taylor and Francis Group.

Jenkins, C. (2017). Journalism and African Americans: Diversity and perspective. In C. Campbell (Ed.), *The Routledge Companion to Media and Race*. New York/Abingdon: Routledge/
Taylor and Francis Group.

Julie, V. (2015, December 29). Millennials gravitate to social, mobile to get their news. *Inves-
tors Business Daily*, p. A04.

Love, D. (2017). Why the black press is more relevant than ever. CNN. Retrieved at: https://
www.cnn.com/2017/11/30/opinions/newsroom-diversity-mainstream-media-opinion-love/
index.html.

Moyer, J. W. (2015, April 29). "Baltimore riots" transforms into "Baltimore uprising." *The
Washington Post*. Retrieved at https://washingtonpost.com/news/morning-mix/wp/2015/04/
29/when-baltimoreriots-became-baltimoreuprsing/?utm_term=.1a4b642fd8f7.

Nielsen. (2016). Young, connected and black. Nielsen. Retrieved at http://www.nielsen.com/
us/en/insights/reports/2016/young-connected-and-black.html.

Pavlik, J. (2000). The impact of journalism on technology. *Journalism Studies, 1*(2), 229–237.

Porter, T. (2004, April 21). ASNE's diversity study: Looking for answers. Message posted to
http://www.timporter.com/firstdraft/archives/000298.html.

Radio Television Digital News Association. (2016, July 16). *RTDNA Research: Women and
minorities in newsrooms*. Retrieved at: https://www.rtdna.org/article/rtdna_research_
women_and_minorities_in_newsrooms.

Richardson, A. V. (2017). Bearing witness while black: Theorizing African American mobile
journalism after Ferguson. *Journal of Digital Journalism, 5*(6), 673–698.

Ruiz, R. R. (2017, September 17). Baltimore officers will face no federal charges in death of
Freddie Gray. *The New York Times*. Retrieved at http://www.nytimes.com/2017/09/12/us/
freddie-gray-baltimore-police-federal-charges.html.

Schwalbe, C. B. (2009). Leveraging the digital media habits of the millennials: Strategies for
teaching journalism courses. *Southwestern Mass Communication Journal, 25*(1), 53–68.

ThinkNow (2015). *African American millennials media and technology and habits report*.
Retrieved at https://www.slideshare.net/ThinkNow_Research/africanamerican-millennials-
media-and-technology-habits-report.

Wilson, C., Gutierrez, F., & Chao, L. M. (2003). *Racism, sexism and the media*. Thousand
Oaks, CA: Sage Publications.

Part II

Representation as Resistance

Chapter Six

The Role of Parody in Decoding Media Text

Saturday Night Live *and the Immigration Narrative*

Daleana Phillips

Just in case any viewers missed news coverage in November of 2018 of the migrant caravan heading toward the United States on the Fox News cable program *The Ingraham Angle,* that week's episode of NBC's *Saturday Night Live* (*SNL*) provided a great synopsis! The "vicious caravan" headed toward the United States was full of "hella Aladdin's," as well as "everyone you've seen in your nightmares" such as "Guatemalans, Mexicans, ISIS, the Mendendez Brothers, the 1990 Detroit Pistons, Thanos, and several Babadooks!" (*SNL*, 2018). *SNL* reported that the caravan also had several women who were nine months pregnant and waiting to "drop anchor" on U.S. soil. And that the vicious caravan was moving quickly toward the United States; in fact, if they "walk at the normal pace of three hundred miles a day, they could be here in time to vote for Election Day!" (*SNL*, 2018).

SNL, largely known for its comedy sketches and political parodies of politicians, has stepped up its political satire in recent years to cover more policy-based issues like immigration. The show's shift from personality parody to political satire parallels the emergence of a rising millennial voting presence and increased diversification in media consumption. *SNL*'s core audience, as of 2018, was between the ages of 18 and 39 (38.3 percent) (Semeraro, 2018). While millennials comprise a large portion of *SNL*'s audience, they are also closely approaching the largest adult voting demographic with 62 million eligible voters (Fry, 2016). Fry (2016) explains, "Millennials, who are projected to surpass Baby Boomers next year as the United States' largest living adult generation, are also approaching the Boomers in their share of the American electorate" (para. 1). Comedy news programs, or "fake news," along with partisan cable news programs may play an increasingly influential role in setting the political agenda for both legal and illegal immigration policies.

The increasing popularity of partisan and "fake news" programs has also arisen alongside technological innovations responsible for diversifying media consumption. Media consumption by young audiences, such as millennials (often regarded as being born between 1981 and 1996) is often selectively filtered into echo chambers through technological algorithms and individual preferences (Dimock, 2019). Foer (2017) argues, "The algorithm is a novel problem for democracy. Technology companies boast, with little shyness, about how they can nudge users toward more virtuous behavior—how they can induce us to click, to read, to buy, or even to vote" (p. 111). This is especially poignant to research on millennials because according to the Pew Research Center (2017) during the 2016 election, young audiences between the ages of 18 and 29 reported social media sites as being their primary source for election news (35 percent) followed by news websites/apps (18 percent), cable TV news (12 percent), radio (11 percent), local TV (10 percent), late night comedy (6 percent), network nightly news (4 percent), and various other sources comprising under 5 percent (Gottfried, Barthel, Shearer & Mitchell, 2016, p. 4).

Based on the Pew Research Center's findings, it is evident that millennials prefer what Katz (1992) once referred to as "New News," which he considered to be "dazzling, adolescent, irresponsible, fearless, frightening and powerful . . . part Hollywood film and TV movie, part pop music and pop art, mixed with popular culture and celebrity magazines, tabloid telecasts, cable and home video" (p. 35). Katz argued that traditional journalism or "Old News" has been "bewildered and paralyzed" by these new postmodern mediums for news consumption (p. 36). "Fake news" programs, such as *SNL*, increasingly use celebrities, music, popular culture and political humor to expose dominant political ideology. Political humor, such as satire, negotiates dominant narratives by poking holes in hegemonic ideologies that are perceived to be incongruous with lived experiences. Rossing (2012) argues that "by holding a fun house mirror to contemporary culture, humor distorts, exaggerates, and reframes in ways that invite audiences to see themselves and society from new vantage points" (p. 46). In a rapidly changing media environment characterized by partisan and "fake news" or "infotainment," parody has the potential to not only problematize dominant news narratives, but also influence further critical analysis and oppositional frameworks for interpreting these discourses.

The purpose of this case study is to examine how parodic techniques used in the *Saturday Night Live* episode's "Caravan Cold Open" (the program's opening skit) complement Stuart Hall's (1980) theoretical framework for decoding media texts in how the techniques encode analyses of illegal immigration, asylum seekers and U.S. immigration policy. First, an overview of Hall's decoding framework (dominant, negotiated, oppositional) is established to provide the necessary theoretical foundation for examining the role of parody in revealing "ideological abuse" found in dominant news narratives (Barthes, 1972, p. 10). Second, because parody requires an initial discourse for its existence, it is necessary to "situate" the original discourse within Hall's dominant or preferred level of analysis. This makes the complementary nature of parodic techniques explicit within the levels of negotiation and opposition. Third, Hariman's (2008) use of the Bakhtinian model for analyzing parody will be employed to reveal how "parody can take any other discourse outside of its given context of assertion and assent to show how things could be otherwise" (p. 260). The *SNL* caravan parody will be analyzed within Hall's (1980) negotiated level of analysis according to the four operations from the Bakhtinian model: doubling, carnivalesque spectatorship, social leveling and decentering discourse. Lastly, a discussion of the limits and potential of political parody in Hall's oppositional reading will conclude the analysis.

Hall's theoretical framework is comprised of three levels of analysis: dominant or "preferred," negotiated and oppositional. A preferred or dominant reading closely resembles the intended message of the media text's producer. A negotiated reading of a media text goes beyond the intended meaning of the producer, allowing for multiple interpretive readings. Hall (1980) explains that within the negotiated level of analysis, the dominant ideology is "shot through with contradictions . . . [that are] . . . only on certain occasions brought to full visibility" (p. 137). Hall (1980) argues that negotiated codes within media texts may become "detotalized" from the dominant reading and "re-totalized" within an alternate framework (p. 138). Hall explains that when events decoded in a "negotiated way begin to be given an oppositional reading [that] . . . here the 'politics of signification'—the struggle in discourse—is joined" (p. 138).

THE INGRAHAM ANGLE: THE DOMINANT READING

SNL's parody derives its primary discourse from an episode of *The Ingraham Angle*, in which host Laura Ingraham focuses on the migrant "invasion" heading toward the United States. Ingraham interviews several politicians and bureaucrats, including former ICE acting director Tom Homan and U.S. House of Representatives majority whip and Republican congressman Steve Scalise, about their concerns regarding the looming "tide" of "illegal aliens" making their way through Central America and into Mexico. This episode aired two weeks before the 2018 midterm elections, in which the Trump administration hoped to capitalize on the illegal immigration platform and sway voters for a Republican majority. This episode also addresses Trump's self-proclaimed identity as a "nationalist," in which Ingraham jumps to Trump's defense against the "outraged liberals." Ingraham cites Merriam-Webster's definition of nationalism as "loyalty and devotion to a nation. In other words, loyalty and devotion to America. So where is the controversy?" she asks (Fox News, 2018, para. 83). Within the context of *The Ingraham Angle,* these two issues are discussed within different segments separated by commercial advertising.

Nielson data released in April of 2018 indicates that "Ingraham has an average audience of 2.5 million viewers, making her the fourth-highest-rated show in cable news and one of the pillars of Fox News Channel's dominance in prime time" (Joyella, 2018). Joyella (2018) further explains that out of the 20 top-ranked cable news programs, Fox News owns fourteen. The popularity of *The Ingraham Angle* reflects a wider systemic return to partisan media in lieu of new media technologies and the expansion of cable networks that cater to niche audiences. While Fox News and *The Ingraham Angle*, in particular, cater to conservative-leaning audiences, it is important to note the impact of these dominant narratives on partisan cable news consumers. Wicks, Wicks and Morimoto (2013) found that individuals who identified as being conservative or liberal were more likely to seek out partisan media and engage in political conversations that support their views. When people become more enmeshed within their political echo chambers, they tend to become more polarized in their political views. Conservatives tended to surround themselves with more traditional media sources like talk radio and Fox News, whereas liberals were more likely to use Facebook, Twitter and blogs for their news sources. Levendusky (2013) argues that partisan media has the potential to affect the democratic process by accelerating "the move toward the 'uncompromising mind' that seeks out gridlock and partisan advantage rather than compromise and consensus solutions" (p. 621). The effects of dominant narratives through partisan news coverage has the potential to effect the livelihood of undocumented migrants within the United States, as well as those attempting to seek asylum.

While *The Ingraham Angle* reflects just one cable news program on a conservative-leaning network, the dominant narrative regarding illegal immigration pulls from a rich history of national news coverage that positions undocumented migrants within threat frames. McQuail (2010) argues that the news media presents socially constructed frames, such as a threat frame, in order to guide audiences toward intended "learning" outcomes (p. 511). Ortega and Feagin (2016) argue that news stories tend to use particular metaphors and language to construct arguments, as well as repetitious phrases that become naturalized for news consumers. Cisernos (2008) argues that metaphors "are some of the principle tools with which dominant ideologies and prejudices are represented and reinforced" (p. 571). Cisernos (2008) provides a list of common metaphors used in existing literature on news coverage of immigrants and immigration: disease, infection, criminal, infestation, invader, burden and flood (p. 572). He adds pollution as a metaphor to this list within his own analysis of CNN and Fox News coverage of the proposed immigration reforms in 2005. Cisernos (2008) found that immigrants were often portrayed in similar ways to news coverage on toxic pollutants during the Love Canal Crisis in the late 1970s and early 1980s:

> Like the barrels [of toxic chemicals] in images of Love Canal, the immigrants are portrayed as unorganized, idle, and aimless—connoting a sense of accumulating danger. Whether sitting under trees or collecting on street corners, these images disrupt a sense of order and safety by portraying immigrants as ticking time bombs of cultural and economic contamination situated throughout our cities (p. 580).

These metaphors become naturalized by news consumers and "form part of our popular consciousness" around immigration through frequent repetition by journalists and politicians (Cisernos, 2008, p. 593).

In *The Ingraham Angle,* Ingraham references many of these metaphors, but her most commonly used are centered on immigrants as invaders and unstoppable floods. Ingraham uses additional creativity to elevate the threat of invasion by regularly referring to the migrant caravan as an "invading horde." Not only does her dominant discourse warn viewers of an invasion, but by adding "horde" she also adds a savage or animalistic aspect to these migrants. Migrants are stripped of human rationality in her narrative, which heightens the fear of their arrival because they are perceived as lawless and ready to devour the nation's natural resources. For example, Ingraham (2018) argues that "this current horde coupled with a number of illegals streaming across the border daily, will overwhelm the infrastructure and cause another crisis that is totally avoidable." She further explains that "as for the invading horde headed our way, they must be intercepted and sent back to their countries of origin." She argues that if these migrants are not stopped they will "swamp" or "mass rush" the border.

Ingraham also uses flood metaphors to describe the migrant caravan. For example, she asks one of her guests how we can "stem the tide" of migrants headed toward the U.S.-Mexico border. In the previous examples of invasion, she also uses the word "streaming" to refer to illegal immigrants entering the United States in smaller numbers to contrast the "horde" making its way through Central America. She also refers to the caravan as "swelling" in size as it moves through Central America and into Mexico, suggesting that more people are joining the caravan. Ingraham's comment is a response to a video clip in which Donald Trump makes a statement about who and what may be found in the caravan, as well as a subsequent response from CNN's

Don Lemon. In the video clip, Donald Trump urges the media to "take your camera, go into the middle and search. You are going to find MS-13, you're going to find middle easterners, you're going to find everything." Don Lemon argues that Trump is "ceasing on unsubstantiated right wing media reports that the caravan has been infiltrated by criminals and unknown middle easterners." Ingraham shuts down Lemon's alternate narrative using sarcasm and referencing a government source to add credibility to her threat narrative. Ingraham (2018) states,

> Well, it turns out the president may be privy to more information than the bright lights at CNN headquarters and their reporters are ever privy to. Tonight, the spokesperson for the Department of Homeland security confirmed that the caravan includes "citizens of countries outside of Central America, including countries in the Middle East, Africa, South Asia and elsewhere are currently traveling through Mexico toward [the United States]" (para. 13).

Ingraham's metaphors generate a dominant threat narrative around the migrant caravan heading toward the United States. This threat narrative is used to generate fear of the migrant's impending "invasion," as well as to pressure her audience to vote for conservative Republican measures to ensure America's safety.

Ingraham's use of metaphors to construct her narratives function in a similar way to the naturalization process critiqued by Roland Barthes (1972) as "myth" and Clifford Geertz (1983) as "common sense." As Cisernos (2008) explains, metaphors function as "cultural indices" from which we build "common sense" understandings and attitudes (p. 570). Because metaphors are interwoven throughout discourse, they become naturalized components of the overall narrative. With the rise of audiences choosing partisan news, these narratives reinforce one another; creating master narratives. Hall (1980) explains that dominant hegemonic definitions of situations "connect events implicitly or explicitly, to grand totalizations, to the great syntagmatic views-of-the-world" which gives master narratives the capacity to appear all-encompassing and inevitable or natural (p. 137).

Master narratives, such as Ingraham's discourse on immigration, become reinforced through other programs on Fox News that share similar views, as well as those of the Trump administration. Master narratives within partisan echo chambers are likely to be decoded by audience members in line with the intention of the media producer because they carry a "stamp of legitimacy" within a particular thought community (Hall, 1980, p. 137). Hill (2013) explains that master narratives become a natural part of our interpretive process, escaping conscious detection as they continually work to organize our perception of the world (p. 327). Hill (2013) further explains that these master narratives influence what an audience comes to define as right or wrong and provides a "template" for how to understand and interpret future narratives (p. 327). In the case of illegal immigration, Ingraham leaves no doubt for her audience that the migrant "horde invasion" making its way toward the United States is bad and must be stopped. Voting for a republican majority is her intended solution to "stemming this tide." Ingram (2018) argues, "But now my friends, it's up to the American people. They will either allow Democrats to continue to ignore the obvious and permit rank lawlessness of the border or you the voters will empower the president with the majority he needs to protect our country" (para. 33).

SNL'S "CARAVAN COLD OPEN": A NEGOTIATED READING

Political humor, such as parody and satire, operate within Hall's negotiated level of analysis because humor "can be used to expose and express the contradictory aspects of life, and to communicate and share this experience with others" (Kuipers, 2008, p. 377). Within a negotiated level of analysis, the cracks or inconsistencies and contradictions within dominant narratives are made visible. Hill (2013) explains that political parody and satire can function as counter-narratives because they aim to "arouse and awaken the perceptions of 'men asleep' by shining the brightest, most piercing light into the gaps present in dominant discourse" (p. 331). Political humor utilizes negotiated codes operating in what Hall (1980) calls a "particular or situated logics" to illuminate the "differential and unequal relation to discourses and logics of power" (p. 137). Within parody, negotiated codes are often "shot through with contradiction" using various techniques that combine imitation and alteration of these codes (Hall, 1980). Hariman (2008) explains that these parodic techniques include "direct quotation, alternation of words, textual rearrangement, substitution of subjects or characters, shifts in diction, shifts in class, shifts in magnitude, etc." (p. 249). These techniques problematize dominant codes and have the potential to engage audiences in a "politics of signification" (Hall, 1980, p. 138).

SNL's political humor has shifted from parodies and satires that are solely based on personality to also include political issues. Boskin (1990), decades ago, argued that American political humor is "more frequently than not a tepid cup of tea" (p. 475). He argued that because political humor was largely centered on personality-based issues that it left political and corporate interests safely "wrapped in a cocoon" (p. 481). Wild's (2015) analysis of *SNL*'s parodies of the 2000 and 2008 election reflect the changes that have occurred in political humor since Boskin's analysis. Wild (2015) found that Will Ferrell's impersonation of George W. Bush, as well as the parodic storyline, largely focused on personality-based issues. While these issues may have made Bush appear less intelligent, they were rarely taken seriously by mainstream media and had little effect on the 2000 election. However, in 2008, Tina Fey's impersonation and parody of Sarah Palin went beyond personality-based issues and has been considered a possible reason for Palin's demise as a politician. Day and Thompson (2012) argue that Fey's parody was so effective because she "largely used Palin's own words and embellished them to highlight their naivety and nonsense, ultimately creating a vision of the politician as hopelessly vapid and uniformed" (p. 179). They argue that this depiction is much more satirical than the majority of previous *SNL* parodies. This switch in focus from personality-based to issue-based parodies gives *SNL*'s political humor more theoretical leverage to illuminate dominant hegemonic ideologies surrounding political policies and economic corporate interests.

Hariman (2008) argues that political humor, such as parody, can contribute to the maintenance of a democratic public culture. Hariman (2008) explains that "parody creates and sustains public consciousness first and foremost by exposing the limits of dominant discourse: it counters idealization, mythic enchantment, and other forms of hegemony" (p. 253). He further explains that parody is especially powerful when it moves beyond functioning as a corrective measure and generates thoughts and discussion in the public democratic sphere. Using the Bakhtinian model, he emphasizes four operations that are necessary for parody to contribute to a democratic public culture: doubling, carnivalesque spectatorship, social leveling and decentering discourse.

Doubling

Comic doubling within a parody opens up an original discourse to more than one meaning or interpretation. This is often accomplished through creating ambiguity and placing the parodic discourse alongside the target discourse. Hariman (2008) explains that "parodic imitation works, appropriately, at more than one level. The parody replicates some prior form and thereby makes that form an object of one's attention rather than a transparent vehicle for some other message" (p. 253). In this sense, it identifies a dominant or hegemonic code/message and negotiates it through parody in order to highlight contradictions in the original message or "transparent vehicle." Comic doubling in parodies is often accomplished through refraction or "making minor alterations to the original text" in order to be interpreted through a new angle or light (Peifer, 2013, p. 166). Peifer (2013) further explains,

> The exaggerated refractions of parody can often expose the underlying absurdities, ridiculousness, or contradictions commonly pervading the political realm . . . the subtle and not so subtle refractions can offer up illuminating interpretations of the unspoken subtext in political rhetoric (p. 167).

Refractions have the capability of moving negotiated messages into a "politics of signification" because rather than just reflecting or imitating, they have the capacity to create new meanings and interpretations outside of the dominant and negotiated codes. Peifer (2013) argues that this is why *SNL*'s parody of Sarah Palin was so powerful: "The comedy sketches were helping to create new and meaningful interpretations of Palin beyond the parameters of immediate 'real life' circumstances" (pp. 170–171). Peifer (2013) does caution that parody cannot accomplish this feat on its own, but must do so through the intertextual nature of dialogical discourse (p. 171).

In the *SNL* sketch "Caravan Cold Open," Kate McKinnon impersonates Laura Ingraham, host of *The Ingraham Angle.* The *SNL* set is transformed to visually appear like the Fox News studio, with the Fox News banner and *The Ingraham Angle* logo on the screen. Kate McKinnon imitates Ingraham's hairstyle, makeup and posture as she sits behind the studio desk wearing a red dress—to emphasize her conservative Republican political leanings. The target discourse and parody both begin with Ingraham introducing herself and the show. *SNL*'s parody also provides comic doubling through its imitation of programmatic style: interviews, live footage, and advertisements.

Parody Ingraham interviews fellow Fox News cable show host Judge Jeanine Pirro, played by Cecily Strong, as well as former Milwaukee County Sheriff David Clarke, played by Keenan Thompson. Ingraham, in the initial discourse, interviews a former ICE director as well as a Republican congressman from Louisiana. *SNL*'s choice to replace these individuals with people who have arguably less knowledge and experience with immigration policy or knowledge about the migrant caravan is an example of an exaggerated refraction. This exaggerated refraction places the establishment of partisan news, in general, under scrutiny. While parody is limited in what it is actually able to "say," one may extrapolate this strategic move as a critique of partisan news in its attempt to pass as "traditional" news. Partisan news is undermined through this comic double because the parody suggests that a host can have politically subjective and unqualified "experts" on their programs to dispense "the news," which is often assumed to be an objective account. Baym (2005) argues that conventional or "old news" asserts an "epistemological certainty" and pretends to already have the truth packaged neatly for consumption (p. 267). Juxtaposing the assumption of objectivity on Fox News' *The Ingraham Angle,* invokes humor, especially for those outside of the Fox News echo chamber, because it is known to be conservatively biased news. Providing parody interviews with Pirro, a fellow Fox News show host, and Sheriff David Clarke, a known Trump cheerleader, provide an exaggerated reading of partisan cable network news.

Carnivalesque Spectatorship

Hariman (2008) argues that parodied objects are cast into carnivalesque spec-
tatorships in which they are "held up to be seen, exposed, and ridiculed. . . .
The key operation is to reveal that what seemed to be identical with a particular mode of articulation in fact is otherwise" (pp. 255–256). He explains that
parody is a particularly effective strategy for externalizing discourse because
it uses "shifts, slippage, and silliness" to illustrate the performance inherent
within both discourses (p. 256). Hariman (2008) explains that as "parodic
techniques coalesce in the construction of carnivalesque spectatorship, institutional forms are revealed to be masks, [and] power and status are shown to
be acts" (p. 256).

    SNL's parody makes a textual shift in the order of the original discourse
to expose the relationship between Trump's announcing that he is a nationalist and his use of threat narratives against illegal immigrants. In the original
discourse, these two topics are separated by commercial breaks and not intended to be a continuation of the same conversation. In the *SNL* parody,
Ingraham says, "Thankfully we have a president who actually protects America. President Trump seen here in an official portrait . . . sent thousands of
troops to the border to stop the caravan" (*SNL*, 2018). The portrait displays
an American flag backdrop with blurry faceless Mexicans wearing sombre-
ros scattered around the bottom half of the photo. Donald Trump appears
front and center as a Rambo-type of action figure. He is accentuated with
exaggerated muscles and shirtless chest wearing a Davy Crocket raccoon-
skin hat. Parody Ingraham continues,

> Of course the liberal media is trying to label President Trump a racist. But
> except for his words and actions throughout his life, how is he a racist? All of
> sudden the term nationalist is bad. The word white is bad. The phrase white
> nationalist is bad. When I hear white nationalist, I just think of a fun Fourth of
> July barbeque. The kind you don't have to call the cops on. (*SNL*, 2018)

Immediately after this dialogue she switches to an interview about the caravan with parody Fox News show host Judge Jeanine Pirro. This shift in
discourse, as well as its silliness, make the relationship between Trump's
racist political discourse and enacting state violence against undocumented
immigrants explicit to the audience. Additionally, parody Ingraham, upon
thanking her sponsors, includes White Castle to further illustrate the point,
"A castle for whites, yes please" (*SNL*, 2018).

Social Leveling

Social leveling occurs when "humor starts with word play but quickly degen-
erates into . . . altering photos or adding voiceovers to represent events that

are patently impossible, interviewing people that are totally nuts, and so forth" (Hariman, 2008, p. 257). *SNL*'s parody provides several examples of social leveling. While Ingraham refers to the migrant caravan as an "invading horde," parody Ingraham refers to the migrants as a "vicious" caravan. Parody Ingraham is alluding to one of Ingraham's earlier statements in which she questioned whether or not the caravan had weapons based on Trump's claim that they were probably armed. Parody Ingraham states, "Tonight we're live from the Arizona border where a vicious caravan and dozens maybe millions of illegal immigrants are headed straight for you and your grandchildren. And that is not fear mongering. That is just the truth" (*SNL*, 2018). While Ingraham never said these words, her original discourse did exaggerate a threat narrative about the migrant caravan. *SNL*'s parody unmasks this ideology by providing heightened exaggeration of the original threat narrative to illustrate its ridiculousness.

Another example of social leveling occurs when parody Ingraham interviews Fox News show host Judge Jeanine Pirro. Parody Ingraham asks parody Pirro what she has heard about the caravan. Pirro responds, "I haven't just heard about it, I've seen it with my own eyes. Take a look at this footage of the caravan from earlier today" (*SNL*, 2018). The footage Pirro shows is Black Friday shoppers storming into a Walmart. The video shows mass chaos as people are rushing and pushing past each other to gather their coveted items. Upon seeing the footage, parody Ingraham gasps and says, "My God. And that is real footage of the caravan?" (*SNL*, 2018). Parody Pirro responds that "it has to be real. I found it on trutheagle.gun" (*SNL*, 2018). This aspect of the parody juxtaposes actual American citizens behaving with an "invading horde" mentality to consume material goods with *The Ingraham Angle's* actual footage of the caravan migrants pulling apart a fence to push through a blockade in Central America. The Black Friday video is far more chaotic and horde-like than the video of the migrants, which *SNL* purposely uses as a social leveling device to problematize the "objectivity" of the news coverage. Pirro's jab about truth and objectivity found on a website called trutheagle.gun further emphasizes the critique of partisan objectivity in news coverage.

The final example of social leveling demonstrates how *SNL*'s parody unmasks neoliberal discourses surrounding illegal immigration in order to reveal their racist undertones. Parody Ingraham asks Pirro who is in the caravan, alluding to the previously discussed video clips between Trump, Lemon and Ingraham. In the original discourse, Ingraham references a Homeland Security report that indicates people from the Middle East, Africa and South Asia are part of the caravan. The parody illustrates how traditional news coverage of illegal immigration is often racialized as a Mexican or Central American issue, by taking the original discourse and exaggerating it beyond realism. Pirro responds to parody Ingraham, "Everyone you've ever seen in your nightmares, Laura. It's got Guatemalans, Mexicans, ISIS, the Menendez Brothers, the 1990 Detroit Pistons, Thanos, and several Baba-dooks" (*SNL*, 2018). The parodic response begins in line with traditional discourses on illegal immigration, but then extends beyond into fictional examples to include comic book and horror villains. The cracks in the domi-nant discourse become evident through this parodic example as the original threat moves from only the migrants to all people of color, whether real or fictional.

This exchange continues, as President Trump is tied back into the dis-course on race and the caravan. Parody Ingraham asks Pirro, "And President Trump said that there are Middle Eastern people as well?" (*SNL*, 2018). Pirro responds, "No question, Laura. This caravan has hella Aladdin's. They took the very common direct flight from Iran to Guatemala. They claimed their elephants as service animals and then rode them straight into Mexico. It makes too much sense" (*SNL*, 2018). The humorous absurdity of Pirro's statement threatens the legitimacy of President Trump and Homeland Secur-ity's claim that the caravan traveling toward the United States from Central America includes people from the Middle East and other entire continents. Pirro's claim that Middle Easterners were taking the "very common direct flight" into Guatemala and riding their elephants into Mexico further pro-blematizes the dominant narratives surrounding the migrant caravan because it would be far more realistic to fly into the United States and overstay a travel visa. De Genova (2002) explains that overstaying a visa is a "discrete act by which very significant numbers of people become undocumented migrants" (p. 436). However, he argues that this is not especially dramatic, which is why "it is precisely 'the Border' that provides the exemplary theater for staging the spectacle of 'the illegal alien' that the law produces" (p. 436). *SNL*'s focus on the U.S.-Mexico border emphasizes the theatrical aspect of this stage, as well as its subsequent racializing effects for migrants.

This section of dialogue ends with parody Ingraham asking what will happen when the caravan arrives. Parody Pirro shows footage from the 2013 movie *World War Z* in which zombie hordes are moving rapidly and crawl-ing over one another to scale a giant wall. As the screen pans out, a zombie horde overturns a large public transit bus and a glimpse of Brad Pitt's profile is shown. When parody Ingraham asks Pirro if that was Brad Pitt, she re-sponds by saying that he was dating the caravan and that people had labeled them "Bradavan." The zombie reference in particular problematizes Ingra-ham's original discourse of referring to the migrant caravan as "an invading horde." Consistent with animal metaphors, hordes can also refer to zombies in popular culture with similar effects. Shifting the metaphor from animal to zombie elevates the threat narrative to a state of pandemic crisis. El Refaie (2001) argues that when illegal immigrants or refugees are no longer re-garded as human, "it becomes quite 'natural' to talk of them as being hunted and caught in a net" (p. 363). These metaphors naturalize state-sponsored violence against illegal immigrants through INS patrols tracking, hunting, rounding up and detaining migrants attempting to cross the U.S.-Mexico border. Whether depicted as a horde of animals or zombies, migrants are stripped of their human agency and rationality through these discourses.

Decentering Discourses

Hariman (2008) argues that "parody nurtures public culture by portraying public life as a dynamic field of competing voices forever commenting on each other. As with leveling, this is part of democracy's social imaginary" (p. 257). A common political argument made by Ingraham, as well as other conservative politicians, is that illegal immigrants take advantage of social welfare policies that end up costing taxpayers billions of dollars. *SNL*'s parody encourages an "opening" up of this debate and narrative through the exaggerated refraction of "dropping anchor" in the United States. When parody Ingraham interviews Sheriff David Clark, he tells her that he has "also learned that all the women in the caravan are more than nine months pregnant. And they are holding the babies in until the exact moment when they cross over the border. And the babies . . . get this . . . are pregnant" (*SNL*, 2018). *SNL*'s parody decenters the dominant narrative and problematizes it through the absurd exaggeration that the pregnant women's babies are also pregnant. Escobar (2008) argues that by suggesting undocumented women "drop anchor" or have "anchor babies," migrant women's reproduction is targeted and criminalized within public welfare discourse. Escobar explains that often in media and political discourses that "migrant women are imagined as crossing the border 'illegally' to secure not only their children's citizenship, but their own eventually, and undeservingly, accessing resources such as healthcare and education" (p. 64). *SNL*'s parody opens up these dominant narratives to multiple interpretations and problematizes hegemonic ideologies underlying immigration policy and its impact on the welfare state.

AN OPPOSITIONAL READING:
THE LIMITS AND POTENTIAL OF PARODY

Parody undoubtedly has the potential to illuminate contradictions within dominant narratives. Rossing (2012) explains that humor distorts, exaggerates, and reframes in ways that invite audiences to see themselves and society from new vantage points [and] . . . distinctively confronts contradictions and constructs possibilities for meaning and social and political repression" (p. 46). Parody is able to de-totalize dominant ideologies, but struggles in its ability to re-totalize them in an alternate framework. Often political parodies are left within the realm of humor and lack the necessary vehicle to join in "the struggle over discourse" in an oppositional framework. Abel and Barthel (2013) explain that "most stories filtered through the comedic domain remain there, but occasionally they are taken back into mainstream news with more critical frames" (p. 2).

SNL's parody of Sarah Palin is an example of how a negotiated reading transcends into an oppositional reading. Abel and Barthel (2013) argue that Palin's initial interview with CBS news anchor Katie Couric received little attention from the press and that Palin's answers during the interview were largely disregarded. However, after *SNL*'s political parody, the original interview was revisited and critiqued in new ways. Abel and Barthel (2013) explain that "after the *SNL* skit aired, journalists and news commentators used Tina Fey's impersonation and/or skit to discuss, reinterpret, or further analyze the Couric interview" (p. 9). Abel and Barthel (2013) argue that news organization's adherence to objective reporting often limit their ability to critically evaluate and analyze news stories, which leads them to reference "soft news" such as comedic "fake news." Campbell (2017) further explains that "soft news" programs like *The Daily Show* indicate "the potential of postmodern media to serve the role that journalists once performed" (p. 206).

It is too soon to evaluate whether *SNL*'s parody "Caravan Cold Open" has been re-totalized in mainstream media. The parody highlights and problematizes many of the dominant media metaphors and narratives surrounding illegal immigration and U.S. immigration policy. It will depend on whether or not journalists evaluate these "contradictions" and offer new critical approaches to discussing immigration. Baym (2005) argues that "the parody pieces ask us to consider just what a reporter's job should be. As such, they ultimately play a diagnostic function, identifying much that is wrong with news in its current form" (p. 270). While parody may remain confined to Hall's level of negotiation, it provides a valuable resource for critical cultural researchers and mainstream journalists to recognize these codes and re-totalize them in alternate frameworks that disrupt harmful hegemonic ideologies.

Journalists who wish to "re-totalize" *SNL*'s "Caravan Cold Open" could do so by examining how news coverage and political debates surrounding immigration are cloaked in neoliberal discourses. Roberts and Mahtani (2010) explain that "neoliberalism effectively masks racism through its value-laden moral project: camouflaging practices anchored in an apparent meritocracy, making possible a utopic vision of society that is non-racialized" (p. 254). By emphasizing meritocracy and individual agency, neoliberal discourses suggest that migrants who "choose" to enter the United States illegally also "choose" to break the law, therefore making them criminals and worthy of harsh treatment such as detention and deportation. Lawston and Murillo (2010) argue that this tautological reasoning "naturalizes" the binary "criminal/noncriminal" and "offers no historical context for migration patterns and trends; it also refuses to recognize the role of racism and white supremacy in the policing, criminalization, and imprisonment of large groups of people" (p. 41). Varsanyi (2008) explains that U.S. neoliberal economic policies such as the North American Free Trade Agreement (NAFTA) coupled with the desire for cheap labor and goods "act as powerful push and pull factors promoting cross-border labor migration" (p. 878). Neoliberal discourses surrounding immigration have effectively obscured the "interventionist" role of the United States in "creating and maintaining political and economic conditions that have driven migration northward" from Mexico and Central America (Lawston & Murrilo, 2010, p. 40).

By centering illegal immigration discourse around the spectacle of the U.S.-Mexico border, constructions of "illegal aliens" become synonymous with Mexicans and Central Americans (Romero, 2008). This has the racializing effect of targeting people of Latin American descent as "illegal" through the use of stereotypes centered on both physical characteristics and any failure to fully assimilate into white mainstream culture, such as continuing to speak Spanish. Dick (2011) argues that "racializing practices mark actors as non-normative by dehumanizing them, representing them as undifferentiated, immoral, dangerous—inherently and irredeemably Other. . . . To be sure, racialization often goes hand-in-hand with criminalization" (p. 40). While the law determines criminality, policing and surveillance are critical elements that assist in the construction of illegal immigrant status. Romero (2008) explains, "The practice of racial profiling demonstrates that citizenship status is inscribed on the body" (p. 28). Whether a person of Latin American descent is an immigrant (legal or illegal) or a citizen, they are often unable to leave the border behind them and often feel coerced to assimilate into white mainstream society. The racialization of illegal immigration discourse is important because "policy recommendations generated from the focus on assimilation maintain the status quo, ignore White privilege, and set the agenda to disadvantage racialized groups even further (Romero, 2008, p. 25). Retotalizing *SNL*'s parody requires journalists to deconstruct and unmask policies appearing to be "race neutral" in order to reveal underlying racist ideology and how it shapes and restricts our discourse on illegal immigration through the confinement of naturalized metaphors.

THE LIMITS OF PARODY TO
CHALLENGING DOMINANT IDEOLOGIES

Millennial's preference for postmodern mediums of news consumption parallels a return to partisan news and the emergence of news as "infotainment" or comedy-based "fake news." Consuming news through postmodern media often encapsulates viewers within particular political echo chambers based on algorithms. The algorithms propagate content similar to what is clicked on or liked most frequently, which is associated with increases in political polarization (Wicks, Wicks & Morimoto, 2014). However, *SNL*'s young audience's political affiliation spans across the political divide, uniting both Democrats and Republicans through political humor (Statistica, 2017). Through political humor, *SNL*'s "Caravan Cold Open" "de-totalizes" dominant ideologies prevalent in discourse on illegal immigration. *SNL*'s parody creates an opportunity for its audience to see the contradictions, exaggerations and inconsistencies within the dominant narrative of *The Ingraham Angle.*

While unmasking ideology through a negotiated reading is a worthwhile endeavor, political humor often fails to become "re-totalized" in an alternate framework. This is especially problematic for discourse surrounding immigration. Common metaphors naturalize and restrict immigration discourse within negative threat frames that serve to police and control their mobility. While political humor identifies and problematizes important elements within the immigration discourse, it is unable to "re-totalize" or shift this discourse within a context of neoliberal U.S. policies that create (often forced) migration, as well as the racist ideologies subsumed under neoliberal ideals of meritocracy and individual agency. Millennials will soon overtake Baby Boomers as the generation with largest voting capacity; this provides journalists with an increased responsibility for paying attention to how comedy-based "fake news" reveals dominant ideologies. Journalists must then engage in a "politics of signification" by establishing an alternate framework that is capable of challenging these dominant ideologies.

REFERENCES

Abel, A. D., & Barthel, M. (2013): Appropriation of mainstream news: How *Saturday Night Live* changed the political discussion. *Critical Studies in Media Communications, 30*(1): 1–16.

Barthes, R. (1972). *Mythologies.* New York, NY: The Noonday Press.

Baym, G. (2005). *The Daily Show*: discursive integration and the reinvention of political journalism. *Political Communication, 22*(3): 259–276.

Boskin, J. (1990). American political humor: Touchables and taboos. *International Political Science Review, 11*(4): 473–482.

Campbell, C. P. (2017). #IFTHEYGUNNEDMEDOWN: Postmodern media criticism in a post-racial world. In Lind, R. A. (Ed.), *Race and gender in electronic media: Content, context, culture* (pp. 195–212). New York, NY: Routledge.

Cisneros, J. D. (2008). Contaminated communities: The metaphor of "Immigrant as Pollutant" in media representations of immigration. *Rhetoric & Public Affairs, 11*(4): 569–602.

Day, A., & Thompson, E. (2012). Live from New York, it's the fake news! *Saturday Night Live* and the (non) politics of parody. *Popular Communication, 10*: 170–182.

De Genova, N. P. (2002). Migrant "illegality" and deportability in everyday life. *Annual Review of Anthropology, 31*: 419–447.

Dick, H. (2011). Making immigrants illegal in small-town USA. *Journal of Linguistic Anthropology, 21*(1): 35–55.

Dimock, M. (2019). Defining generations: Where millennials end and generation Z begins. Pew Research Center. Retrieved from: https://www.pewresearch.org/fact-tank/2019/01/17/where-millennials-end-and-generation-z-begins/.

El Refaie, E. (2001). Metaphors we discriminate by: Naturalized themes in Austrian newspaper articles about asylum seekers. *Journal of Sociolinguistics, 5*(3): 352–371.

Escobar, M. (2008). No one is criminal. CR10 Publications Collective (*Eds.) Abolition now! Ten years of strategy and struggle against the prison industrial complex*. Oakland, CA: AK Press (pp. 57–70).

Foer, F. (2017). *World without mind: The existential threat of big tech*. New York, NY: Penguin.

Fox News. (2018). What can US do to stop migrant caravans? Ingraham Angle Transcript. Retrieved from https://www.foxnews.com/transcript/what-can-us-do-to-stop-migrant-caravans.

Fry, R. (2016). Millennials approach baby boomers as America's largest generation in the electorate. Pew Research Center. Retrieved from http://www.pewresearch.org/fact-tank/2018/04/03/millennials-approach-baby-boomers-as-largest-generation-in-u-s-electorate/?amp=1.

Geertz, C. (1983). *Local knowledge: Further essays in interpretive knowledge*. New York, NY: Basic Books.

Gottfried, J., Barthel, M., Shearer, E., & Mitchell, A. (2016). The 2016 presidential campaign—a news event that's hard to miss. Pew Research Center. Retrieved from http://www.pewresearch.org/wp-content/uploads/sites/8/2016/02/PJ_2016.02.04_election-news_FINAL.pdf.

Hall, S. (1980). Encoding/Decoding. In Centre for Contemporary Cultural Studies (Ed.): Culture, Media, Language: Working Papers in Cultural Studies, 1972–79. London: Hutchinson, pp. 128–138 ("Encoding and Decoding in Television Discourse," 1973).

Hariman, R. (2008). Political parody and public culture. *Quarterly Journal of Speech, 94*(3): 247–272.

Hill, M. R. (2013). Developing a normative approach to political satire: A critical perspective. *International Journal of Communication, 7*: 324–337.

Joyella, M. (2018). Surging MSNBC puts added pressure on Fox News to defend Laura Ingraham. *Forbes*. Retrieved from https://www.forbes.com/sites/markjoyella/2018/04/03surging-msnbc-puts-added-pressure-on-fox-news-to-defend-laura-ingraham/#6136689c1c3d.

Katz, J. (1992). Rock, rap, and movies bring you the news. *Rolling Stone* 625 (pp. 33–45, 40, 78).

Kuipers, G. (2008). "The sociology of humor." In Raskin, V., & Ruch, W. (Eds.), *The primer of humor research*. New York, NY: Mouton de Gruyter.

Lawston, J. M., & Murillo, R. R. (2010). The discursive figuration of U.S. supremacy in narratives sympathetic to undocumented immigrants. *Social Justice, 36*(2): 38–53.

Levendusky, W. S. (2013). Why do partisan media polarize viewers? *American Journal of Political Science, 57*(3): 611–623.

McQuail, D. (2010). *Mass communication theory*. (6th ed.) Los Angeles, CA: Sage.

Ortega, F. J., & Feagin, J. R. (2016). The undying white racial frame. In Campbell, C. P. (Ed.), *The Routledge companion to media and race*. (pp. 19–30). New York/Abingdon: Routledge

Peifer, J. T. (2013). Palin, *Saturday Night Live*, and framing: Examining the dynamics of political parody. *The Communication Review, 16*: 155–177.

Pew Research Center. (2017). Defining generations: Where millennials end and generation Z begins. Retrieved from http://www.pewresearch.org/fact-tank/2019/01/17/where-millennials-end-and-generation-z-begins/.

Roberts, D. J., & Mahtani, M. (2010). Neoliberalizing race, racing neoliberalism: Placing "Race" in neoliberal discourses. *Antipode, 42*(2): 248–257.

Romero, M. (2008). Crossing the immigration and race border: A critical race theory approach to immigration studies. *Contemporary Justice Review, 11*(1): 23–37.

Rossing, J. P. (2012). Deconstructing postracialism: Humor as a critical, cultural project. *Journal of Communication Inquiry, 36*(1): 44–61.

Saturday Night Live. (2018, November 3). Caravan Cold Open. Season 44, episode 6, 2018. Retrieved from https://www.youtube.com/watch?v=kG7szS15O8Q.

Semeraro, E. (2018). Here's who's watching *Saturday Night Live*—and where they are watching it. Retrieved from https://www.broadcastingcable.com/.amp/news/heres-whos-watching-saturday-night-live-where-theyre-watching-it.

Statistica. (2017). How often do you watch *Saturday Night Live* (*SNL*)? By political affiliation. Retrieved from https://www.statista.com/statistics/681955/snl-viewership-frequency-political-affiliation/.

Varsanyi, M. W. (2008). Rescaling the "Alien," rescaling personhood: Neoliberalism, immigration, and the state. *Annals of the Association of American Geographers, 98*(4): 877–896.

Wicks, R. H., Wicks, J. L., & Morimoto, S. A. (2014). Partisan media selective exposure during the 2012 presidential election. *American Behavioral Scientist, 58*(9): 1131–1143.

Wild, N. M. (2015). Dumb vs. fake: Representations of Bush and Palin on *Saturday Night Live* and their effects on the journalistic public sphere. *Journal of Broadcasting & Electronic Media, 59*(3): 494–508.

Chapter Seven

#DCNative: Examining Community Identity, Representation and Resistance in Washington, D.C.

Loren Saxton Coleman

On May 14, 2018, the *Washingtonian* magazine launched a preview to its T-shirt marketing campaign, "I'm not a tourist. I live here," via Instagram. The campaign guaranteed new subscription holders T-shirts and encouraged them to share their "#Imnotatourist" stories on Instagram. The preview featured young white Washingtonians posing in tourist locations in the city. In the first 24 hours of its launch, the campaign's preview received significant criticism for its lack of racial diversity. Instagram users posted negative feedback that questioned the magazine's decision to only feature young, white models in the campaign's photoshoot (Lambert, 2018).

A local activist, Tony Lewis, Jr., reposted one of the campaign's images with this comment:

> PLEASE TAKE A LOOK AT @washingtonianmag's DEPICTION OF WHO 'LIVES HERE'—NOT ONE BLACK FACE IN THE ENTIRE PIECE. BLACK PEOPLE STILL MAKE UP 47% OF THIS CITY. THIS IS DISRESPECTFUL, CARELESS, AND RACIST. (YEAH I SAID IT, RACIST.) THIS IS VERY REPRESENTATIVE OF HOW WE FEEL IN OUR OWN CITY. THAT WE ARE INVISIBLE. THAT WE DON'T EXIST. THAT PEOPLE THAT MOVE HERE HAVE MORE VALUE THAN THOSE BORN HERE. THAT WHEN WE DIE IN THE STREETS IT ISN'T IMPORTANT. THAT THE NEW RESTAURANT OR CONDO SUPERSEDES OUR EXISTENCE.

Other Instagram users echoed Lewis' sentiment by circulating across social media outlets that the *Washingtonian* had failed to launch an inclusive campaign that was representative of Washington, D.C (Lambert, 2018). The overwhelming amount of criticism and outrage on Instagram and across other media outlets led the *Washingtonian* magazine to cancel the campaign and issue a formal apology. The *Washingtonian*'s CEO and president, Catherine Merrill Williams, wrote:

> As a native Washingtonian, I am very sorry that our latest "I'm Not a Tourist" marketing campaign did not represent the wonderfully diverse city in which we live. . . . We always appreciate feedback and are glad that people take the time to point out when we let them down, as we did this time. I apologize on behalf of our entire team. (*Washingtonian* staff, 2018)

Although this apology was issued and the campaign never launched, the damage appeared to be done. On the same day the *Washingtonian* launched its preview of the campaign, Lewis announced an alternative photoshoot called "Native. I'm From Here." He invited "folks who were born, raised, and educated in this city," according to his Instagram post on May 14, 2018, to meet at Union Market. This counter photoshoot was intended to "provide a counter image that not every person living in this city is a white millennial," according to Lewis' Instagram post.

The Washingtonian campaign's preview and most importantly, the counter photoshoot raised the following questions: (1) How do black Washingtonians in D.C. create and maintain community during revitalization efforts, and (2) How do black Washingtonians use social media to challenge revitalization efforts across the city? In this chapter, I will explore the "Native. I'm From Here" photoshoot as an exemplar of how black Washingtonians pursued spatial justice via media practice. Guided by historical cultural (geographical) materialism, this textual analysis will investigate how black Washingtonians resisted exclusion and produced a counternarrative to the "white millennials" as native Washingtonians portrayed in the *Washingtonian*'s T-shirt campaign's photoshoot.

DEFINING THEORY: CULTURAL HISTORICAL (GEOGRAPHICAL) MATERIALISM

In cultural and critical studies, communication and culture are both constitutive and active processes, rejecting the viewpoint that culture is a static object, or separate from political and economic structures (Klaus, 1993). Raymond Williams (1961/2000) defined communication as the continued process of re-creating meaning among individuals in society. Meaning exists and is shared on both an individual and collective level and works to form community (Williams, 1961/2000). Cultural theorists also define culture as active historical processes. For Williams (1961/2000), culture is intertwined and inseparable historical processes, and human activity, such as communication, is central to those processes. With an emphasis on human activity, historical cultural materialism accounts for levels of fluidity, movement and, therefore, change, in culture and society via communication.

Communication forms are primarily contextualized in social space (Shin, 2009). Individuals are historically and socially located in space (Williams, 1973). As Marx and Engels observed, "Men are producers of their conceptions, ideas, etc.—real, active men, as they are conditioned by a definite development of their productive forces" (1845–46/1970, p. 47). Here, Marx and Engels highlighted how people participate in the making of their own social and physical environments while constantly being conditioned by those produced material forces. Physical environments help shape human behavior, influencing political action, civic engagement and democratic practice, among other cultural and social practices (Shin, 2009).

Prior to the 1960s and 1970s, space and spatiality was largely defined by empirical geographies (Soja, 2010). Henry Lefebvre and Michel Foucault helped shift the geographical conversation from the "physical" and "empirical" to the socially produced and producing concept of space. For the purpose of this chapter, I will focus on Lefebvre's definition of spatiality (social space).

Lefebvre's (1991) concept of space emphasized human practice and the re-constitution of space. He emphasized this point in his discussion on the spatial triad. There are three points on the spatial triad—spatial practice, representations of space and spaces of representation. Lefebvre (1991) defined spatial practices as the means by which material spaces are made, and human activity that use and transform those spaces. Representations of space are the social relations in which spatiality is produced. Lastly, spaces of representations are the spaces in which people live through complex images and symbols. All three points of the triad exist in unity and are simultaneously contradictive. Lefebvre's spatial triad highlights how people participate in the production of specific geographies, conditioned by specific practices of social life.

Soja's (1989) socio-spatial dialectic is rooted in Lefebvre's spatial triad. This dialectic continued to help move empirical geographies towards more critical analyses of space and spatial structures' role in the construction of social life. For Soja, space is both political and ideological, conditioned by historical and social processes. People create geographies within particular geographic, political, cultural and social constraints that then shape human action (Soja, 1989). Cultural geographer Manuel Castells (1983) observed that "space is not a reflection of society, it is society. . . . Therefore, spatial forms, at least on our planet, will be produced, as all other objects are, by human action (p. 4). Here, Castells emphasized that space is constitutive of society. Since it is produced by humans, it is conditioned by complex power relationships and will also express those power relationships, shaped by gender and class structures. Soja (2010) contends that those power relationships can also be determined by racial structures.

A materialist perspective on space takes into consideration that space is shaped by historical processes and those processes are political. These processes often contribute to uneven development, which is inherent to capitalism (Harvey, 1976; Soja, 2010). Walker (1981) examined the uneven development in urban spaces. He highlighted how social relations create restraints and pressures that inform particular forms of spatial organization. Harvey (1976) and Walker (1981) investigated the production of built environments such as urban cities as divisional and often discriminatory practices. However, Castells (1983) and Soja (2010) argued that uneven development can also serve as the foundation of resistance.

Historical cultural (geographical) materialism, coupled with Lefebvre's spatial triad, will inform this chapter's analysis of the "Native. I'm From Here" campaign as portrayed on Instagram via the hashtag #dcnativephotoshoot. I locate this hashtag within a space of representation, and I argue that the photoshoot is a form of spatial resistance. As such, this textual analysis will interrogate the production of #DCNativephotoshoot as a counternarrative of native Washingtonians in Washington, D.C.

DEFINING AND LOCATING THE TEXT: WASHINGTON, D.C. AND THE "NATIVE. I'M FROM HERE" PHOTOSHOOT

Like other urban areas across the nation, Washington, D.C. is a site of uneven cultural, economic and political geographies. From 1950–2000, Washington, D.C. experienced a steady decline in population (Hyra, 2015). In accordance with other "back-to-the-city" movements, also known as urban renewal, across the nation between 1990–2010, D.C.'s population has increased steadily since 2000 (Hyra, 2015). However, one key distinction about D.C.'s "back-to-the-city" movement was that the population increase was driven largely by incoming white residents. The city, formerly known as "Chocolate City," lost more than 39,000 black residents, resulting in a more racially diverse, more educated and affluent city (Hyra, 2015).

This demographic shift happened at the same time as several predominantly black low-income neighborhoods in the city were gentrified. Gentrification is a highly debated area of study (Hyra, 2015). For the purpose of this chapter, I use Zuk et al.'s (2018) conceptualization:

> Gentrification has been seen as a tool, goal, outcome, or unintended
> consequence of revitalization processes in declining urban neighborhoods,
> which are defined by their physical deterioration, concentrations of poverty,
> and racial segregation of people of color (p. 32).

Here, the authors established a clear relationship between revitalization and gentrification. This conceptualization of gentrification also highlighted the consistencies in the spaces ripe for revitalization. Most importantly, it specifically called attention to how these spaces are racially constructed.

Unintended consequences of revitalization can be both positive and negative. For example, an influx of high-income residents can lead to an increase in grocery store options, increased police presence and more diverse restaurant and entertainment options (Hyra, 2015). Similarly, Zuk et al. (2018) stated that high-income residents with higher levels of education demand certain amenities in their neighborhoods, such as job and recreational opportunities and, sometimes, the "authentic" urban experience. Hyra's (2015) work in the historic Shaw/Howard and U Street Corridor in Washington, D.C. found that while current residents can benefit from revitalization in the neighborhood, these changes also foster feelings of resentment and alienation.

One exemplar of this resentment and alienation can be understood through the backlash the *Washingtonian* received after previewing its "I'm Not a Tourist. I live here" T-shirt campaign. This campaign's tone-deaf imagery of Washington, D.C. is consistent with scholarship that has found that traditional media often support the political and economic interests of the city (Brown-Saracino & Rumpf, 2011). Traditional media have been found to support efforts that support the city as a "growth machine," or a place desirable or in need of revitalization.

Tom Slater (2006) noted that traditional media serve urban elite interests, prioritizing a narrative about a city that appeals to tourists and deprioritizes local residents and the spaces where they live. Similarly, Slater (2006) noted that traditional media, like the *Washingtonian*, often promote an "urban authenticity" that appeals to gentrifiers. Although D.C. residents were shown wearing "I'm Not a Tourist" T-shirts, the models were all young and white, posing in or near tourist attractions. T-shirts were sent to people with some of "D.C.'s most popular Instagram accounts" to help raise awareness and generate enthusiasm about the *Washingtonian* campaign (Cohen, 2018).

This analysis departs from research on traditional media coverage of gentrification in that it focuses on the counter campaign, the "Native. I'm From Here" photoshoot. I examine the photoshoot as an act of resistance and locate it in the space of representation. As such, using textual analysis, I examine the ways in which this counter campaign helped create community and re-create the meaning of native Washingtonian.

The study of culture in cultural studies is the study of fluid and transformative practice via the abstraction of forms from various texts (Storey, 1996). Culture is not static, nor reflective (Johnson, 1986/1987). Therefore, textual analyses in cultural studies highlight the constitutive role of culture in the production of our social, political, economic and spatial world. Stuart

Hall (1975) stated that textual analyses should investigate the social process-es of production and consumption of texts. In his introduction to *Paper Voices*, he described the intricate process of textual analyses of newspapers as cultural artifacts. A cultural artifact has a "culture" of its own, meaning it has a set of distinct produced meanings and practices (du Gay et al., 1997). This textual analysis will examine a specific cultural artifact, #dcnativephot-oshoot, an Instagram hashtag used to help document the photoshoot "Native. I'm From Here."

Instagram is one of the most popular social networking sites worldwide. As of June 2018, there were one billion active users per month (Statista, 2018). On this social networking site, users can edit and share photos and videos. Hashtags, a keyword or combination of words denoted by a hash (#), are used as a search function, and also to increase visibility of tagged content (Oh et al., 2016). According to Smith (2018), adding one hashtag on an Instagram increases its reach by 12.6 percent. Zappavigna (2015) also noted that hashtags can also help build relationships among Instagram users. In this case, hashtags can be used to address users or convey specific evaluative meaning about a post. In the following analysis, I will examine #dcnative-photoshoot as a cultural artifact to interrogate how this hashtag helped create community among native black Washingtonians.

Hall (1975) stated that immersion is the first step in cultural analyses. In this phase the researcher is able to hone in on a narrow and specific area to help select meaningful and significant evidence. Two key historical moments guided the immersion process of the textual analysis—the preview of the *Washingtonian*'s "I'm Not a Tourist" campaign posted to its Instagram page on May 14, 2018, and the counter-campaign "Native. I'm From Here" photo-shoot on May 20, 2018.

During the immersion process, I used the keyword "DCNative" to search hashtags on Instagram. The top two hashtags in the results were: #dcnative with 9,498 posts and #dcnativephotoshoot with 41 posts. The goals of this analysis are to examine the space of representation of the "Native. I'm From Here" photoshoot and how a community of resistance was formed and spatial justice pursued in response to the *Washingtonian*'s "I'm Not a Tourist" cam-paign. The text, #dcnativephotoshoot hashtag, was selected because it pro-vided evidence of how the campaign created community via media and spa-tial practice.

Consistent with Hall (1975) and Johnson's (1986/1987) prescription for cultural analyses, my analysis examined the images, tone of comments, style and treatment of the 41 public posts using the hashtag #dcnativephotoshoot. Critical analyses do not have concern with breadth and objectivity; instead, a cultural analysis focuses on context (Hall, 1975). After the long preliminary soak (Hall, 1975), three themes were identified: "I'm So D.C.," "We're not Tourists. We've Been Here" and "Change is Evolution, not Exclusion." Although separated for analysis, thematic categories are not mutually exclusive and should be understood as working together as a complex whole cultural artifact.

REPRESENTATION AS RESISTANCE IN #DCNATIVEPHOTOSHOOT

"I'm So D.C."

The "Native. I'm From Here" photoshoot was announced on May 14, 2018, on Tony Lewis, Jr.'s Instagram account. In his response to the *Washingtonian*'s campaign, he and @thespicesuite, local black entrepreneur and chef Angel Anderson, called for all native Washingtonians to meet at the old Florida Avenue Market in Northeast D.C., now known as Union Market. They asked attendees to wear all black or "Native" t-shirts. His post stated, "No more conceding to these false campaigns." Here, Lewis was specifically referencing the *Washingtonian*'s "I'm Not a Tourist" campaign. The magazine's failure to include any black models in the photoshoot was explicitly noted here as a false campaign about Washington, D.C. and what it means to be a native Washingtonian.

The comment was accompanied by an image of a flyer for the photoshoot. It listed the date and time, location, who was invited, dress code and contact information. The location on the flyer was listed as Union Market, which is described on its website as "a place where businesses scale and grow—where neighbors, students, DC transplants, artists and tourists come to find a community they can shape and call their own" (About Union Market, 2019). However, the flyer was set on the backdrop of an image of the D.C. Farmers Market, also known as the Florida Avenue Market.

D.C. Farmer's Market first opened in 1931 as the Union Terminal Market (D.C. Office of Planning, 2009). For three decades the market housed meat and produce vendors and served as a local wholesale distributer (D.C. Office of Planning, 2009). In the 1960s, D.C. officials banned the sale of meat and eggs outdoors. The ban, coupled with industrial deterioration, contributed to the market's decline in business until the city included the warehouse district in the city's 2006 Comprehensive Plan that called for a revitalization of the Florida Avenue Market. The plan stated that its goal was to create a "regional destination" that featured residential, entertainment, dining and wholesale food uses (D.C. Office of Planning, 2009). The "regional destination" was realized in 2012 when the revitalized D.C. Market reopened as Union Market.

The photoshoot's flyer is representative of what Soja (2010) highlighted as an uneven geography and a contested space. Andrew Herod (2011) and Soja (1985) both stated that spatiality is intricate, unevenly developed and constantly remade. In Lewis's post of the photoshoot's flyer, the "old" (D.C. Farmer's Market) and "new" (Union Market) spaces were shown in opposition to one another, and simultaneously being used as a rallying call for those "Native Washingtonians" who Lewis defined as being "born, raised and educated in D.C." Here, the inclusion of the "old" D.C. Farmer's Market image challenged the dominant signification of the "new" Union Market. Lewis used the image of the "old" D.C. Market as a sign of remembrance. Users identified with this space by commenting, "throw back pic" and "for the culture" on Lewis's post. Although Union Market was open, this counter photoshoot's location was reclaimed on the flyer. More specifically, in the space of representation, this flyer is representative of a creation of an alternate cultural geography that celebrated and commemorated the memory and history of black native Washingtonians.

Other posts in this theme featured images and comments consistent with this alternate cultural geography. For example, in one black female's post, she included an image of herself wearing a "Native" T-shirt in all black standing in one of the city's intersections. This image contrasted the *Washingtonian*'s campaign imagery that featured many white millennial models in the city. The black female Instagram user commented,

> "I'm not a tourist, I live here" . . . in fact, I was born, raised, educated and still live in #DC. That's right, not the #DMV! It's not an "anti-anything" movement, just a group of #chocolatecity #DCnatives showing love and the #pride for our #hometown.

Here, this Instagram user described herself as a D.C. native. In her comment, she referenced a clear distinction between Washington, D.C. and the DMV (D.C./Maryland/Virginia). It seemed important for her to make it clear to her followers that she was from D.C. specifically, not any of the surrounding suburbs in Maryland or Virginia. Similarly, she explicitly referenced Washington, D.C. as "Chocolate City," a nickname given to the city by funk band Parliament in 1975 (Asch & Musgrove, 2017). In the 1970s, "Chocolate City" symbolized and celebrated black culture and consciousness in the city (Asch & Musgrove, 2017). It also highlighted that Washington, D.C. was a predominantly black city, making up about 70 percent of the city in the 1970s. Although those numbers have declined recently, black residents still make up 47 percent compared to 45 percent white residents (U.S. Census Bureau, 2018). In this post, the hashtag #chocolatecity seemed to be used to remind users that D.C. is still "Chocolate City," and black Washingtonians, like herself, continue to be proud of their hometown. Again, this post is an exemplar of how spaces of representation can use symbols such as "Chocolate City" to counter dominant narratives of racial exclusion and segregation often associated with revitalization efforts.

Other posts included images of black men and women wearing T-shirts and hats with different symbols that communicated "I'm So DC." In one post, two older black men are pictured with the hashtag #lovemycity in the image. In the picture one man wears an "I'm So DC" hat and the other man is shown wearing all black with his fist raised. The comment included an additional hashtag, #westandtogether. Similarly, two additional posts include images of people wearing T-shirts with D.C. flags and "I'm So DC" T-shirts.

One black female Instagram user posted a video of the crowd after the photoshoot with go-go music playing in the background. The video showed some attendees in all black dancing to the music. The video was accompanied by the comment, "of course #gogo after the #dcnativephotoshoot." Here, the Instagram user used go-go music to help define what it means to be a D.C. native.

Go-go music originated in Washington, D.C. in the mid-1970s and can be conceptualized as an alternative and counter discursive reality that has endured via D.C.'s black communities (Hopkinson, 2012). As the city's demographics changed, new laws were developed to minimize its presence in the city, because it was often associated with drugs, crime and violence (Hopkinson, 2012). However, go-go music endured and as included in this Instagram users' post can be understood as a symbol of longevity, persistence and, most importantly, authenticity, among native black Washingtonians.

Another Instagram user posted an image of what appeared to be an aerial view of the back of the photoshoot crowd. Majority attendees are shown wearing all black and seem to be awaiting instruction on how to organize for the photo. The significance of this post is in the background, which includes a dilapidated building and what appears to be a high-rise under construction. The photo was accompanied by the hashtag, #dcornothing and the *Washingtonian*'s handle, @washingtonianmag.

The visual contrast of the run-down building and the new high-rise conveyed the uneven development in the city. The people at the photoshoot shown amidst economic renewal and reinvestment conveyed a reclaimed and reformed space of resistance. In this image, the #DCNativephotoshoot appeared to have created community in spatial struggle to help combat the *Washingtonian*'s singular racialized imagery of "authenticity" in the city.

"We're Not Tourists. We've Been Here."

The *Washingtonian*'s use of "white millennial" models, as pointed out by Lewis, provides evidence of how traditional media use specific imagery to represent an urban "authenticity" that can appeal to newcomers, signaling the city as a place suited for renewal, revitalization, and thus, gentrification (Slater, 2006). The counter campaign, "Native. I'm From Here," responded to a campaign that failed to depict the diversity in Washington, D.C. and, more importantly, failed to include and celebrate black native Washingtonian communities. As such, the counter campaign, tagged by #dcnativephotoshoot, not only showed pride among native black Washingtonians, but also referenced spaces and symbols that indicated that black Washingtonians are an integral part of the city's past, present and future. The counter campaign highlighted the role that black Washingtonians have played and continue to play in the production of the city's historical, cultural, political and economic life.

In several posts in this category, Instagram users mentioned specific spaces, such as schools, and specific quadrants of the city (Northeast, Northwest, Southeast, Southwest) that provided evidence of being "born and raised" in D.C. For example, one black female Instagram user posted an image of herself and her sister. Both women wore black T-shirts with different symbols that represented being a D.C. native. One wore a shirt with the words "202 Born Raised" and the other wore a T-shirt with the D.C. flag and "Dunbar Alumni." "202" is the Washington, D.C. area code and Dunbar is a public high school, one of two public high schools for African Americans in the city (Fitzpatrick & Goodwin, 1999). The comment accompanying the image stated:

> #dcnativephotoshoot ready with my sister #bornandraised #SEDC #Anacostia #FortDupont #DunbarDC #dcornothing #Eastern # JeffersonJHS #AnneBeers #AnthonyBowen.

In this comment, the Instagram user explicitly stated that both women pictured were born and raised in the city, specifically in the Southeast quadrant of the city. The hashtags in this post are locations in the city, and names of elementary, junior high and high schools in the D.C. Public School system. This post validated this campaign as an act of resistance as it constructs a counter narrative of celebration and positivity about public schools located in the area.

Other posts categorized under this theme featured images of black men and women in various T-shirts that include different symbols and language that communicate D.C. is home. For example, one black male user posted an image of himself and a coworker at work. Although shown at work, the user was still able to participate in the counter campaign via the photoshoot's hashtag. The user commented:

> We're not tourists. We've been here. In solidarity with brother @MrTonyLewisJr and all the true natives at #dcnativephotoshoot #chocolatecity

Another black female Instagram user posted herself with a black T-shirt with a blue D.C. flag on it. Her comment stated:

I'm not a tourist. I'm a #DCNative #dcornothing #dcasfuck #dcig #dcigers # dcblogger #dcstyle #weariwent

In the aforementioned posts, Instagram users explicitly reclaimed the language, "I'm not a tourist" from the *Washingtonian*'s campaign. Here, this statement was used to convey an alternative representation of D.C. natives. In the first post, "we've been here," also seems to convey longevity and endurance, unlike the message conveyed by models in the *Washingtonian*'s campaign. Also, this Instagram user identified as a true, or more authentic, native than those pictured in the *Washingtonian*'s campaign.

Authenticity was also signified in other Instagram posts in this theme. Instagram users posted images that conveyed multigenerational D.C. native families. For example, one black female Instagram user posted an image of herself and what appeared to be her mother and daughter. All three black women were wearing black. The user stated:

Born here, lives here, and gonna die here. #dcnativephotoshoot #dcornothing #nedc #nevergonnaleavenowwhat.

Here, this Instagram user emphasized her family's history in Northeast D.C. and explicitly stated that they're not going to leave. Another black female Instagram user posted an image of herself and her mother, who wore a Ms. District of Columbia sash. The user's comment indicated that her mother was crowned Ms. Senior D.C. Similarly, another black female Instagram user posted a picture of a woman and her two daughters wearing black T-shirts with the words "Native" written on them in white. The outline of the map of DC was superimposed as the "A" in "Native."

Another black female Instagram user posted an image of her family, stating, "#dcnatives BORN N RAISED IN DC! #dcnativephotoshoot #mycity #chocolatecity." This user also posted a video that showed photoshoot organizers asking children to come to the front of the crowd. In the video, it appeared that the organizers wanted to take a picture of majority black D.C. native children. Children helped construct a counternarrative of growth and longevity.

Washington, D.C. Ward 8 City Councilman Trayon White also participated in the counter photoshoot via the hashtag. He posted an image of himself wearing a "DC Native" hat with the D.C. flag on it. His comment stated:

My family and many like mine endured a lot to survive and stay in this DC we see today. We will never be silent about claiming our city! There was a lot of blood shed, triumph, and heart breaks that allows me to do what I do so I/we owe up. I stand with my family against the @washingtonianmag! We will never allow you to change our narrative #dcnative #dcnativephotoshoot

#GreaterSEBorn #TheRealDC @thespicesuite @jimmieblackjr @ silasgrant @ robertwhite_dc @cm_mcduffie

Although the image of White was not at the physical location of the photo-shoot, the use of the hashtag allowed him to engage with other users partici-pating in the larger counter campaign. His comment about the "DC we see today" pointed to the contested spaces between "old" and "new" D.C. Yet White's position as a young, black councilman, coupled with his emphasis on the struggle and survival of black families in the "D.C. we see today," can be conceptualized as an act of resistance against the cultural and political displacement that Hyra (2015) stated are common consequences in neighbor-hoods undergoing urban renewal. Despite the economic pressures and changes during revitalization, White highlighted that his family, and others like his, have endured and remain active in the city. His post communicated that his family and community were fighting against a narrative of displace-ment and exclusion, like the one perpetuated in the *Washingtonian* campaign.

Several Instagram users posted the "official" photo from the "Native. I'm From Here" photoshoot. For example, one Instagram user posted the image that included black people gathered in the old Warehouse District of the Florida Avenue Market. The two organizers, Tony Lewis, Jr. and Angel Anderson, are pictured standing in the front and center of the crowd holding a D.C. flag. Lewis is shown with a raised fist, and Angel is shown making a peace sign. The post's comment stated:

> We are from here and still live in the Nation's Capital. Just a glimpse of the people that remain and have thrived in this city. A magazine and gentrification can't erase us from the narrative of our home. The official photo came out great! Four quadrants, three stars, two bars, one city. #DCNative #DCNative-Photoshoot #DCorNothing.

Here, the Instagram user's comments rejected the *Washingtonian*'s represen-tation of the city. More importantly, even though this user called out the *Washingtonian* as trying to erase black Washingtonians from the city's narra-tive, the tone of this comment is one of inclusivity. In the last statement, "four quadrants, three starts, two bars, one city," the user highlighted how the city's narrative should encompass the stories and images that represent the rich cultures in D.C., not just white millennials.

"Change is Evolution, not Exclusion"

The "Native. I'm From Here" photoshoot was planned to provide a counter narrative to the *Washingtonian*'s "I'm Not a Tourist" T-shirt campaign. In-stagram users' posts that were categorized in this theme highlighted the flawed *Washingtonian* campaign but, most importantly, called for a more diverse representation of the city that includes all of the city, specifically black Washingtonians, in plans for growth and progress.

One Instagram user posted the official photograph from the "Native. I'm From Here" photoshoot and a candid shot of the crowd. In both images, a majority of black people wearing all black filled the frame. The user posted this comment.

> The Washingtonian magazine published an campaign called "I'm not a Tourist, I Live Here" and not a single person in it was black, despite the fact that African Americans are the largest ethnic group in DC . . . hundreds of people born and raised in DC converged on Union Market in solidarity . . . today was a great day in DC . . .

Here, this Instagram user pointed out that the *Washingtonian* excluded black people from its campaign. For this user, the omission of black Washingtonians in its campaign was inconsistent with the city's demographics. This user praised the counter photoshoot's organizers and their ability to create a space where people can gather to produce more inclusive representation of the city.

Another Instagram user also praised the counter photoshoot for planning an event that helped remind others that D.C. is not monolithic. The black female Instagram user posted an image of Lewis and Anderson, both draped in D.C. flags, and another picture with Lewis posing with other photoshoot attendees. The first half of her comment stated:

> When two people decided we aren't and will not be forgotten! Hundred show up in all black. Washington, DC was once known as "Chocolate City" but with gentrification came an increase in high income "others" and the push out of low/high income "chocolate" seeking affordable housing in MC and VA.

Here, this Instagram user illustrated the racial and class tension in the city. As such, consistent with Soja's (2010) assertion that uneven development is essential for capitalism, this user highlighted the economic, racial and spatial injustices produced via "gentrification" in the city as she emphasized how the influx of high-income "others" resulted in the lack of affordable housing for "chocolate," or assumed black residents, even those with high incomes. The second half of her comment stated:

> After @washingtonianmag published a pictorial depicting DC as White, @mrtonylewisjr and @thespicesuite decided to take a stand. Thank you for spearheading a dope movement. There's room for all of us in my beloved city, but DO NOT pretend that we don't exist, we will unite quick to remind you!

Although, Soja (2010) and Herod (2011) both highlight that uneven development and spatial injustices are embedded in capitalism, Soja (2010) pointed out that uneven development can create conditions for spatial justice. In the second part of this comment, the Instagram user highlighted how the *Washingtonian*'s representation of uneven development served as a catalyst for the creation of a counternarrative of the city, and the formation of community among native black Washingtonians. Also, this user explicitly stated that the "movement" was about inclusion, as she stated that "there's room for all of us."

In another Instagram post, a black male Instagram user posted an image of himself with Lewis. The Instagram user wore a black T-shirt with "DC AS FUCK" on the front, and Lewis is pictured wearing a black T-shirt with "Native" written in red letters, with the DC flag superimposed on the "e." Both black men are smiling in the photo. The Instragram user posted this comment.

> I was about to make a long post about my once vibrant city, being reduced to a humdrum hub that caters to the sensibilities of folk that have 0 connection to it's roots. . . . Instead, #blackmensmiling. S/O to @mrtonylewisjr for making this event happen. This dude is real inspiration to lil black boys that come from nothing, doing great work in our communities.

Here, this user begins his comment with a critique of changes in his once "vibrant" city. For this user, it seemed that these changes have resulted in a reduction of culture, as he referred to the city as a "humdrum" hub. However, the tone of this comment shifted as he ended with a celebration of black men in the community. As such, it seemed the Instagram user conveyed that amidst changes that result in cultural displacement there is still work being done by and for black men and boys in the city.

Users' posts that were categorized in this theme conveyed gratitude and celebration for the photo shoot's organizers. There was specific emphasis on thankfulness for the organizers uniting a community for a common cause, which was to provide a more diverse representation of D.C. One black male Instagram user posted a video of Tony Lewis Jr. standing above the crowd as he shouted: "D.C. Natives," "We ain't going nowhere," and "Welcome to DC." Each time he yelled, the crowd repeated the phrase back to him. As he shouted and the crowd responded, the video panned the crowd. The user's comment stated:

> Dear @Washinigtonianmag. . . . Today was beyond amazing. Change is evolution not exclusion #DCorNothing #DCNativePhotoshoot (emoji) @mrtonylewisjr & @thespicesuite for bringing all the tribes of the village together (emoji) #ittakesavillage…#justcuriouslife

The user's video, coupled with his comment, conveyed that the photoshoot was in support of inclusive change in the city, in contrast to the *Washingtonian*'s perceived exclusive campaign. Further, the tone of this post illustrated the celebration of a community united for a common cause, which was to help produce a counternarrative of what a native Washingtonian looked like. Like other users' posts categorized in this theme, this black male user praised the photoshoot's organizers for creating a space for community-building and uplift. Here, it seemed that evolution called attention to the needs for more diverse representation of the city in the *Washingtonian* and for more opportunities for the various "tribes" that represent the city's black multitude to gather together to build and uplift the community.

LOCATING "NATIVE. I'M FROM HERE" IN THE SPACE OF REPRESENTATION

This textual analysis, guided by historical cultural (geographical) materialism, investigated how black native Washingtonians produced a counter narrative of inclusivity via media practice in what Lefevbre (1991) defined in the space of representation. Levebfre (1991) iterated that people live through complex symbols and images in the space of representation and, while symbols and images in this space can work to reinforce dominant classist and racist structures, this space can also include the production of counter-hegemonic symbols and images. Historical cultural (geographical) materialism emphasizes the roles we play in the production of our cultural and material world (Williams, 1961/2000). More specifically, this theoretical framework accounts for the fluidity and transformative nature of cultural production and, therefore, provides a framework to explore the historical and material conditions in which counter-hegemonic spatial and media practices can emerge.

This textual analysis provides evidence that the hashtag #dcnativephotoshoot is counter-hegemonic practice, as it was a participatory act of subversion among black native Washingtonians. As such, the analysis specifically examined the hashtag #dcnativephotoshoot as a cultural artifact, to explore how black native Washingtonians created community, challenged and resisted dominant representations of native Washingtonians. The analysis provided evidence of three prominent themes: "I'm So DC," "We're not Tourists. We've Been Here" and "Change is Evolution, not Exclusion."

Each Instagram post within the "I'm So DC" theme exhibited pride black Washingtonians have in their city, by users specifically referencing spaces, such as the D.C. Farmer's Market. Users' posts in this theme also referenced signs such as "Chocolate City" and go-go music that are embedded with social relations of struggle and subversion to signify authenticity. For these users, authenticity was communicated via their connection to and participation in the production of historical social spaces and practices.

Posts categorized in the "We're not Tourists. We've Been Here" theme provided an alternative narrative to the "I'm Not a Tourist. I Live Here"

campaign, as it specifically related to identity. Posts in this theme emphasized how black Washingtonians still live in the city, despite revitalization
efforts that often left them feeling displaced or alienated. Instagram users'
posts that conveyed narratives of multigenerational black families living and
thriving in D.C. told stories of resistance, survival and persistence. Black
native Washingtonian identity and ownership and, therefore, I argue, also
power, was communicated via users' reclamation and celebration of spaces
indicated in hashtags, such as D.C. public schools and the Southeast and
Northeast quadrants of the city. While these spaces are generally labeled as
underperforming (schools) or violent and dangerous (neighborhoods), posts
in this theme seemed to specifically name these spaces to challenge stereotypical narratives and also highlight the necessity and willingness to struggle
and endure for the good of the whole community.

Lastly, posts in the "Change is Evolution, not Exclusion" theme raised
awareness of the political, cultural and economic consequences of gentrification and explicitly called out the *Washingtonian* for its participation in promoting and perpetuating exclusion. While many of the posts in this category
criticized the *Washingtonian*, the tone of the messages was not antagonistic.
Instagram users' posts conveyed unification and solidarity, and the movement of people towards a common goal—to include native black Washingtonians in the (r)evolution of the city's social and physical landscapes.

Located in the space of representation, #dcnativephotoshoot produced an
online and offline space for native black Washingtonians to unite and create
an alternative narrative and meaning of native Washingtonian that included
and prioritized black culture, black family and black communities. The Instagram hashtag helped users amplify the alternative inclusive narrative among
followers and helped produce a digital, social and physical space that sub-
verted cultural displacement and (mis)representation of black native Washingtonians.

While this research is not generalizable and is only based on public posts
on Instagram, it has several implications as it relates to media and millennials, the role of media in revitalization, and the pursuit of spatial justice. This
research calls into question the symbol of white millennials in media coverage of revitalization efforts and gentrification. "Native. I'm From Here" was
largely in response and resistance to the prioritization of white millennial
subjects and what they represented in the *Washingtonian* magazine's T-shirt
campaign's photoshoot. The analysis suggested that white millennials in this
campaign represented exclusion and displacement to black native Washingtonians. Future research should explore ways in which media use white millennials to promote authenticity and the need for "progress" as urban renewal
and back-to-city movements continue across major metropolitan areas. More
importantly, future research should continue to investigate the ways in which

black communities are using media to create counter narratives that challenge white "urban authenticity."

The Instagram campaign's hashtag #dcnativephotoshoot created social and offline connections that enabled a co-creation of a subversive geography that challenged practices of exclusion and alienation that are embedded in revitalization and gentrification. As gentrification remains a popular topic of research across various disciplines, this research calls on media studies scholars to interrogate how social media can be used to subvert gentrification, not just promote and support it. The analysis of Instagram hashtags as cultural artifacts allows for a rich investigation of the relations of production in not just the technology or tool, but also in community formations and transformations. As a native black Washingtonian, I call on scholars to prioritize the communities, counter narratives *and* cultural geographies in the periphery that are engaging in media practice to pursue social justice, with an understanding that, as Soja writes,

> Space—like justice—is never simply handed out or given, that both are socially produced, experienced, and contested on constantly shifting social, political, economic, and geographical terrains, means that justice—if it is to be concretely achieved, experienced, and reproduced—must be engaged on spatial as well as social terms. (2010, p. 28)

REFERENCES

About Union Market. (2019). Retrieved January 10, 2019, from https://unionmarketdc.com/the-history-of-union-market/.

Asch, C. M., & Musgrove, G. D. (2017). *Chocolate city: A history of race and democracy in the nation's capital*. Chapel Hill, NC: The University of North Carolina Press.

Brown-Saracino, J. & Rumpf, C. (2011). Diverse imageries of gentrification: Evidence from news coverage in seven U.S. cities, 1986–2006. *Journal of Urban Affairs*, *33*(3), 289–315.

Castells, M. (1983). *The city and the grass roots*. Berkeley and Los Angeles: University of California Press.

Cohen, M. (2018, May 14). *Washingtonian* apologizes after botched "I'm not a tourist. I live here." T-Shirt Campaign. Washington City Paper. https://www.washingtoncitypaper.com/news/city-desk/blog/21005049/washingtonian-apologizes-after-botched-im-not-a-tourist-i-live-here-tshirt-campaign.

Delesa, E. (2018, May 14). *Washingtonian* mag under fire for lack of diversity in "I'm Not a Tourist" campaign photoshoot. https://wpgc.radio.com/blogs/joe-clair-morning-show/washingtonian-mag-under-fire-lack-diversity-im-not-tourist-campaign.

District of Columbia, Office of Planning. (2009). *Florida Ave. market study*. Retrieved from https://planning.dc.gov/sites/default/files/dc/sites/op/publication/attachments/famreduced.pdf.

Du Gay, P., Hall, S., Janes, L., Mackay, H. & Negua, K. (1997). *Doing cultural studies: The story of the Sony Walkman*. London: Sage.

Fitzpatrick, S., & Goodwin, M. R. (1999). *The guide to black Washington: Places and events of historical and cultural significance in the nation's capital*. New York: Hippocrene Books, Inc.

Hall, S. (1975). Introduction. In A. C. H. Smith, E. Immirzi & T. Blackwell (Eds.), *Paper voices: The Popular press and social change* (pp. 11–24). Totowa, NS: Rowman & Littlefield.

Harvey, D. (1976). Militant particularism and global ambition: The conceptual politics of place, space, and environment in the work of Raymond Williams. *Social Text, 42,* 69–98.

Herod, A. (2011). Company towns in America. In O. Dinius & A. Vergara (Eds.), *Geographies of Justice and Social Transformations* (pp. 21–44). Athens, GA: The University of Georgia Press.

Hopkinson, H. (2012). *Go-go live: The musical life and death of a chocolate city.* Durham, NC: Duke University Press.

Hu, Y., Manikonda, L., & Subbarao Kambhampati. What we Instagram: A first analysis of Instagram photo content and user types International AAAI Conference on Wed and Social Media, North American, Mau. 2014. Available at https://www.aaai.org/ocs/index.php/ICWSM/ICWSM14/paper/view/8118.

Hyra, D. (2015). The back-to-the-city movement: Neighbourhood redevelopment and processes of political and cultural displacement. *Urban Studies, 52*(10), 1753–1773.

Klaus, G. (1993). Cultural materialism: A summary of principles. In W. J. Morgan & P. Preston (Eds.), *Raymond Williams: Politics, Letters, Education* (pp. 88–104). New York: St. Martin's.

Lambert, E. (2018, May 14). *Washingtonian* apologizes for "I'm Not a Tourist. I live here" ad campaign for lack of diversity. http://www.fox5dc.com/news/local-news/washingtonian-apologizes-for-im-not-a-tourist-i-live-here-ad-campaign-for-lack-of-diversity.

Lefebvre, H. (1991). *The production of space.* (D. Nicolson-Smith, Trans.) Oxford, UK: Blackwell Publishing. (Original work published in 1974).

Lefrak, M. (2018, May 20). Black D.C. natives respond to *Washingtonian*'s "I'm not a tourist" campaign with counter photo shoot. https://wamu.org/story/18/05/20/black-d-c-natives-respond-washingtonians-im-not-tourist-campaign-counter-photo-shoot/.

Johnson, R. (1986/1987) What is cultural studies anyway? *Social Text, 16,* 38–80.

Marx, K. & Engels, F. (1845–1846/1970). Part one: Feuerbach. In C. J. Arthur (Ed.), *The German Ideology* (pp. 42–49, 64–67). New York: International Publishers.

Oh, C., Lee, T., Kim, Y., Park, S., & Suh, B. (2016). Understanding participatory hashtag practices on Instagram: A case study of weekend hashtag project, presented at CHI 2016, San Jose, CA, 2016. New York, NY: Association for Computing Machinery.

Rofe, M. (2004). From "problem city" to "promise city": Gentrification and the revitalisation of Newcastle. *Australian Geographical Studies, 42*(2), 193–206.

Shin, Y. (2009). Understanding spatial differentiation of social interaction: Suggesting a conceptual framework for spatial mediation. *Communication Theory, 19,* 423–444.

Slater, T. (2006). The eviction of critical perspectives from gentrification research. *International Journal of Urban and Regional Research, 30*(4), 737–757.

Smith, M. (2018). Why it's time to update your Instagram hashtag strategy. Retrieved from https://www.adweek.com/digital/why-its-time-to-update-your-instagram-hashtag-strategy/.

Soja, E. (1985). Regions in context: Spatiality, periodicity, and the historical geography of the regional question. *Environmental and Planning D, 3,* 1975–1990.

Soja, E. (1989). *Postmodern geographies: The reassertion of space in critical social theory.* London: Verso.

Soja, E. (2010). *Seeking spatial justice.* Minneapolis: The University of Minnesota Press.

Statista. (2018). Number of monthly active Instagram users from January 2013 to June 2018. Retrieved January 10, 2019, from https://www.statista.com/statistics/253577/number-of-monthly-active-instagram-users/.

Storey, J. (1996). *Cultural studies and the study of popular culture.* Athens, GA. University of Georgia Press.

U.S. Census Bureau. (2018). *Quickfacts District of Columbia.* Retrieved from https://www.census.gov/quickfacts/dc.

Walker, R. (1981). A theory of suburbanization: Capitalism and the construction of urban space in the United States. In M. Dear and A. Scott (Eds.), *Urbanization and Urban Planning in Capitalist Society* (pp. 383–429). London: Metheun.

Washingtonian Staff. A Statement from Our CEO and President (May 14, 2018). https:// www.washingtonian.com/2018/05/14/statement-ceo-president/.

Williams, R. (1961/2001). *The long revolution.* New York: Columbia University Press.

Williams, R. (1973). *Country and the city.* New York City: Oxford University Press.

Zappavigna, M. (2015). Searchable talk: The linguistic functions of hashtags. *Social Semiotics, 25*(3), 274–291.

Zuk, M., Bierbaum, A. H., Chapple, K., Gorska, K., & Loukaitoy-Sideris, A. (2018). Gentrification, displacement, and the role of public investment. *Journal of Planning Literature, 33*(1), 31–44.

Chapter Eight

Calling out Racism for What It Is

Memes, BBQ Becky and the Oppositional Gaze

Jessica Maddox

Much has been written in internet studies about the ways race and racism are complicated, exacerbated and celebrated online (Daniels, 2012; Nakamura & Chow-White, 2012). Whereas people of color can use, and have used, digital spaces to resist racism and dominant whiteness (Everett, 2012) and to cultivate communities (Brock, 2012), they are also subject to more frequent occurrences of racism and racial violence through online anonymity and trolls (Phillips, 2015). One avenue that has been popular with digital scholars is examining the intersections of race and internet memes in order to explore how these popular image macros celebrate race or promote racism. It is well documented that memes and online images can further aggravate racism (Nakamura, 2014; Boxman-Shabtai & Shifman, 2013). However, memes can also promote social justice (Milner, 2016).

Herein, I interrogate the intersection of race and internet memes in order to understand how these popular digital image macros can simultaneously be tools of entertainment and resistance. Specifically, I am interested in how black individuals use memes to challenge the racism they experience and resist white supremacy. In order to push at these theoretical margins, I examine internet memes made by black individuals through the lens of bell hooks' oppositional gaze (1992) and interrogate how memes can function as a tool of said gaze. According to Boylorn (2008), "The oppositional gaze resists intended and embedded ideologies that are based on racist and internalized racist views" (p. 414). Boylorn's work expands hooks' foundational concept, in that the oppositional gaze is a set of "looking" relations imbricated in looking, being looked at, images, media and representations. Media of the oppositional gaze not only challenge dominant whiteness, but also call out said whiteness for its oppressive tendencies. Memes have a particular ability to subvert and comment on dominant power structures and ideologies. Combined with their incorporation of images and representations, this essay is concerned with adding memes to discussions of the oppositional gaze.

At the core of this discussion are questions of race, space and place, and how black millennials and black meme-makers can wield memes to actively comment on and critique a dominant whiteness that seeks to regulate black individuals to social margins. Memes can be a powerful tool for social commentary (Milner, 2016; Petray & Collin, 2017), and when a meme targets specific social problems, and is unapologetic for that identification, the meme has power to usher in change. Scholars have long-since examined the power of digital tools and technologies for creative resistance (Brock, 2012; Everett, 2012), and the digital comes to function as another type of third space for black communities, akin to barber shops and beauty salons (Daniels, 2012). This digital third space provides an avenue for examining the power that can come out of these communities, and meme-making is no exception. To specifically examine this, this chapter explores this radical potential of specific internet memes by analyzing them through the lens of the oppositional gaze, and, in doing so, seeks to understand how these radical, change-inducing memes can function as a tool of the oppositional gaze.

Like the movies and television shows hooks (1992) describes in her foundational work on the oppositional gaze, memes function as texts. Cultural studies, as well as critical race theory, has long been preoccupied with using texts as avenues to explore the interstices of media, culture and society, as well as the text's relationship to and within various power structures. In analyzing social life, Antonio Gramsci said that we should look in the "ensemble of the system of relations in which these activities . . . have their place within the general complex of social relations" (2014, p. 8). Therefore, this work uses memes as a textual avenue in which to examine broader, macro-level relations that allow for the internet meme to function as a tool of the oppositional gaze. A specific case study was needed to ground the examination of this relationship, and that is the meme of BBQ Becky.

BBQ Becky, also known as the White Woman Calling the Cops, refers to a Photoshopped meme of a woman calling the police on a group of black individuals having a cookout in a park in Oakland, California. This event actually took place on April 29th, 2018, and in the video of the incident, that ultimately went viral, a white woman is seen calling the cops after asking a group of black individuals to leave the park. The subsequent "meme-ification" of the event occurred against the backdrop of several other recent notable instances in which non-white individuals were policed (sometimes quite literally) for simply being in public. The first iteration of the meme appeared shortly after the video spread (KnowYourMeme, 2018). On the left in the image is Chadwick Boseman, the actor who played T'Challa in the

2018 blockbuster *Black Panther*. Boseman was the guest speaker at the historically black Howard University in 2018, and meme speaders Photoshopped BBQ Becky into the image, next to Boseman (KnowYourMeme, 2018). By combining the woman, "BBQ Becky," with his image, black individuals began to comment on how difficult it is to be black in public in America when they are always already subject to a white supremacist gaze. Within this context, the BBQ Becky meme spread, with individuals Photoshopping the woman on the cell phone into various gatherings of black individuals in public spaces. The BBQ Becky meme is an ideal textual avenue for examining the internet, race and memes, because it wields resistance power and struggle against dominant groups and ideologies.

In order to fully interrogate the BBQ Becky meme as a tool of the oppositional gaze, I must also lay a groundwork that problematizes several of the ontological, color-blind and "white savior" problems that Daniels (2012) describes as existing within internet studies. According to Daniels (2012), "We must resist longing for a color-blind internet and eschew a white-framed internet studies" (p. 711). While I am a white woman, and I make no claim to shed that baggage, I begin this work by making a claim that internet scholars have definitely incorporated since Daniels' (2012) foundational work, yet it is worth reminding ourselves of again and again: Whiteness is in fact a race and not a default preset. Oftentimes, to speak colloquially of "the internet" means just speaking of white practices, objects and attitudes (Phillips, 2015), and internet scholars must avoid speaking of the internet in such general terms.

We must problematize idiomatic assumptions that lead to white-dominated digital spaces. I emphatically make this claim here in order to begin to paint a picture of the backdrop memes like BBQ Becky exist against—it is only understanding BBQ Becky in this way, and against a colloquially white-dominated internet, that we can understand memes as tools of the oppositional gaze. Furthermore, I emphasize eschewing a conception of simply "the internet," because there is no such thing as simply "the internet." What there is online is a multitude of internets, consisting of individuals interacting, spreading content and creating communities within their own stocks of meaning and cultures. There are no firm boundaries and typically no definitive racial divides (though certain websites and social media sites do try), and strong communities of people of color, such as Black Twitter, frequently blend into other communities and areas of digital cultures. The BBQ Becky meme epitomizes this, as it became a mainstream internet meme that grew out of its critique of whiteness and white supremacy. Most importantly, *it did not lose its criticism of whiteness* as it spread and gained popularity, which demonstrates the powerful potential of the oppositional gaze.

This chapter moves in four parts. First, I discuss the ways internet, race and racism have intersected in the past, setting up groundwork on which to understand contemporary memes like BBQ Becky. Second, I further explain the ability of the internet meme to challenge racism in conjunction with the oppositional gaze. Third, I move into specific discussions of how the BBQ Becky meme—and certain memes in general—can function within the oppositional gaze. Finally, I discuss implications of BBQ Becky and broader issues at stake in the meme. Examples of the BBQ Becky meme are interwoven throughout in order to emphasize key points and bolster evidentiary claims.

INTERNET RELATIONS AND RACE

Assumptions of the contemporary internet have a whiteness problem. Discussion and comments referring to simply "the internet" typically mean discussions and comments of the *white* internet (Phillips, 2015). Everyday digital sociality is always gendered, classed and raced (Kanai, 2016), and it is near to impossible to divorce these relations from digital content and objects—nor should we strive to do that. When we refer to the digital cultures and spaces in such sweeping terms as "the internet," we lose sight of how there are myriad users of all races, sexes, classes, genders, religions and ethnicities using digital spaces to interact, communicate, resist, submit, create and share.

Often, when a notable sub-community emerges, it gains recognition and popularity in reference to the group it represents—the most notable being Black Twitter. And while it is absolutely worthwhile to study the ways marginalized groups intermingle and form creative, interactive clusters online, the more and more we understand digital cultures through specific subgroups, it is worth asking what is left to simply be "the internet." Though some may take a conception of "the internet" to refer to the overarching experience of all subgroups, combined, "the internet" is less often referenced in this way and more understood as digital culture painted in the broadest strokes. In understanding digital cultures and spaces on the utmost macro-level, only the loudest and biggest strokes stand out, thus the finer nuances and marginalized voices and spaces are overlooked.

Problems further emerge within this extreme macro-conception of the internet, however, when we do consider what is left when digital cultures are divvied into subgroups, and how dominant ideologies regulate such groups further to the margins. This becomes a question of identities, that is, who formulates identity and under what conditions. In his work on Black Twitter, André Brock (2012) points out that "White participation in online activities is rarely understood as constitutive of White identity; instead we are trained to understand their online activities as stuff 'people' do" (p. 534). As such, we come to understand certain subgroups as giving us insight into Black

Twitter, or LGBTQ practices on Instagram, or Latinx representations on Snapchat. However, we rarely come to understand white practices online as indicative of white community. Instead, the practices of white individuals on the internet simply come to be understood as "the internet."

The process of white digital cultural practices coming to be understood as indicative of macro-level internet practices is not simply synchronicity. There are strong social and racial precedents that lend themselves to this prevailing assumption. Whiteness has always been "considered normal and neutral, the yardstick against which other races are measured" (Petray & Collin, 2017, p. 2; Carr, 2016). Because many white individuals do not view themselves as having a race (Hill, 1995), they come to understand their practices as indicative of practices and general, the things "everybody" does or should do. In terms of practices on the internet and social media, Brock (2012) calls this online "fixity": "online fixity is the assumption that online visitors either occupy an online 'normal' identity: White, male, middle class, and hetero; or they are so diverse that their cultural origins cannot (or should not) be ascertained" (p. 538). Online fixity is a crucial component of this work and understanding how BBQ Becky functioned vis-à-vis the oppositional gaze, because it is precisely online fixity that is challenged through the spread of such a meme.

A further problem with coming to understand typically white internet practices as indicative of simply "internet practices" is that much of the content that gains popularity amongst white internet users has been appropriated from online sub-groups such as Black Twitter. Lauren Michele Jackson has written extensively on this matter, particularly in conjunction with reactions GIFs, and how they form what she calls "digital blackface." She elaborates:

> But even a casual observer of GIFing would notice that, as with much of online culture, black people appear at the center of it all. Or, images of black people, at least. *The Real Housewives of Atlanta*, Oprah, Whitney Houston, Mariah Carey, NBA Players, Tiffany Pollard, Kid Fury, and many, many other known and anonymous black likenesses dominate day-to-day feeds, even outside online black communities . . . if you've never heard the term before, "digital blackface" is used to describe various types of minstrel performance that became available in cyberspace . . . while often associate with Jim Crow-era racism, the tenets of minstrel performance remain alive today in television, movies, and music, and, in its most advanced iteration, on the internet. (Jackson, 2017)

Non-black individuals using GIFs of black individuals to engage in networked sociality amounts to digital blackface—adopting an identity that is not their own by pretending to be that person in the GIF. White individuals frequently use black culture, identities, practices and bodies to cultivate a likeable, and sometimes laughable, internet presence.

What's at stake in these issues I have discussed are issues of identity. Myriad—though not all—content that gains popularity in communities like Black Twitter can be hijacked by white individuals for their own purposes. Communities like Black Twitter are important for many reasons, but Everett (2012) explains, "at issue is the question of how viral media and new digital media technologies simultaneously challenge and reinforce the nation's racialized body politic" (p. 147). Furthermore, DuBois (1903) has famously written that "personal Black identity is the intersection between Black communal solidarity and a national White supremacist ideology." Taken together, these two quotes, written over 100 years apart, prompt us to think through the ways black identity is formulated online, through and within digital media technologies and cultures, and how the ability to resist white supremacist ideology is a part of that. This brings me to BBQ Becky.

BBQ BECKY AND INTERNET MEMES

Memes exist, are created and spread within and against the backdrop discussed above. Limor Shifman defines a meme as "a group of digital items sharing common characteristics . . . that are created with awareness of each other . . . and shared via the internet by many users" (2014, p. 41). Because memes can never be divorced from their social, cultural and historical context, "meme-making is always a meaning-making process" (Frazer & Carlson, 2017, p. 1). Memes are always intertwined in the circumstances around them, even though, as Phillips argues, "online content is rarely presented in full political, material, and/or historical context" (Phillips, 2015, p. 12). There is a tension in the statements just presented: Memes cannot be divorced from their cultural origins and contexts, but they are often not presented or spread in full context. Just because memes are not *presented* in full context does not mean the context and origins vanish; it simply means a return to context is necessary in spreading memes online. Because content from specific online, and typically black, communities often gets appropriated by white internet users in the dominant vein of digital cultures, the content becomes decontextualized. However, memes are not immaculately conceived; they are purposefully created in response to certain social, cultural and historical events.

Frequently, memes are created in response to certain social, cultural, and historical events that are broadcast on the news. This is a prime example of convergence culture (Jenkins, 2006) and demonstrates how "within minutes, a story can migrate from a TV set to a computer and then to a mobile phone, assuming new forms in the process" (Boxman-Shabtai & Shifman, 2013, p.

523). One common way these stories migrate is through the form of internet memes, since memes encourage people to "play with the news" (Tay, 2012, p. 45) in malleable ways. This does not equate to the phenomenon of "fake news," in that these memes are not concerned with re-presenting stories. What they are concerned with is "treat[ing] the news as an open text, reinterpret[ing] it in a language that one can make sense of, and experiment[ing] with its meanings" (Tay, 2012, p. 46). In this way, memes function as less of a different kind of news reporting and more as social commentary on news. (It should be noted that memes can also be pulled from news broadcasts and come to have nothing to do with the news story in question—the famous "Disaster Girl" meme is a prime example. See Zittrain, 2014). This chapter, however, is concerned with what happens when a news event gets memed and how the subsequent meme serves as social commentary on the original event. According to Frazer and Carlson (2017), "When memes comment on 'serious' issues, they often do so humorously . . . memes, humor, and politics often mix playfully" (p. 1). Thus, the cycle of a meme works like so: An event happens. Through the conditions set by convergence culture, the meme moves from the offline, to the TV or internet, and, in the process, becomes a meme that reveals some kind of social commentary vis-à-vis humor.

The social commentary that began the BBQ Becky meme is specifically a social commentary about racism and race relations in America. BBQ Becky is certainly not the first meme to comment on this or to have been subject to analysis. Just like how conceptions of various internets and race have a complex relationship, memes and race also have a complicated history. Nakamura (2014) has looked at the ways in which racist content gets memed and further perpetuates racism. Phillips (2015) accomplishes something similar in her ethnography on internet trolls by looking at the ways trolls justify their racism or color-blindness "for the lolz." But memes can function as a type of social commentary that speaks truth to power in humorous ways. For instance, Petray and Collin (2017) analyzed the text-only #WhiteProverbs meme on Australian social media and found it functioned as a way for social media to comment on and challenge experiences of racism.

Meme-ing White Fragility

When it comes to social commentary on race relations and racism, BBQ Becky accomplishes something similar to #WhiteProverbs: both comment on race through poking fun at white fragility, a phenomenon Robin DiAngelo (2011) defines as follows:

> White people in North America live in a social environment that protects and insulates them from race-based stress. This insulated environment of racial protection builds white expectations for racial comfort while at the same time lowering the ability to tolerate racial stress. (p. 54)

This insular protection afforded by whiteness, combined with centuries of white supremacy and oppression of others, leads many white individuals to being incapable of peacefully co-existing in public spaces with people of color. This notion is a crux of BBQ Becky. For instance, one popular BBQ Becky meme Photoshopped the woman into a scene from the 2018 block-buster *Black Panther*, and featured her decrying: "Hello, police? My neighbors are black panthers" (Imgflip, 2018). The point of this particular meme highlighted how many white individuals have difficulty co-existing with black individuals, even when it is the white individual moving into a space where black individuals have been peacefully minding their own business. As the BBQ Becky meme spread, the woman was no longer separately edited into the image. Instead, she was edited straight into an image—in this case, a gathering scene from the movie *Black Panther*. This meme's message articulates how black individuals cannot be in their own spaces, minding their own business, without a white woman coming along and calling the police. Because of white fragility, many white individuals are not accustomed to interacting with black individuals in ways that counter stereotypical notions they may have. Instead, white individuals view black individuals in horribly stereotypical, and thus prejudicial, ways, thus leading to instances like the one that spawned the BBQ Becky meme.

Around the time the BBQ Becky meme spread, there were numerous stories in the news regarding the public mistreatment of people of color by white individuals. In May of 2018, a video of a man named Aaron Schlossberg went viral after he went on a xenophobic rant in a New York City café, telling Spanish-speaking patrons that "This is America" and "If they have the balls to come here and live off my money, I pay for their welfare . . . I pay for their ability to be here. The least they can do . . . is speak English" (Rosenberg & Eltagouri, 2018). A few weeks prior, two black men were arrested at a Philadelphia Starbucks while waiting for a friend to arrive, simply because they wanted to wait for their friend before placing an order. These horrific instances are unfortunately not rarities. According to DiAngelo (2011), "The direction of power between Whites and people of color is historical, traditional, normalized, and deeply embedded in the fabric of U.S. society" (p. 55). White individuals hold the power, and while DiAngelo (2011) defines white fragility as the inability of white individuals to handle even the most minute racial stress, the above-mentioned examples demonstrate that simply co-existing in public with people of color can be stressful for white individuals. BBQ Becky specifically comments on this white fragility.

As previously mentioned, the BBQ Becky meme took off after a white woman called the cops on a group of black individuals having a cookout in Oakland, California, in April 2018. The entire exchange was filmed and put on YouTube, and within days, the BBQ Becky meme began to spread. Though the woman who called the cops was not in fact named Becky, the meme became known as such through the cultural notion of white women as "Beckys." According to Whitehead (2016), the term Becky refers to "a white woman who is clueless, who is kind of racist, [and] who makes statements without knowing what she's saying." It is important to note, as Whitehead says, that Becky is not a racial slur against white individuals, given the power dynamics of racial relations and white supremacy in America. Whitehead elaborates that names of black culture, like DeShawn, often carry with them preconceived prejudicial notions of race and class in broader society, while names like Becky do not. That being said, the meme in question, BBQ Becky, came to be known as such because of one, its alliterative pithiness, and two, how the ability of the simple name of the meme is able to reveal a lot about what it is commenting on: a white woman who is unable to co-exist in public with black individuals because of white fragility. In this way, BBQ Becky simultaneously refers to the meme as a whole, as well as the individual woman who called the cops.

Individuals began Photoshopping the woman, BBQ Becky, into various situations in which black individuals were gathered. The point of this was to demonstrate how uncomfortable white individuals are with the presence of black individuals in public spaces. In this way, this leads to "barbecuing while black" being a crime, as is "going to Starbucks while black." Such an interation merged with a popular news event at the time, that of the royal wedding between Harry, Prince of Wales, and American Megan Markle, who is now the Duchess of Sussex. Markle is biracial, and her mother, shown in the cathedral in this meme, is black (Afropunk, 2018). BBQ Becky, the woman, was Photoshopped into this meme in order to make a key point: In the view of BBQ Becky, black individuals are not allowed in certain situations, and it would be unusual to BBQ Becky to see black women in this situation.

Another popular version of the BBQ Becky meme features BBQ Becky Photoshopped into Barack Obama's presidential inauguration, with BBQ Becky behind Michelle Obama as she holds the Bible (KnowYourMeme, 2018). This meme is similar to the Royal Wedding iteration in that it comments on how white individuals—on some level, explicitly or implicitly—take issue with black individuals in perceived "white" spaces—such as the British Royal Family or the United States presidency. It has been well-documented how many individuals staunchly believed the United States to be "postracial" (that is, race "doesn't matter" anymore) after the election and re-election of President Barack Obama. In reality, instances of racism and racial violence against black individuals actually increased during this time (Lacy & Triece, 2014). With this in mind, now that I have established the ways the BBQ Becky meme pokes fun at white fragility, it is worth examining how, and to what extent, the meme genre influences these conversations about race.

BBQ Becky and the Photoshop Meme

The style of the BBQ Becky meme is not new. It is referred to as a Photoshop meme, in which an out-of-place character is Photoshopped into an image or scene to make a (typically humorous) statement. According to Highfield and Leaver (2016), "Photoshop memes and templates involving visual juxtaposition and composition, such as Texts from Hillary, Pepper Spraying Cop, and McKayla Is Not Impressed, variously offer humor and commentary with often very obvious clues that this is not an actual scene being depicted" (p. 52). BBQ Becky functions in a similar way—we know that BBQ Becky the woman was not at the Royal Wedding, and the rudimentary style of editing clues us in to the fact that this is *definitely* not a real image, but one that has been altered.

However, BBQ Becky, the meme, functions on a deeper level of social commentary than Pepper Spraying Cop and the other memes mentioned above—BBQ Becky, the meme, is solely concerned with commenting on how white individuals, and, more specifically, white womanhood and the white female gaze are pervasive and can be actively detrimental to black individuals in public spaces. Additionally, the Photoshopped juxtaposition Highfield and Leaver (2016) speak of is not quite juxtaposition in this case. While BBQ Becky, like Pepper Spraying Cop, is graphically inserted into a variety of situations, the placement of BBQ Becky into situations of gatherings of black individuals demonstrates the pervasiveness of white supremacy and the white gaze that is always surveilling black individuals. While there is juxtaposition in this meme in the sense of inserting a woman into a situation she was not originally in, there is not juxtaposition in the sense that black individuals must be watchful and negotiate the omnipresent white gaze.

In this way, BBQ Becky, while bearing similarities to Photoshop meme, may be better understood as what Milner (2016) refers to as a memetic lingua franca. According to Milner (2016), "Memetic logics and grammar underscore a lingua franca—a shared social vernacular prevalent within and across participatory media collectives" (p. 84). In other words, when it comes to memes, the meaning of the post is not simply "there" waiting to be discovered, but there is often a "lightbulb moment" (Kanai, 2016) that relies on an individual's stock of meanings to interpret and understand the meme. In this case, BBQ Becky was able to resonate with many black individuals because it spoke to similar experiences many have had. In doing so, BBQ Becky also provided an outlet for black individuals and meme spreaders to comment on the pervasiveness of the white supremacist gaze.

THE OPPOSITIONAL GAZE AND
"BARBECUING WHILE BLACK"

Black content—and, more specifically, black culture and black bodies—dominate digital public spaces. It is often such black content and images, words, phrases and ideas from communities like Black Twitter that "go viral" and receive commendation by white internet users (Brock, 2012; Jackson, 2017). Black culture may be what is most popular and desirable in digital spaces, but actual black individuals are regulated to the margins in digital and physical public spaces. BBQ Becky speaks to this cultural moment—a cultural moment in which black men cannot sit in Starbucks waiting for a friend; Latino individuals cannot speak Spanish in public without being victims of a verbal assault; and in which black individuals cannot barbecue in Oakland, California, without having the cops called on them.

bell hooks's (1992) conception of the oppositional gaze is useful to understanding the BBQ Becky meme. More specifically, the oppositional gaze is useful for understanding the ways in which individuals subvert oppressive white tactics and assumptions of digital cultures. hooks (1992) defines the oppositional gaze as:

> A site of resistance for colonized black people globally. Subordinates in relations of power learn experientially that there is a critical gaze, one that "looks" to document, one that is oppositional. In resistance struggle, the power of the dominate to assert agency by claiming and cultivating "awareness" politicizes "looking" relations—one learns to look a certain way in order to resist. (p. 116)

The oppositional gaze defies the dominant, white supremacist gaze. It allows for a space that celebrates black culture and black individuals while critiquing and resisting whiteness. In this spirit, one iteration of the meme had BBQ Becky, the woman, animated to create a cartoon version. BBQ Becky is inserted into a popular Disney Channel sitcom, *The Proud Family*, that ran from 2001–2005 (Afropunk, 2018). Even today, *The Proud Family* is hailed for its cultural significance, Afrocentrism, and inclusivity. This particular meme serves all the functions discussed thus far but also adds a new dimension—not just the commenting on white fragility, but the active resistance of it.

According to hooks (1996), the oppositional gaze is not just looking relations, but looking relations that actively resist white supremacy. Some of the most common and everyday arenas in which this plays out are the realms of media and representation. Gazes and looking relations are imbricated in such arenas because "issues of race and media directly touch issues of ideology" (Hall, 2011, p. 81). hooks (1996) elaborates on this, writing, "to stare at the television, or mainstream movies, to engage its images, was to engage its negation of black representation. It was the oppositional gaze that responded to those looking relations by developing independent black cinema" (p. 96). Most mainstream and popular forms of media, including memes, favor dominant whiteness, but the oppositional gaze is a space and set of looking relations in which black individuals do not have to outright accept whiteness. The oppositional gaze is a space of resistance and a terrain to counter white supremacy.

Furthermore, people of color have long since used gazes and screens as opportunities for creative resistance. hooks (1996) elaborates:

> Given the real-life public circumstances wherein Black men were murdered/ lynched for looking at white womanhood, where the black male gaze was always subject to control and/or punishment by the powerful White Other, the private realm of television screens or dark theaters could unleash the repressed gaze. (p. 96)

Presently, phone and computer screens offer the same ability for resisting dominant whiteness. By using the privacy of screens in public ways—be it in physical publics, like movie theaters, or digital publics, like on Twitter—black individuals hone agency and resiliency in the face of white-dominated social structures. Entertainment spaces, media and images have long since been used as tools of oppression, but they have also been sites of resistance, struggle and agency. The creation and spread of memes are no exception.

BBQ Becky speaks to the reality of being black in America—and, more specifically, being black in public in America. Like Frazer and Carlson (2017) found in their work on #WhiteProverbs, memes have a powerful function in their ability to comment on white supremacy and white privilege, as well as the ways white racial identity hinges on the subordination, marginalization and surveillance of other racial groups. BBQ Becky differs from #WhiteProverbs, however, since #WhiteProverbs were only concerned with text, and BBQ Becky incorporates images within a traditional meme format to move broadly into the realm of representations. As hooks (1996) writes, "One learns to look a certain way in order to resist" (p. 96). Looking in this context is literal seeing and being seen relations—black individuals can look back at the white supremacist gaze in a way that does not accept it.

One of the most powerful iterations of the BBQ Becky meme combined a popular song by rap artist Childish Gambino (a.k.a Donald Glover). The song and music video for Childish Gambino's "This is America" dropped right around the time the BBQ Becky meme was gaining popularity, and the following meme emerged as a screen grab from "This is America," and, as discussed above, individuals Photoshopped BBQ Becky into the image to demonstrate white fragility at large groups of black individuals gathering in public (Semajblogeater, 2018). But there is more at stake in this meme when we consider the context of Childish Gambino's song. The song itself is a commentary on what it is like to be black in America, but it also delves into the radical nature of looking and be looked at while black. In the song, Childish Gambino raps, "Watch me move/This is a celly/That's a tool/On my Kodak/" (Glover & Göransson, 2018). Celly, in this context, refers to cell phone, and more specifically a cell phone camera (as indicated by the reference to Kodak). This is noteworthy, because the cell phone camera has been the tool that has been used to document instances of police brutality against unarmed black individuals, and, in the case of BBQ Becky, was used to film her racist actions against the folks "barbecuing while black" in Oakland, California. This BBQ Becky meme, in conjunction with "This is America," speaks to the power of looking relations. "This is America" is itself a product of the oppositional gaze, and, combined with BBQ Becky, critiques white supremacy on a double level. This meme does not just resist. It actively calls out racial intolerance and the violence of dominant whiteness.

Actively identifying racism and white supremacy is a key component of the oppositional gaze. In this way, BBQ Becky demonstrates how, as hooks has observed, "spaces of agency exist for Black people, wherein [they] can both interrogate the gaze of the Other, but also look back, and at one another, naming what [is seen]" (1996, p. 96). This is the crux of the BBQ Becky meme: not only does the meme speak to the realities of being black in public in America, it actively calls out white supremacy and *names racism for what it is*. A slightly different version of the BBQ Becky explicitly names such racism. Such a meme mimics the style of many popular dating apps that currently exist for mobile phones. In this meme, BBQ Becky, the woman, is "matched" with a man named earlier in this chapter—Aaron Schlossberg, the lawyer who went viral for publicly chastising Spanish-speaking individuals (Trendsmap, 2018). Because these two instances of white fragility and white supremacy occurred around the same time, this meme maker actively called out both Shlossberg and BBQ Becky, the woman, for their racism. The meme even explicitly states, "Quick! Don't miss out on a lifetime of bigotry together." The meme implies these two individuals would have a lot in common over their very public displays of racism. This particular meme also shows that even though there are almost always elements of BBQ Becky that black individuals would find humorous, this humor does not detract from the social commentary. In fact, according to Boxman-Shabtai and Shifman (2013), "the narratives of such jokes often reflect the perceived failings of majority groups" (p. 22). BBQ Becky is a terrain in which individuals could creatively resist racism, stare back at the white supremacy that led to the "barbecuing while black" incident in the first place, and name prevailing racism and white supremacy in American for what it actually is.

SPEAKING TRUTH TO POWER:
NO BECKY ALLOWED

At the core of the BBQ Becky meme is a discussion of how black individuals are policed and surveilled for simply co-existing in public with white fragility. As many of the instances discussed above demonstrate, "public space is constructed by intense monitoring of non-white speakers" (Brock, 2012, p. 541). Part of the reason the "barbecuing while black" video and subsequent meme spread the way it did was because they demonstrated how people of color are always monitored and always surveilled, as well as how white fragility almost always escalates a simple situation (barbecuing while black) to a level that involves the police and risks police brutality against black individuals. Part of the reason white fragility escalates in public situations—in Starbucks, or in a café, or barbecuing while black—is because white-perceived public spaces are "a morally significant set of contexts in which whites are invisibly normal, and in which racialized populations are visibly marginal" (Hill, 1995, p. 62). Therefore, what BBQ Becky really speaks to is who is allowed to take up public space in America, and who is allowed to exist peacefully in public space.

This issue of peacefully existing in public is compounded by the way black culture, images and bodies are often appropriated in *digital* spaces. Once again, citing Jackson (2016):

> It is a long fact of Black cultural production that our creative endeavors are always at risk of being severed from the community that wrought them. Not only can the origins of many memes be found in Black creators or online Black communities (Black Twitter, Black Tumblr, Black nerd culture at large), memes appear to model the circulatory movement of Black vernacular itself. Black folks are hardly the sole proprietors of internet memes, yet it's undeniable that memes at their liveliest—that is, what allows them to keep living—is in fact indebted to Black processes of cultural survival.

Black culture is essential to what I have criticized as that sweeping monolithic block known as "the internet," but black individuals are regulated to the margins of physical and digital cultural spaces. BBQ Becky speaks to both the physical and digital marginalization: The meme comments on how difficult it is to be black in public in America under the white supremacist gaze, but the meme also refuses to let itself be co-opted by the so-called "internet" to succumb to the white gaze, for critiquing whiteness is an active component of the image. BBQ Becky comments on physical marginalization while refusing to let itself become digitally hijacked and marginalized. This is the oppositional gaze of BBQ Becky, and the power of the oppositional gaze to be found in other types of social commentary memes. When a meme actively pinpoints social problems and is unapologetic for that identification, a meme has immense potential to spur radical change.

Perhaps this is why Everett (2012) posits that "it is difficult to not be optimistic about the myriad ways youths of color today successfully appropriate digital media tools to speak truth to power" (p. 148). As discussed, even though black culture and black individuals are appropriate by white individuals on "the internet," it is striking and monumental to examine the ways black individuals co-opt these same tools for creative resistance and resiliency. Digital spaces have always been beneficial to people of color, and "in some ways, the internet functions as a kind of third space . . . similar to the way Black barber shops and beauty salons allowed private spaces for identity discourse between Black men and women" (Daniels, 2012, p. 699). Eschewing an extreme, generalized, macro-level conception of "the internet" means opening up scholarly and practical space for understanding the ways people of color create their own public spaces online.

Communities on the internet, digital media tools, and memes wield their own unique powers in commenting on racial and social problems. This is what leads me to suggest that the most striking element regarding the BBQ Becky meme and the oppositional gaze is in fact its active criticism of white privilege. By this, I mean the BBQ Becky meme, through the oppositional gaze, ultimately speaks to race, space and place. The "barbecuing while black" incident that led to the meme's creation demonstrate how white fragility and white supremacy make it difficult for white individuals to co-exist in public with black individuals. BBQ Becky, the woman, did not want to share space with people of color. However, by Photoshopping BBQ Becky into myriad memes, black meme makers comment on the ease and freedom to which white individuals can enter any type of space they want, free of criticism from others, and subsequently critique others who were already there. By playing with place, the BBQ Becky meme shows how white individuals can often do whatever they like in the public sphere, as well as enter and exit freely. The meme speaks truth to power, as meme makers creatively resist, comment on, and point out the failings of dominant whiteness. This is a meme of solidarity and power for communities of color. It comes from a space with a vibrant, powerful community of black individuals. It comes from a digital space where people of color speak truth to power. It comes from a space of creative resistance. There, there is no Becky allowed.

REFERENCES

Afropunk. (Producer). (May 16, 2018). Megan Markle at the royal wedding. Retrieved from: https://afropunk.com/2018/05/the-best-of-cookout-beckie-the-wildest-memes/.

Afropunk. (Producer). (May 16, 2018). BBQ Becky proud family. Retrieved from: https://afropunk.com/2018/05/the-best-of-cookout-beckie-the-wildest-memes/bbqbeckie6/.

Boxman-Shabtai, L., & Shifman, L. (2013). When ethnic humor goes digital. *New Media & Society, 17*(4), 520–539.

Boylorn, R. M. (2008). As seen on TV: An autoethnographic reflection on race and reality television. *Critical Studies in Media Communication, 25*(4), 413–433.

Brock, A. (2012). From the blackhand side: Twitter as a cultural conversation. *Journal of Broadcasting and Electronic Media, 56*(4), 529–549.

Carr, P. R. (2016). Whiteness and white privilege: Problematizing race and racism in a "color-blind" world, and in education. *International Journal of Critical Pedagogy, 7*(1), 51–54.

Daniels, J. (2012). Race and racism in Internet Studies: A review and critique. *New Media & Society, 15*(5), 695–719.

DiAngelo, R. (2011). White fragility. *International Journal of Critical Pedagogy, 3*(3), 54–70.

du Bois, W. E. B. (1903). *The souls of black folk.* New York: A. C. Hamburg and Co.

Everett, A. (2012). Have we become postracial yet? Race and media rechnology in the age of President Obama. In L. Nakamura & P. A. Chow-White (Eds.), *Race After the Internet* (pp. 146–167). New York: Routledge.

Frazer, R., & Carlson, B. (2017). Indigienous memes and the invention of a people. *Social Media + Society, 3*(4), 1–12.

Glover, D., & Göransson, L. (2018). This is America. mcDJ RCA.

Gramsci, A. (2014). *Selections from the Prison Notebooks* (Q. Hoare & G. N. Smith, Trans. Reprint ed.). New York: International Publishers Co.

Hall, S. (2011). The whites of their eyes: Racist ideologies and the media. In G. Dines & J. M. Humez (Eds.), *Gender, race, and class in media: A critical reader* (pp. 81–84). Los Angeles: Sage.

Highfield, T., & Leaver, T. (2016). Instagrammatics and digital methods: Studying visual social media, from selfies and GIFs to memes and emoji. *Communication Research and Practice, 2*(1), 47–62.

Hill, J. H. (1995). Language, race, and white public space. *American Anthropologist, 100*(3), 680–689.

hooks, b. (1992). *Black looks: Race and representation.* Boston: South End Press.

hooks, b. (1996). The oppositional gaze: Black female spectators. In J. Belton (Ed.), *Movies and mass culture* (pp. 247–265). New Brunswick, NJ: Rutgers University Press.

Imgflip. (Producer). (June 15, 2018). Hello, Police? My neighbors are Black Panthers. Retrieved from: https://imgflip.com/i/2aqyfj.

Jackson, L. M. (2016). The blackness of meme movement. *Model View Culture,* (35). Retrieved from https://modelviewculture.com/pieces/the-blackness-of-meme-movement.

Jackson, L. M. (2017). We need to talk about digital blackface in reaction GIFs. *Teen Vogue.* Retrieved from https://www.teenvogue.com/story/digital-blackface-reaction-gifs.

Jenkins, H. (2006). *Convergence culture: Where old and new media collide.* New York: New York University Press.

Kanai, A. (2016). Sociality and classification: Reading gender, race, and class in a humorous meme. *Social Media + Society, 2*(4), 1–12.

KnowYourMeme. (Producer). (June 1, 2018). BBQ Becky at the Obama inauguration. Retrieved from: https://knowyourmeme.com/photos/1372317-bbq-becky.

KnowYourMeme. (Producer). (June 1, 2018). Hi, I'd like to report a graduation. Retrieved from: https://knowyourmeme.com/memes/bbq-becky.

Lacy, M. G., & Triece, M. E. (2014). Introduction: Gramsci, race, and communication studies. In M. G. Lacy & M. E. Triece (Eds.), *Race and hegemonic struggle in the United States: Pop culture, politics, and protest.* Madison, NJ: Fairleigh Dickinson University Press.

Milner, R. (2016). *The world made meme: Public conversations and participatory media.* Cambridge, MA: MIT Press.

Nakamura, L. (2014). "I WILL DO EVERYthing that am asked": Scambaiting, digital showspace, and the racial violence of social media. *Journal of Visual Culture, 13*(3), 257–274.

Nakamura, L., & Chow-White, P. A. (2012). Introduction—race and digital technology: Code, the color line, and the information society. In L. Nakamura & P. A. Chow-White (Eds.), *Race After the Internet.* New York: Routledge.

Petray, T. L., & Collin, R. (2017). Your privilege is trending: Confronting whiteness on social media. *Social Media + Society, 3*(2), 1–10.

Phillips, W. (2015). *This is why we can't have nice things: Mapping the relationship between online trolling and mainstream culture.* Cambridge, MA: MIT Press.

Rosenberg, E., & Eltagouri, M. (2018). Lawyer who threatened to call ICE about Spanish speakers is now target of complaint. *The Washington Post.* Retrieved from https://www.washingtonpost.com/news/politics/wp/2018/05/17/lawyer-who-threatened-to-call-ice-about-spanish-speakers-is-now-target-of-complaint/?utm_term=.bdf292701bec.

Semajblogeater. (Producer). (June 14, 2018). BBQ Becky and "This is America." Retrieved from: http://semajblogeater.blogspot.com/2018/06/bbq-becky-update-on-that-oakland-video.html.

Shifman, L. (2014). *Memes in digital culture.* Cambridge, MA: MIT Press.

Tay, G. (2012). Binders full of LOLiitics: Political humor, internet memes, and play in the 2012 US presidential election (and beyond). *European Journal of Humour Research, 2*(4), 46–73.

Trendsmap. (May 23, 2018). BBQ Becky joins Tinder. Retrieved from: https://www.trendsmap.com/twitter/tweet/996921703337988097.

Whitehead, K. W. (2016, April 28) *Is "Becky" really a racist stereotype against white women?/Interviewer: S. Weiss.* Complex Pop Culture.

Zittrain, J. L. (2014). Reflections on internet culture. *Journal of Visual Culture, 13*(3), 388–394.

Chapter Nine

Latina/o Millennials in a Post-TV Network World

Anti-Stereotypes in the Transmedia Edutainment Web TV Series East Los High

Celeste González de Bustamante and Jessica Retis

On June 3, 2013, Hulu aired Hollywood's first and only series with an all-Latino cast: *East Los High* (*ELH*). The 24-episode first season became one of the top-five shows on hulu.com and attracted more than one million unique visitors to its Latino page each month (Population Media Center, n.d.). In 2019, the show had 31,000 followers on its Instagram account "eastloshigh," 10,600 followers on the Twitter account "@EastLosHighShow," and vibrant activity on its Tumblr and Facebook accounts (eastloshigh). Population Media Center (PMC) joined forces with Latina executive producer Katie Elmore Mota to introduce transmedia storytelling to reach a target audience—young Latina/os—and they incorporated an approach of entertainment-education, in an effort to address teen pregnancy and other health-related, political, cultural and social issues. Transmedia approaches go beyond multiplatform storytelling by creating a wide-variety of content using multiple platforms through storylines that are separate and complete from the umbrella programming, in this case, *East Los High* (Ramasubramanian, 2016). For example, during the first month of *East Los High*'s airing, more than 27,000 people used a Planned Parenthood widget available on the series's website, more than 98 percent of those who watched the episodes and used its transmedia elements said they found its resources very helpful, and 60 percent of viewers said they referred those resources to a friend (Population Media Center, n.d.).

This chapter interrogates the connections among changing demographics, patterns of media production, distribution and consumption in a post-TV

157

network era (Molina-Guzmán, 2018). Using the web-TV series *East Los High* as a case study, we examine, first, how the growth of a young Latina/o bilingual population is influencing the relationship between media and advertising/marketing that seeks to attract these groups that, despite their increasing political and economic power, are usually portrayed in mainstream media in stereotypical ways and as apolitical. Second, the study concentrates its analysis on new approaches to media production, focusing on programming that incorporates transmedia narratives and which provide audiences with web-only content. Third, we examine the unique approach of *East Los High*, which utilizes an entertainment genre and transmedia storytelling to educate Latina youth to promote and effect social change. We view the *East Los High* transmedia approach as a contemporary effort to create content that develops anti-stereotypical female figures, specifically as relates to the issue of unwanted teenage pregnancy.

Our theoretical approach uses Molina-Guzmán's and Valdivia's work (2004) on Latina icons (Salma Hayek, Jennifer Lopez and Frida Kahlo) as a conceptual departure point, linking the concepts of Latinas as the embodiment of hybrid spaces and production (Bhabba, 1994; Anzaldua, 1987; Garcia Canclini, 1995), along with pioneers and contemporary Feminist Media Studies scholars (Anzaldúa, 1987; Cepeda, 2016; Fregoso, 1993; Molina-Guzmán, 2010; Moraga & Anzaldúa, 1984; Valdivia, 1995; Vargas, 2009, 2006), through the lens of Latinx critical race theory (LatCrit) and Latinx in communication studies (Anguiano & Castañeda, 2014; González de Bustamante & Retis, 2016), or what Anguiano & Castañeda (2014) call "Latina/o Critical Communication Theory" (p. 109). Our examination concentrates on the social and historical context and "deep structure" (Ramírez Berg, 2002) of a post-network TV program with an all Latina/o cast, *East Los High* (2013–2017). We concentrate on geographical emphases and this production's location, enabling us to interrogate how geography, gender, class, race and media representation might intersect to influence hybrid constructions of *latinidad*, described by Laó-Montes's (2001) as "an analytical concept that signifies a category of identification, familiarity, and affinity. In this sense, *latinidad* is a noun that identifies a subject position (the state of being Latino/a) in a given discursive space" (p. 3).

Through this highly focused investigation, we advance the work of Molina-Guzmán and Valdivia by introducing the concept of *scale-shifting* (Livingston & Asmolov, 2010; González de Bustamante & Relly, 2014) as a way to understand how a new generation of media producers might bypass traditional media structures that are in place to construct *latinidad* on their own, enabling more nuanced, complicated, and hybrid images of Latinas to emerge. In other words, as a result of new avenues for production, and a restructuring of the media landscape, Latina millennial producers, somewhat distinct from Latina actors and media producers of the past, are able to "scale-shift" (Livingston & Asmolov, 2010) beyond traditional media and power structures to further their individual and collective goals. One of the ways that Latina/o producers are scale-shifting is through the implementation of transmedia strategies (Wang & Singhal, 2016). In other words, Latina/o producers are going beyond legacy media to convey and reaffirm culturally relevant and politically specific messages through television programming and social media. In advancing this argument, we acknowledge that despite some evidence of "scale-shifting," there are limits to the potential for moving beyond the power of legacy media and power structures that historically have been in place. We ask both how are Latina millennials choosing to represent themselves in the digital era, and what strategies are they using? In short, are they able to side-step big media, and if so, how are they scale-shifting? In addition, we examine how, in the midst of these efforts to self-represent, *latinidad* is racialized, gendered and hybridized by Latina millennials (Molina-Guzmán & Valdivia, 2004). Further, we argue that when producers and community partners collaborate through a transmedia edutainment approach, and key elements of the "deep structure" are considered in the media production, as in the case of *East Los High*, the potential for collective action and social change might increase, and the risk of stereotypical representations of Latina/os might be diminished.

In the next section, we present the conceptually and methodologically relevant scholarship that treats intersections among Latina millennials, gender, geography, entertainment media, and the potential for collective action. Then, we turn to our analysis of *East Los High*, utilizing a methodology adapted from Ramírez Berg's (2002) call to examine the "deep structure" of media production, and focusing specifically on the issue of unwanted teenage pregnancy. In the last section, we provide some concluding thoughts and suggestions for continued research.

MEDIATING LATINA/OS AND *LATINIDAD*

Since the pioneering work of the 1980s and 1990s in Latina/o media feminist studies (Anzaldúa, 1987; Moraga & Anzaldúa, 1984; Fregoso, 1993; Valdivia, 1995), several important strands of research have captivated scholars' attention, ranging from transnationalism and hybridity (Cepeda, 2016; Valdivia, 2004; Vargas, 2009, 2006) to inquiries and studies related to constructions and representations of the body (Beltrán, 2002; Cepeda, 2016; Molina-Guzmán, 2010; Molina-Guzmán & Valdivia, 2004). Latina/o media feminist studies' emphasis on transnational processes such as concepts and constructions of identity to cross-national media flows and production allow the field to expand beyond Western-oriented scholarship (Cepeda, 2016; Piñon & Rojas, 2011; Patil, 2013). In the case of *East Los High*, many of the characters have familial ties to Mexico. The notion of transnationalism obligates recognition of the hybrid processes that are underway as new migrants arrive and consume and produce in the U.S. context (Valdivia, 2004; Garcia Canclini, 1995) and as historically present Latina/o groups access and contribute to content.

Scholars examining Latinas and the media have turned to Critical Race Theory as a way to examine issues of representation and self-representation (Anguiano & Castaneda, 2014; Molina-Guzmán, 2018; Vargas, 2009). Molina-Guzmán argues that a certain form of "hipster racism" on twenty-first century entertainment television has enabled the perpetuation of negative stereotypes (2018). Anguiano and Castañeda (2014) note that Latina/o Critical Race Theory in communication can be applied to examine "U.S. Latina/o communicative practices, rhetoric approaches, media spaces, audience responses, and public policy implications, to name just a few" (p. 108).

We contribute to the scholarship by examining, specifically, the subject of unwanted pregnancy, as this issue continues to be a part of a stereotypical trope in mainstream entertainment. As Molina-Guzmán noted (2018, p. 90), the "self-sacrificing, almost virginal Latina mother is a staple of Hollywood dramas." Ramírez Berg (2002) identified the harlot, female clown, the dark "hot" lady and the subservient mother as stereotypes usually assigned to Latinas. The motherhood/unwanted pregnancy issue enables an opportunity to investigate whether "anti-stereotypes" emerge when casts are primarily Latina/o and when the programming is written, produced and directed by Hispanics. Further, the issue of unwanted pregnancy remains salient, given that teen pregnancy rates for Latinas and African American women are still more than twice as high as white female teens, despite declines in teen pregnancy in all U.S. states among all racial/ethnic groups (Power to Decide, 2018). Finally, more than 19 million women live in "contraceptive deserts" where they do not have reasonable access to public clinics that provide all forms of contraceptives (Power to Decide, 2018).

Geographies of *Latinidad*

Despite mainstream media's more recent tendency to construct female *latinidad* as a light brown, non-Afro-Latina, and somewhat ethnically ambiguous, with curvaceous bodies and dark hair (Molina-Guzmán, 2008), we acknowledge, as Valdivia (2005), just as diversity exists among Latina/os there is diversity among Latina/o scholars. For example, scholars have not arrived at a consensus on whether to continue to use the "umbrella category" of *latinidad* or to rely on more specific terms of Chicano, Boricua, and Cuban American studies, among others (Valdivia, 2005). Valdivia (2005, p. 315) explains how mainstream media have portrayed Latinas differently, depending on their heritage and place in the United States. The phenomenon of mainstream producers to create a *latinidad* that is not "too brown" and ambiguously hybrid in part has led to the displacement of both Afro-Latina/os and Mexican Americans from the media landscape, though they are the largest group among Hispanics in the United States.

The discourses of *latinidad*, in Spanish language media, for the past three decades have pointed to Miami as the "global center for the growing integration of the Latina and Latin American entertainment industry" (Dávila, 2012, p. 143). At the same time, in Spanish-language media, authentic *latinidad*'s source tends to be more connected to Latin America, rather than the "deterritorialized" United States (Dávila, 2012, p. 145). It is in this context that we acknowledge Baéz's (2018) call for place-based study of Latina/os, given that the lived experiences are not always consistent with mainstream or Spanish-language media constructions of *latinidad*. The chapter contributes to this stream of scholarship by advancing understandings of a particular form of *latinidad*—one located and constructed by the residents and lived experience of Angelenos in East LA who have a distinct history and culture from Latina/os in other parts of the United States.

EDUTAINMENT AND THE POTENTIAL FOR COLLECTIVE ACTION IN THE POST-TV NETWORK ERA

This chapter examines the potential for collective action among producers and actors of *East Los High* through a process called "scale-shifting." In Tarrow's (2005) definition, scale-shifting involves "a change in the number and level of coordinated contentious actions to a different focal point, involving a new range of actors, different objectives and broadened claims. It can also generate a change in the meaning and scope of the object of the claim" (p. 121). While Tarrow (2005) and Livingston and Asmolov (2010) were concerned with the potential for activists to side-step bona-fide political actors and structures in nation-states, we focus our attention on the structural issues involving the entertainment industry and the ability of Latina/o producers and actors to circumvent traditional power structures to contribute to collective-action to effect social change. Livingston and Asmolov (2010) argue that "the growth of networked non-state actors and scale shifting sometimes bypasses both states and traditional news organizations" (p. 751). We ask in this post TV-network era whether approaches involving transmedia and edutainment strategies (Ramasubramarian, 2016; Wang & Singhal, 2016) and/or the use of social media by entertainment actors as activists may contribute to create a sense of collective action.

We are living times where media content is continuously changing in order to adapt to the post-TV network era, defined by five C's: choice, control, convenience, customization and community (Lotz, 2007). Producers are increasingly creating content that engages audiences by using various techniques to develop synchronized stories across multiple platforms in a trend largely known as transmedia storytelling (Jenkins, 2006). As Jenkins noted, transmedia storytelling "represents a process where integral elements of a fiction get dispersed systematically across multiple delivery channels for the purpose of creating a unified and coordinated entertainment experience. Ideally, each medium makes its own unique contribution to the unfolding of the story" (Jenkins, 2010, p. 944). Although transmedia storytelling has been gaining more prominence in recent decades, what is suggestive in this case study is the fact that the series *East Los High* implemented this creative narrative to disseminate educational content in an entertainment production, also called edutainment.

As Wang and Singhal (2016) explain, edutainment programs are grounded in theories of narrative persuasion that explain the factors and processes that facilitate changes in audience members' knowledge, attitudes and behaviors. Decades ago, edutainment programs used radio and television dramatic serials in Latin America, Asia and Africa to entertain and educate on a variety of topics; however, edutainment programs in North America and Europe face stiff competition in their media-saturated environments. Many edutainment programs use social cognitive theory, an agentic framework of psychosocial change with a dual path of influence: direct exposure to media models and indirect social learning through interpersonal discussions. In their analysis on how *East Los High* promoted sexual and reproductive health, Wang and Singhal (2016) identified three contributions: cultural sensitivity, transmedia edutainment and collaborative multilateral partnership.

THE EXPLANATORY POWER OF
USING A TV PROGRAM AS A CASE STUDY

After outlining the theoretical and conceptual debates that undergird the chapter we now turn to questions regarding our methodological approach. The decision to focus analysis on a program or a few programs as a case study enables several explanatory payoffs: Programs as case studies provide a research scenario in which deep analysis can occur; programs as case study allow the researchers to examine specifically one or two issues, instead of casting a wide net to examine superficially many phenomena; and, this type of analysis lays the groundwork for future work on other similar or distinct programs. Navar-Gill (2018), for example, examined the manner in which television entertainment writers for female-centered programs including *Jane the Virgin* used Twitter to engage with audiences. That qualitative study found that @JaneWriters' tweets tended to concentrate on promotion rather than engagement with audiences.

In the shaping and reshaping of ethnic identity by news and entertainment media, women's bodies become a "a stand-in for nation" (Molina-Guzmán, 2006, p. 234). In a case study of the film *Frida*, Molina-Guzmán analyzed the cinematic production of ethnic identity and compared the film's construction of ethnic identity with news coverage of the movie and online chats about Hollywood production. The study found that while the producers of the movie attempted to present an "authentic Frida," and one that was hypersexualized and therefore more familiar to mainstream audiences, audiences had more "fluctuating constructions of ethnic identity and culture" (2006, p. 247).

Some previous studies have used *East Los High* as a case study to analyze its targeted health messages and the transmedia storytelling approach of the series. Wang and Singhal (2016) noted that *East Los High* was "the first culture-centric intervention that was designed to use trans-media edutainment to promote sexual and reproductive health, especially among Latina adolescent girls and young women" (p. 1008). The researchers found that in season one alone, "tens of thousands" of visits occurred, and that visitors arrived at the site from all fifty U.S. states. Ramasubramanian's (2016) study focused on the social media and interactive elements of *East Los High*, and findings suggested that a transmedia edutainment approach can foster social change and "larger community goals such as health, and social justice" (p. 340).

Our qualitative analysis contributes to the literature by attempting to *locate* (a concept used by feminist scholars to identify the politics of women's representation) Latina millennial *latinidad* in *East Los High* and pays specific attention to the issue of unwanted pregnancy. In addition, we examine the edutainment and transmedia strategies of *East Los High* producers in an effort to identify the potential for collective action through scale shifting (Livingston & Asmolov, 2010; González de Bustamante & Relly, 2014).

We adapt Ramírez Berg's (2002) suggestion to go beyond simple content analysis and to first examine and explain the social and historical context in which the program was produced (e.g., the "post network TV" era). Second, we follow Ramírez Berg's suggestion to examine the "deep structure" of TV programming. To narrow our focus, we analyze specifically the topic of unwanted teen pregnancy. In our investigation, we are interested, too, in identifying how *East Los High* producers construct a specific version of *latinidad* for Latina millennials. In other words, we seek to identify the "signifiers" of *latinidad* in a Los Angeles urban-based context. In addition, we also look at these elements to determine if and how an anti-stereotypical aesthetic or anti-stereotypes might take shape (Ramírez Berg, 2002).

Ramírez Berg suggests an analysis that includes multiple factors: the star system (recruiting top-billed stars to play leads), casting, screenwriting, camera angles, shot selection, direction, production design, editing, acting conventions, lighting, framing, makeup, costuming and *mise-en-scène*. It is part-ly as a result of the pressures of the Hollywood star-system that Latina/os rarely are selected to play lead roles in mainstream films and that, in 2013, "despite being 17 percent of the population, Latinos comprised none of the lead actors among the top ten movies and scripted network shows" (Negrón-Mutaner et al., 2014). In our attempt to identify signifiers for *latinidad*, we focus our analysis on: casting, makeup and costuming (as they relate to Latina bodies) and screenwriting.

Second, as part of the "deep structure," we examine the production teams (Molina-Guzmán, 2018) of these two programs. Who is behind the pro-grams' development and distribution, and what are their goals? Third, we analyze the edutainment and transmedia strategies of producers of *East Los High* in an effort to determine the potential for collective action through scale-shifting strategies.

THE EMERGENCE OF
ANTI-STEREOTYPES AND *EAST LOS HIGH*

East Los High began as a Hulu series in 2013 and broke ground as "Holly-wood's first and only series with an all Latino cast" (Population Media Center, n.d.). The series ran for five seasons, and the first season was a collaborative production between Wise Entertainment and Population Media Center. Teen pregnancy represented a central topic in story lines, especially during the first season. The dramatic series, based on students in a fictional high school located in East Los Angeles that was established in 1972, depicts the struggles and triumphs of Mexican-origin, working-class teens. Though episodes were released on Hulu, additional media content, known as trans-media, was pushed through Vimeo, Facebook and Twitter.

The innovative approach of *East Los High* was not only its efforts for uniting an all Latina/o cast on screen, but an all Latina/o crew working behind the scenes, and filming predominantly in East Los Angeles, one of the neighborhoods with the highest presence of Latina/o residents in L.A. (97 percent) (*Los Angeles Times*, n.d.). Over the four years and seasons the production aired, it followed a telenovela-like entertainment genre targeted for teens; promotion material hyped, "Love. Sex. Revenge. High school like you have never seen it—at EAST LOS HIGH." On the other hand, the program provided educational and informative content aimed at the fastest-growing ethnic group in the United States: Latina/o millennials.

Demographically, Latina/os are the youngest major racial or ethnic group in the United States. According to the Pew Research Center (Krogstad et al., 2016), about one third, or 17.9 million, of the nation's Hispanic population is younger than 18, and about a quarter, or 14.6 million, of all Latina/os are millennials. The disproportionately young profile of Latina/os in the United States is driven by the overwhelming youth of U.S.-born Hispanics. With a median age of 19, nearly half (47 percent) of U.S.-born Latina/os are younger than 18. Latina/o millennials make up almost half of all Latina/o eligible voters and will be the main driver of growth over the next two decades, constituting by far the largest source of growth for the Hispanic electorate (Krogstad et al., 2016).

Aside from their potential political power, Latina/o millennial consumers will play an integral role in spending trends over the next 20 to 30 years (Nielsen, 2016). The average age of Latina/os in the United States is 27, much younger than the average age of their non-Hispanic white counterparts, which is 42 (Nielsen, 2018). Latina/os' young median age means many have grown up as digital natives. As a result, they are more likely to use technology than other segments of the population (Nielsen, 2018). Hispanics 18 and older are 9 percent more likely to own a smartphone, 11 percent more likely to own a game console, and 13 percent more likely to own a smartwatch than non-Hispanic whites. Young Latina/os acquire particular importance because of their projection as potential commercial customers and political clients; it is estimated that 800,000 Latina/os turn 18 each year. However, access to higher education is still lower than other groups, so social mobility through education remains an obstacle to overcome for many young Latina/os, particularly for Spanish-heritage speakers (Retis & Badillo, 2018).

As Latina/o millennials are among the fastest-growing, most sought-after consumers, several advertising and marketing enterprises are in continuous pursuit of their attention, alongside media and entertainment industries. A July 2015 report in *The Atlantic* titled, "Billenials are the Cultural Chameleons," described them as the most coveted consumers who often live with their parents, prefer English, but when talking with their *abuela*, speak in Spanish. Coined by Univision, the word "billennial" is a synthesis of bilingual and millennial, a nod to how many young Latina/os speak both Spanish and English (Phippen, 2015). The reason companies are so determined to appeal to billennial interests is not only because of their sheer numbers, but also because of what they have the potential to become. Billenials are largely the first generation that doesn't have to decide if they want to be solely Latina/o or American. By not choosing, they have changed the way marketers appeal to them, the way giant corporations think of them, and they will undoubtedly alter American culture (Phippen, 2015).

After several decades of continual Latina/o immigration to the United States and through the second decade of the twenty-first century, research has increased in an effort to analyze these demographic changes as well as "Latina/o media booms." Critical studies are delineating comparative and interdisciplinary approaches to better understand the influences of the transnationalization of Latino/a media markets and the gendered dimensions of *latinidad* (Cepeda, 2016). In addition, the transformation of the industry requires new theoretical and methodological approaches in order to advance analysis of production, distribution and consumption of U.S. media that target Latina/os. As Dávila (2014) notes, discussions regarding new TV channels abound as Latina/os are widely celebrated as *the* new media market, and the entry of big media players is anticipated to transform what we understand as Latino media:

> Addressing "Latino media" means analyzing at least two industries: one with roots in Latin America and the other with roots in Hollywood, not to mention two industries that are also linked to at least three distinct language media worlds in Spanish, in English, and in Portuguese (translated to Spanish). (Dávila, 2014, p. 2)

Further, technological innovations, transmedia narratives or multiplatform storytelling and the emergence of social networks are opening new avenues for socially significant media content such as edutainment programs that are making their way into a highly saturated media environment (Sherry, 2002; Wang & Singhal, 2016).

The series *East Los High* takes place in East Los Angeles, California, a 7.47 square mile unincorporated area made up of several neighborhoods in Los Angeles County. It is one of the most densely populated areas of the county, with 16,863 people living per square mile (*Los Angeles Times*, n.d.). Just over 85 percent of the residents living in East LA are of Mexican origin, and 96 percent of residents are Latina/o (*Los Angeles Times*, n.d.; World Population Review, 2019).

The last two years of the series were released at a time of increased tensions and political polarization in the United States and noted a break from a post–civil rights era in which most politicians avoided overtly racist and misogynistic language to a new epoch fomented by President Donald Trump's vitriolic discourse, which signaled the acceptance of using racist and derogatory language to refer to gender-based and ethnic groups.

It is important to note that Latina/os have long been a part of California's history. Prior to the early nineteenth century, the area that now comprises the state of California was Alta California and made up part of New Spain. After Mexican independence, Alta California remained part of Mexico from 1821 to 1848, when it was forced to cede more than half of its land to the United States through the Treaty of Guadalupe Hidalgo.

More than 160 years later, through a collaboration between Population Media Center and the series directors and producers, a myriad of additional "stand-alone" edutainment content was created and hosted on the *East Los High* website. Web visitors could access photos, music and videos related to the themes throughout the four seasons. They could also click on the "take action" tag, where they have access to a list of links grouped in 16 topics: voting, mental health/substance abuse, bullying/sexting, immigration, dating violence, sexual abuse, plan for your future, sexually transmitted infections, affordable care act, public services, activism/advocacy, LGBTQ, parents, abortion, pregnancy/parenting and sex/birth control.

The list of partners that joined this groundbreaking production confirms how it became possible to produce content for, by and with young Latina/os utilizing an approach distinct from stereotypical representations of Latina/o-otherness: Advocates for Youth, California Family Health Council, Exhale, It Gets Better Project, Planned Parenthood, Bienvenidos—Healing Children and Their Families, XQ, AltaMed, California Latinas for Reproductive Justice, Ford Foundation, National Latina Institute for Reproductive Health, Population Media Center Acting for Change, Voto Latino, Zero to Three, Bedsider, Catholics for Choice, GSA Network, The National Campaign to Prevent Teen and Unplanned Pregnancy, Rape Abuse & Incest National Network, Art Global Health Center, Sex, etc., Common Sense, Glaad, The National Domestic Violence Hotline, Stay Teen, Youth Build, Break the Circle Empowering Youth to End Domestic Abuse, Define American, Ignite Political Power in Every Young Woman, Planned Parenthood, East Los Angeles Women's Center and United We Dream. In other words, *East Los High* as a transmedia edutainment web series represents a significant case study to analyze how in a post-TV network world how "anti-stereotypes" might emerge.

THE DEEP STRUCTURE OF *EAST LOS HIGH* AND THE FORMATION OF ANTI-STEREOTYPES

While most Hollywood-generated films and TV programs tend to focus on perpetuating a star-system that privileges well-known, usually white actors, who can potentially draw large audiences, *East Los High* included a cast of lesser-known Latina/o actors. The following section focuses on key "deep structure" elements: scene-setting, casting, costume and makeup and screenwriting. It is through analysis of these elements that we begin to understand how *ELH* directors, producers and actors worked in concert to develop an anti-stereotypical aesthetic (Ramírez Berg, 2002) of East Los Angeles and its residents.

Scene Setting

Throughout the series, directors paid close attention to the geographical iconography of East Los Angeles and sought to form a sense of working-class *latinidad* strongly influenced by Mexican tradition and culture. Frequently, directors filmed establishing shots on the bustling streets of East LA. Opening scenes routinely included shots of older model cars from the 1980s and 1990s, mainly pickup trucks and working vans. Shots included storefronts with signs referencing Mexican states such as Guerrero, along with *taquerías* (taco shops). Wide shots of the streets depicted a distinctly Latina/o neighborhood with signs written in Spanish. Additional material culture included exterior and interior shots of the main characters' homes, which were portrayed as lower-middle class through shots of modest furniture and sparsely decorated rooms that often included Virgen de Guadalupe (Mexico's patron saint) statues or candles. Scenes that featured the campus of *East Los High* included almost all Latina/o extras. All of these shot decisions served to create a set of "geographical signifiers" that formed a *latinidad* heavily influenced by Mexican cultural traditions and iconography.

Casting

As mentioned, the *East Los High* series was the first English-language streaming show with an all Latina/o, but not necessarily Mexican, cast. For example, one of the characters who becomes pregnant, Ceci, played by Danielle Vega, describes herself as multiethnic (Spanish, African, Anglo-Saxon and American Indian). Janine Larina, who plays Jessie, another teen who gets pregnant in season one, has dark hair and "Latina-like" features, but her ethnicity is not listed on IMDB. Curiously, according to the show's webpage, only one of the main female actors, Noemi Gonzalez, a Mexican American Latina from Desert Springs, is from Southern California, and not one Latina main actor is from East Los Angeles (EastLosHigh.com, n.d.).

Makeup and Costume

Some, though not all female characters, are highly sexualized through the use of heavy makeup and provocative dress/costume in the series. Other female teen characters, such as Soli, who plans to be a journalist after she graduates, dress more conservatively. Ceci, who is a member of the high school dance group called the "Bomb Squad," wears large, hooped earrings, crop tops, short shorts, heavy makeup, false eyelashes, bright pink lipstick and well-defined eyebrows. After she has her baby, Ceci's attire becomes more conservative. Most of the female characters, including those who are less sexualized, yet distinctly feminine, have long dark-brown or black hair. Female characters dress casually for school and outside of school, reflecting both their age as well as socio-economic status.

Screen Writing

Despite the highly sexualized and feminine attributes assigned to the female roles through makeup and costume, these same characters demonstrate that they are intellectualizing and fully aware of what transpires in their lives. Through dialogue and behaviors, female leads make decisions on their own, after consultations with health experts and other older more experienced female supporting characters.

The series follows sensational telenovela-like plots of "sex, revenge, and love," but woven into the story lines are educational messages. Many of the plots in season one episodes focused on the topic of unwanted pregnancy. Two Latina teens have unprotected sex, become pregnant and then must decide whether to continue with or end the pregnancy through abortion. The episodes that focused on unwanted pregnancy centered on two main points, the issue of choice and the use of condoms to prevent pregnancy and sexually transmitted infections. After consulting with friends and a health professional at a neighborhood clinic, Ceci, who came from a family with little economic resources and support, decided to carry the baby to full term. In contrast, Jessie gained support from her professionally successful aunt, Paulina, who told her the story about her having an abortion when she was a teenager. Jessie, who has dreams of becoming a doctor, after being inspired and encouraged by a Latina doctor, decided to end her pregnancy through a surgical procedure. In both cases of unwanted pregnancy, the teens go to a health clinic to speak with a health professional before making the decision. Though both girls are influenced by family and friends, they make the decision on their own. Season one culminated with Jessie stating a clear message: "Make sure you really, really, really know a guy before you have sex with him, and, oh, use a condom."

Aside from the plots, language and dialogue played important roles in creating a show that resulted in realistic, rather than stereotypical, portrayals of East L.A. residents, especially teens. Directors consulted with East L.A. youth to ensure that the language used in scripts was as "authentic" as possible. Most of the dialogue is spoken in English, though some Spanish terms and phrases are used to indicate the bilingual/bicultural identity of the characters. The accents that actors use are distinctly West Coast Latina/os from a specific socioeconomic level, age and place in Southern California—East L.A. In this regard, the producers and directors help to create characters that are indicative and reflective of those who live in neighborhoods that make up East L.A. This decision, along with other production and directorial choices, foster the development of an anti-stereotypical aesthetic.

TRANSMEDIA AND ADDITIONAL EDUTAINMENT STRATEGIES

Beyond the series that streamed on Hulu, producers created additional multimedia content housed on the *ELH* website to further educate viewers and, in some cases, call them to action. In "Ceci's VLOG #1," for example, Ceci talks to her "primos" (cousins) in Durango, Mexico, telling them that she is three-months pregnant, and that "I wish I was back with y'all, but instead I'm in this shelter for pregnant teens. . . . But, HELL, if I was going to give my baby to some white lady who can't even dance!" In the VLOG, Ceci explains how important it is to eat healthful foods such as "fruits, vegetables, iron," while pregnant, and she recommends that pregnant teens not smoke or drink alcohol because it could harm the baby. At the bottom of the screen, a text-based crawl moves across the screen inviting web visitors to "chat with someone live at plannedparenthood.org." The video post ends by asking viewers to "send Ceci your stories or questions about pregnancy in the comments below."

Beyond vlogs, *The Siren*, the fictional student news outlet of East Los High, represents another form of edutainment content that is located on the series website. The stories published in *The Siren* allow viewers to keep up with the series and characters as well as to learn more about important issues that are discussed ranging from teen pregnancy and voting to undocumented immigration and HIV education. In one story, written by Soli Gomez, who wants to go on to study journalism at a university, readers learn that Ceci gave birth to a baby girl at her friend Jessie's house and that Jessie helped to deliver the baby before the ambulance could arrive. The story concluded on an inspirational note, stating, "sounds like someone is ready for a career in the medical profession." In addition, the newspaper included a story that featured Ceci and the struggles of being a teen mom and tips on how to prevent teen pregnancy in the first place as well as how to cope with the challenges of being a teen mom. The story on the website has links to actual resources such as Planned Parenthood.

Beyond an all Latina/o cast, *East Los High*'s producers, writers and crew are almost all Latina/o. In an interview Katie Elmore Mota, executive producer of *East Los High* and co-founder of Wise Entertainment, which produced the dramatic series, stated that the show is intended to get its audience to take action: "It's about giving a voice, about how to make sense of complex issues, and then hopefully give something to the audience that they can engage with it, beyond the screen" (Elmore Mota, 2016). In an interview at Oxnard College, *ELH* director Carlos Portugal, who co-wrote much of the series with Kathleen Bedoya, stated that through the series, "we're telling our own stories" (Portugal, n.d.).

THE EMERGENCE OF THE ANTI-STEREOTYPES
IN THE POST-TV AND TRANSMEDIA ERA

This chapter answers Ramírez Berg's (2002) call for more systematic studies of Latina/os in entertainment media and for scholarship that goes beyond content analysis. Through this case study, we contribute to others (Navar-Gill, 2018; Molina-Guzmán, 2006; Ramasubramanian, 2016; Wang & Singhal, 2016) who found this approach useful as a way to study formations and representations of *latinidad* and who conclude that transmedia storytelling is an effective tool to assist in achieving entertainment and educational goals.

Our examination of the socio-historical context in which *East Los High* was produced, in conjunction with analysis of key deep structure elements, enabled us to identify Latina millennial *latinidad* in a hyper-local geographical place in the United States. Examining the socio-historical context alongside contemporary phenomena, including technological and industry changes, we found that Latina/o producers created an environment in which they could explore new approaches, in this case, the edutainment "experiment" of *East Los High*. We found, similar to Livingston and Asmolov (2010) and González de Bustamante and Relly (2014), that the contemporary context of new technologies and new avenues for entertainment media (web-TV via Hulu and transmedia) have enabled scale-shifting to occur and increased the potential for social change and collective action.

Focusing on the deep structure of *East Los High* enabled the authors to identify and observe how through scene-setting, casting, makeup/costume and screenwriting, directors, writers, producers and actors have worked to create an anti-stereotypical aesthetic of *East Los Angeles* and Angelenos living in East L.A. Rather than flat or oversimplified caricatures, the female leads tended to play more nuanced characters who experienced a complicated set of positive and negative events that unfolded in their lives. In this way, Latina/o producers of *East Los High* worked to "disrupt the conditions of Latina/o invisibility" (Anguiano & Castañeda, 2014, p. 107) and provide a more accurate portrayal of young Latinas.

Beyond the creation of anti-stereotypes, those involved in the production of *East Los High* through their transmedia and edutainment approach successfully scale-shifted traditional media structures and institutions to increase the potential for collective action and social change. Similar to what Wang and Singhal (2016) and Ramasubramanian (2016) concluded, we note that when intentional efforts are made to not only create programming that speaks to issues related to Latina youth, positive social impacts can be made. We suggest that when producers and community partners collaborate through transmedia edutainment approaches, and the collaboration considers the importance of key elements of the "deep structure," as in the case of *East Los*

High, the potential for collective action and social change increases, and the risk of stereotypical representations of Latina/os diminishes.

The anti-stereotypical aesthetic of East L.A. and its residents that directors, producers and actors developed in the series helped to illustrate that *latinidad* is itself a hybrid and remains in flux. What we refer to and found in the *East Los High* series was both similar and distinct from forms and formations of *latinidad* in the 1990s (Molina-Guzmán & Valdivia, 2004). The notable influence of Mexican tradition and contemporary culture through various elements of the deep structure, particularly through scene-setting, casting and scriptwriting (including language and dialog), helped to create an authentic set of geography and class, ethnicity and gender-based iconography that reflected the lived experiences of East L.A. youth. Further, these constructions of *latinidad*, informed by a sense of *mexicanidad*, demonstrated the transnational/cross-border experiences of East L.A. residents, and emphasized the two cultural and linguistic worlds between which Latina billennials shift seamlessly (Phippen, 2015).

At the beginning of our conclusion we used the word "experiment" to describe the unique approach of *East Los High* because, despite the success of the series, the production remains an outlier and there are few transmedia series and cases that combine entertainment and education and have enjoyed such acclaim. In short, the series remains exceptional rather than indicative of an industry and societal trend. We suggest that there is room and need for more programming similar to *East Los High* that incorporates the dual function of entertaining Latina youth at the same time educating them about significant and relevant social issues. We re-emphasize the continued significance of this growing and economically powerful market niche as a rationale to foster more collaborative, transmedia/edutainment storytelling endeavors because of its potential to promote collective action and social change.

As Latina millennials become more economically and culturally relevant to society, we advocate for continued research on the geographies of *latinidad*. One avenue of research includes comparative work with other post-TV network programming such as *Jane the Virgin* and films such as *Miss Bala*, both of which star emerging Latina icon Gina Rodriguez, who through Instagram and social media is creating an anti-stereotype. Analyses of *Jane the Virgin* and *East Los High* with a focus on the issue of unwanted pregnancy would enable a continued focus on Latina millennials who are at opposite ends of the United States. More recently, Latina leads have been written into TV comedies such as *One Day at a Time*. The cross-general series that features three generations of Latinas has treated a wide variety of topics that deviate from stereotypical representations of Latinas, such as LGBTQ issues among Lesbian youth and Latina mothers as veterans. Such studies would further advance the goal of researchers to interrogate how geography, gender, class, race and media representation might intersect to influence hybrid constructions of *latinidad.*

REFERENCES

Anguiano, C., & Castañeda, M. (2014). Forging a path: Past and present scope of critical race theory and Latina/o critical race theory in communication studies. *Review of Communication, 14*(2), 107–124.

Anzaldúa, G. (1987). *Borderlands/La frontera: the new mestiza.* San Francisco: Spinsters/Aunt Lute.

Baéz, J. M. (2018). *In search of belonging: Latinas, media and citizenship.* Champaign, IL: University of Illinois Press.

Beltrán, M. (2002). The hollywood latina body as site of social struggle: Media constructions of stardom and Jennifer Lopez's "cross-over butt." *Quarterly Review of Film and Video, 19*(1), 71–86.

Bhabha, H. (1994). *The Location of Culture.* London: Routledge.

Cepeda, M. E. (2016). Beyond "filling in the gap": The state and status of Latina/o Feminist Media Studies. *Feminist Media Studies, 16* (2), 344–360.

Dávila, A. (2014). Introduction. In A. Dávila & Y. Rivero (Eds.), *Contemporary latina/o media. Production, circulation, politics* (pp. 1–20). New York, NY: New York University Press.

Dávila, A. (2012). *Latinos, inc.: The marketing and making of a people.* Berkeley, CA: University of California Press.

EastLosHigh.com. (2019). Wise Entertainment.

Elmore Mota, Kate. (2016). Panel. Beverly Hills, CA: USC Annenberg Norman Lear Center. Retrieved from: https://www.youtube.com/watch?v=YoVTmfNpgUc.

Fregoso, R. L. (1993). *The bronze screen: Chicana and chicano film culture.* Minneapolis, MN: University of Minnesota Press.

Garcia Canclini, N. (1995). *Hybrid cultures: Strategies for entering and leaving modernity.* Minneapolis: University of Minnesota Press.

González de Bustamante, C., & Relly, J. E. (2014). Journalism in times of violence: Social media use by U.S. and Mexican journalists working in northern Mexico. *Digital Journalism 2*(4), 507–523.

González de Bustamante, C., & Retis, J. (2016). Latinas: Underrepresented majorities in the digital age. In Christopher Campbell (Ed.). *The routledge companion to media and race* (pp. 222–233). Abingdon, UK: Routledge.

Jenkins, H. (2010). Transmedia storytelling and entertainment: An annotated syllabus. Continuum: *Journal of Media & Cultural Studies, 24*(6), 943–958.

Jenkins, H. (2006). Searching for the origami unicorn: The matrix and transmedia storytelling. In H. Jenkins (Ed.), *Convergence Culture: Where Old and New Media Collide* (pp. 93–130). New York, NY: New York University Press.

Krogstad, J., Lopez, M. H., Lopez, G., Passel, J. S., & Patten, E. (2016). Millennials make up almost half of latino eligible voters in 2016. Washington, DC: Pew Hispanic Research Center. Retrieved from: http://www.pewhispanic.org/2016/01/19/millennials-make-up-almost-half-of-latino-eligible-voters-in-2016.

Laó-Montes, A. (2001). Introduction. In A. Laó-Montes & A. Dávila (Eds.), *Mambo montage: The latinization of New York* (pp. 1–53). New York, NY: Columbia University Press.

Livingston, S., & Asmolov, G. (2010). Networks and the future of foreign affairs reporting. *Journalism Studies, 11*(5), 745–760.

Los Angeles Times. (n.d.). East Los Angeles. *Los Angeles Times.* Retrieved from: http://maps.latimes.com/neighborhoods/neighborhood/east-los-angeles/.

Lotz, A. D. (2007). Conclusion: Still watching television. In A. D. Lotz (Ed.), *The television will be revolutionized* (pp. 241–256). New York, NY: New York University Press.

Molina-Guzmán, I. (2018). *Latinas and latinos on TV: Colorblind comedy in the post-racial network era.* Tucson, AZ: University of Arizona Press.

Molina-Guzmán, I. (2010). *Dangerous curves: Latina bodies in the media.* New York, NY: New York University Press.

Molina-Guzmán, I. (2008). Chapter 13: Mapping the dynamic terrain of US Latina/o media research. In Havidán Rodríguez, H., Sáenz, R., & Menjívar, C. (Eds.), *Latinas/os in the United States: Changing the face of América* (pp. 199–209). Boston, MA: Springer.

Molina-Guzmán, I. (2006). Mediating Frida: Negotiating discourses of Latina/o authenticity in global media representations of ethnic identity. *Critical Studies in Media Communication, 23*(3), 232–251.

Molina-Guzmán, I., & Valdivia, A. N. (2004). Brain, brow, and booty: Latina iconicity in US popular culture. *The Communication Review, 7*(2), 205–221.

Moraga, C., & Anzaldúa, G. (1984). *This bridge called my back: Writings of radical women of color.* Watertown, MA: Peresphone Press.

Navar-Gill, A. (2018). From strategic retweets to group hangs: Writers' room twitter accounts and the productive ecosystem of TV social media fans. *Television & New Media, 19*(5), 415–430.

Negrón-Mutaner, F., Abbas, C., Figueroa, L., & Robson, S. (2014). The Latino media gap: A report on the state of Latinos in U.S. media. NALIP, The Center for the Study of Ethnicity and Race at Columbia University, National Hispanic Foundation for the Arts, SSRC, National Latino Arts Education and Media Institute.

Nielsen. 2018. The database: Young, digital and social-connecting with today's Hispanic consumers. Episode 15. Demographics, 09-24-2018.

Nielsen. 2016. Getting a flavor for what attracts Hispanic Millennial shoppers. Demographics. 05-31-2016.

Patil, V. (2013). From patriarchy to intersectionality: A transnational feminist assessment of how far we've really come. *Signs 38*(4), 847–867.

Phippen, W. (2015, July 31). Billenials are cultural chameleons. *The Atlantic.* Retrieved from: https://www.theatlantic.com/politics/archive/2015/07/billenials-are-cultural-chameleons/43 2453/.

Piñón, J., & Rojas, V. (2011). Language and cultural identity in the new configuration of the US Latino TV industry. *Global Media and Communication, 7*(2), 129–147.

Population Media Center. (n.d.). East Los High, United States. South Burlington, VT: Population Media Center. Retrieved from: https://www.populationmedia.org/projects/east-los-high/.

Portugual, Carlos. (n.d.). Interview at Oxnard College. Oxnard, California. Retrieved from https://vimeo.com/105400455.

Power to Decide. (2018). Declines in teen pregnancy and childbearing lead to billions in public savings. Washington, DC: Power to Decide. Retrieved from: https://powertodecide.org/about-us/newsroom/declines-teen-pregnancy-and-childbearing-means-billions-in-public-sav ings.

Ramasubramanian, S. (2016). Racial/ethnic identity, community-oriented media initiatives, and transmedia storytelling. *The Information Society, 32*(5), 333–342.

Ramírez Berg, C. (2002). *Latino images in film: Stereotypes, subversion and resistance.* Austin: University of Texas Press.

Retis, J. & Badillo, A. (2018). *Los latinos y las industrias culturales en espanol en Estados Unidos.* Madrid: Real Instituto Elcano.

Sherry, J. L. (2002). Media saturation and entertainment—education. *Communication Theory, 12*(2), 206–224.

Tarrow, S. (2005). *The new transnational activism.* Cambridge: Cambridge University Press.

Valdivia, A. N. (2004). Latinas as radical hybrid: Transnationally gendered traces in mainstream media. *Global Media Journal, 3*(4), 4.

Valdivia, A. N. (2005). Geographies of latinidad. In W. Crichlow (Ed.), *Race, identity, and representation in education* (pp. 307–317). Abingdon, UK: Routledge.

Valdivia, A. N. (1995). Feminist media studies in a global setting: Beyond binary contradictions and into multicultural spectrums. In A. N. Valdivia (Ed.), *Feminism, multiculturalism, and the media: Global diversities* (pp. 7–29). Thousand Oaks, CA: Sage Publications.

Vargas, L. (2009). *Latina teens, migration, and popular culture.* New York, NY: Peter Lang.

Vargas, L. (2006). Transnational media literacy: Analytic reflections on a program with Latina teens. *Hispanic Journal of Behavioral Sciences, 28*(2), 267–285.

Wang, H., & Singhal, A. (2016). East Los High: Transmedia edutainment to promote the sexual and reproductive health of young Latina/o Americans. *American Journal of Public Health, 106*(6), 1002–1010.

World Population Review. (2019). Los Angeles, California, Population 2019. http://world populationreview.com/us-cities/los-angeles-population/.

Chapter Ten

#DontTrendOnMe

Addressing Appropriation of Native
Americanness in Millennial Social Media

Ashley Cordes and Debra Merskin

An image by Muksin (2018) circulating on Instagram, a popular social media platform, depicts a peculiar but all too apropos remixed representation of Native Americanness. Disney's Pocahontas' and Snow White's faces are edited onto two music festival-goers' bodies, who are coyly interacting with one another. Wearing a tight, short, lace dress and Native-inspired jewelry, "Pocahontas" is consistently reproduced in popular culture as a symbol or problematic stand-in for Native women—beautiful, sexualized, close-to-earth, and sacrificially available to white people (see Greene, 1975; Morigeau et al., 2018). She is now recast as the *festival princess*. Attendees of the Coachella Valley Music and Arts Festival (CVMAF), or those viewing social media images of it, witness an abundance of participants, particularly white women, wearing outfits constructed out of disjointed signifiers based on various mis-representations of Native Americanness.

CVMAF is an annual (since 1999) event at which many millennial attendees (defined roughly as those born between 1981 and 1996 (Dimock, 2018)), enact race as a performance, seemingly apart from an awareness of the problematic nature of cultural appropriation. The festival qualifies as a media and popular culture spectacle, defined as "those phenomena of media culture that embody contemporary society's basic values, serve to initiate individuals into its way of life, and dramatize its controversies and struggles, as well as its modes of conflict resolution" (Kellner, 2003, p. 2). Music festivals in general, and CVMAF in particular, fall squarely within the logics of media spectacle and have become peripheral expressions of the given zeitgeist.

This chapter explores re-presentations of woman Native Americanness at the 2018 CVMAF. We consider politics of representation and cultural appropriation, as well as the lived and felt experiences of Native American people about these displays. The "Coachella look" (hypersexualized outfits paired with bricolage of headdresses, feathers, beads, and other markers of Native Americanness) is widely appropriated by millennials at CVMF. At the same time, a new wave of Indigenous and ally millennials speaks back to these racial and cultural "rip offs" that are experienced as "felt" attacks on indigenous cultures and identities. Examples of the latter include a slew of memes, hashtags, and culture jams on social media platforms that aim to re-articulate and revise the problem. These social media strategies function as corrective responses and can be categorized as digital resistance to acts of cultural appropriation on social media. Furthermore, we examine how some millennials, often self-proclaimed as part of the awakened or "woke" generation in terms of cognizance of social justice issues, simultaneously have a blind spot when it comes to cultural appropriation. There was hope that millennials would have more racial awareness and distaste for racism, sexism, and ableism, as demonstrated in their overwhelming disapproval of Donald Trump in the 2016 election period (McCaskill, 2016). Yet their sensibilities about race and gender as it pertains to representation does not seem to prevent them from culturally appropriating.

Representation, which regards the selective, mediated presentation of another culture, and appropriation, which regards taking elements of the other culture, while different, are also intertwined as the introductory Pocahontas anecdote describes. Hall's (1997) concept of representation (which he also describes as *re-presentation*, a term we will use in this essay) is used theoretically to predict that fashion-as-performance is in fact a re-presentation informed by dominant cultural ideology. Coachella attendees are not simply appropriating and copying exact styles of Native American culture, but more commonly taking and drawing from Native Americans re-presented in media and mixing and matching them with other hybridized cultural items. This can be typified as disrespectful enactments of continued colonialist fantasies in "playing Indian," or performing Native Americanness (Deloria, 1998).

The findings of this study are important to indigenous people in general, and Native women in particular; they are at least two times more likely to suffer sexual violence than members of the non-Native population (Deer, 2015). Sexualizing appropriations of Native Americanness does nothing to help eliminate the disproportionate pervasiveness of sexual violence towards Native American women. Million's (2008) *felt theory* predicts that cultural appropriation impacts those whose likeness, lifeways, and artifacts are appropriated by outsider cultures.

This study examines 1) how woman Native Americanness is re-presented in millennial music festivals such as Coachella; 2) the markers of woman

Native Americanness in fashion and form at the 2018 CVMAF; and the social media activity created by indigenous millennials (and their allies) that addresses, resists, and/or revises stereotypical or appropriative re-presentations. The following sections discuss media and other popular culture re-presentations of woman Native American-ness and briefly discuss cultural appropriation. This is followed by a discussion of CVMAF, the psychology of the millennial generation, a textual analysis of examples of cultural appropriation at the festival, and social media responses.

NATIVENESS AND REPRESENTATION

Torgovnick's *Primitive Passions* (1997) discusses how Native Americans are often viewed in terms of their perceived connection to what she calls the trope of the primitive. While the primitive is typically framed as feminine, rooted in collectivity and the ecstatic, civilization is coded as masculine and individualist. Native American people are often problematically re-presented in media as noble savages, which regards an axis of values (used to position cultural outsiders within an axis of distance) that predicts whether Native Americans are readily included in mainstream culture or, instead, used as an opposition to mainstream culture to justify neocolonial relations (Deloria, 1998). This helps to explain how Native Americans can be both valorized *and* disrespected—condemned for negative stereotypes, while also widely appreciated or envied for their aesthetic preferences and perceived ties to nature, romanticism, and tradition. Gender then maps onto Native American-ness, typically creating binary gendered stereotypes. Re-presentations of Native American women in particular tend to focus on exoticism, materialism, nobility, and beauty, but can also be more negative, based on the binary of the princess and the squaw (Merskin, 2010). White imagination of Native American women, for example, is linked to a representation of the "noble Princess tied to 'America' and to sacrificial zeal, she has power as a symbol" (Greene, 1997, p. 713). In this vein, Native American femininity is typically re-presented as exotic, but conquerable. On the other hand, specific racist terms and stereotypes, including "squaw," "frame a version of female-ness consistent with the historical colonial construct of Native Americans as animalistic, savage, and sub-human" (Merskin, 2010, p. 346). This problematizes the way Native women are seen as "real" in comparison to these powerful media re-presentations (Marubbio, 2006).

Public displays of Nativeness have ranged from the early Wild West shows to contemporary music festivals. Typically, the display is created through the lens of colonizer culture. While purporting to sell the idea of a commodified, egalitarian ecstatic, music festivals are primarily commercially driven events designed to generate revenue for promoters. Thus, self-selected attendees re-present themselves in ways that are read as consistent with the spectacle's aesthetic. This is true at the annual CVMF.

COACHELLA AS SPECTACLE

Ask any millennial what Coachella is and they will most likely tell you it is a trendy music festival. It is also a place where indigenous people, including some bands of the Cahuilla Indians, call their ancestral homelands. The city of Coachella is located in the Coachella Valley of Southern California in what was once a sandy wasteland in the Colorado River basin. Populated primarily with greasewood and mesquite, this area became inhabited by whites in the late 1800s when Jason L. Rector and his brother, Lon B. Rector, tapped into underground artesian well water ("History," 2018). Originally named Concilla (Spanish for little shells), a printing error produced the name Coachella ("History," 2018).

In this wide-open desert setting with a rich history now often forgotten, the CVMAF premiered in 1999. CVMAF was launched by the entertainment company Goldenvoice, a subsidiary of Anschutz Entertainment Group, and masterminded by promoter Paul Tollett (Pettas, 2016). Originally an inexpensive spring event with single-day tickets over a single weekend, it featured performers such as Rage Against the Machine and Beck as well as up-and-coming indie groups. Since then, some of the biggest names in the industry have performed here including Beyoncé, Radio Head, Kendrick Lamar, Kanye West, Daftpunk, Tïesto, Paul McCartney, Prince, Red Hot Chili Peppers, as well as more niche acts. It is now a two-weekend event, no single-day passes are technically available, with a three-day pass costing $429 for general admission, and a VIP pass costing $899 (Battan, 2016; Leonhardt, 2018). Coachella is attended by more than 200,000 people per year (Mitchell, 2018), but for fans unable or unwilling to pay the steep ticket prices, the festival is accessible through a live stream on their YouTube channel, significantly expanding its reach.

CVMAF has also become the to-be-seen scene of the rich and famous. The Urban Dictionary (2017) defines Coachella as a place where people "'independently come completely together' while being from every single opposite corner of every grooming/fashion style and music genre that exists, while strictly conforming to trends that do not conform." The festival is described as a "star studded," "celebrity hot spot" (O'Leary, 2019), as well as "a fully formed aesthetic, a lightning rod of aspiration, a way of being" (Battan, 2016, para. 1). CVMAF is comprised of art exhibits, five or more stages, and centers on music genres including hip-hop, electronic, indie, and rock.

What exactly does Coachella stand for? Battan (2016) asks this question, reflecting on other big music festivals such as Woodstock, which has the vibe of "peace and free love" in the context of hippiedom; "fire and rage" in 1999; Lilith Fair, which was based on "touchy-feely inclusivity and feminist solidarity;" and Burning Man, which stands for "radical self-reliance" and "techno-utopianism." Coachella is "aestheticized striving for desert hippiedom, divorced from any ideology." The CVMAF is not a space that Schmidt (2015) typifies as a boutique festival, which is smaller in scale and a site of subcultural identity-making and interpersonal connection, but rather is a "unifying mass [spectacle] of large events—crystalized in, say, the throngs of people cramming together to view a headliner" (p. 37). CVMAF is a mass, commercialized spectacle. It is marked, as is society, by the confluence of electronic and digital media, capitalism, and various forms of connectivity and surveillance (particularly via social media), in a constant state of spectatorship.

Debord (1967) explained how spectacles unify society and culture by pacifying the masses and engaging them in the commodification of life and leisure. Media in particular, he argues, is among the most glaring examples of spectacle reaching and creating mass culture. Kellner (2003) notes this influence by focusing on celebritydom, witnessed in a powerful mechanism that constantly begs for our attention. The "logic of the spectacle" is evidenced in the interlocking components of an event, such that it "reverberates through radio, television, CDs and DVDs, computer networks, and extravagant concerts. Media culture provides fashion and style models for emulation and promotes a celebrity culture that provides idols and role models" (p. vii). Instead of CDs and DVDs, Coachella reverberates mainly through the social media sphere and by the liking, re-posting, and re-tweeting of content by millennial, also nicknamed the "selfie-generation," obsessed with self-image and sharing.

Millennials readily consume the culture and brands that capitalize on their market potential. From HP to AMEX to Victoria's Secret taking advantage of publicity at the event, Coachella is defiantly commercialized. But it is also a consumer-oriented fashion moment in its own right

> a place to see live music, but it is also a place to witness a ritualized parade of beautiful people embracing their inner bohemians for a few days. From a distance, it looks less like a haven of free-spiritedness than a catwalk of people who have decided that free-spiritedness looks good on them. (Battan, 2016)

This is particularly the case for women, prompting retailers such as H & M to create the Coachella collection of flowy skirts, fringy vests, and flower crowns reminiscent of the '60s and '70s signature style. Yet something more is happening at the festival where more than 50 percent of attendees are millennials and more than 85 percent are white people (Khawaja, 2017). Given the staggering percentage of white millennial attendees, it is bizarre yet predictable and unoriginal that while enjoying the desert environs, music and celebritydom, many also participate in a racialized fashion phenomenon, that of cultural appropriation.

PRIVILEGE AND CULTURAL APPROPRIATION

Appropriation is defined in different ways, depending on interests and what is at stake. For example, in art, to appropriate is to use existing images or objects with little to no transformation of them. In business, the term means a setting aside, as in funds, and in law appropriation is the use of a "plaintiff's name, likeness, or image without his or her permission for commercial purposes" ("Legal Information Institute," 2018). A more general definition is taking "something for one's own use, typically without the owner's permission" ("Appropriate," n.d.) and includes a cultural aspect, that of a belonging or right to whatever the material is to someone.

Cultural appropriation expands the definition to include less the concept of ownership and more the ethical idea of inherent belonging to, as in lifeways and practices. According to Coombe (1998), cultural appropriation is "shorthand for cultural agency and subaltern struggle within media-saturated consumer societies" (p. 207). This definition identifies that hegemonic power exists and is served by mainstream institutions such as the mass media and popular culture. What media choose to represent, or, according to Hall (1973), re-present, is thereby consistent with dominant ideology that is created from and intended for a primarily white audience. Thus, taking of markers of a minority group (such as language, regalia, art or fashion) by majority culture is an example of cultural appropriation.

A form of colonialism, use of these elements without regard to history, context, appropriateness, or using them in ways that distort or lose the original significance and context are disrespectful and offensive to the culture of origin, regardless of legal definitions. Thus, exoticizing clothing or artifacts, or use of symbols, hairstyles, regalia, body modifications or "dressing up as" in Halloween costumes, for example, are racist acts, regardless of the intention of the person doing so. "Playing Indian," for example, such as a "sexy squaw" or "ruthless savage" not only makes mockery of present and past peoples, but also contributes to long-standing racist stereotypes that reduce a people to a type. It also conceals the very real daily humiliations, discrimination, and violence experienced by the people being represented, such as the sexual violence Native women experience at a much higher ratio than that of any other racial group (Deer, 2015).

Cultural appropriation falls within the view of representation ethics that describes "who has the right to represent others and under what circumstances" (Johnston, 2000, p. 73). This right falls within Article 31 of the United Nations *Declaration on the Rights of Indigenous Peoples* which states:

> Indigenous peoples have the right to maintain, control, protect and develop their cultural heritage, traditional knowledge and traditional cultural expressions, as well as the manifestations of their sciences, technologies and cultures, including human and genetic resources, seeds, medicines, knowledge of the properties of fauna and flora, oral traditions, literatures, designs, sports and traditional games and visual and performing arts. They also have the right to maintain, control, protect and develop their intellectual property over such cultural heritage, traditional knowledge, and traditional cultural expressions. (UNESCO, n.d.)

Those in a position of privilege are able to take on (and take off) the trappings of another's identity. While to do so may not be illegal (unlike unlawful use of the image of a person or logo or moniker), there are significant cultural implications. These "struggles over signification" (Coombe, 1998, p. 9) have significant psychological, emotional, and physical implications for those who are being mimicked, imitated, and parodied, even if through a lens believed as "honoring" or "appreciating." While appreciation can seem, to those doing so, to be benign, it is in fact not an altruistic endeavor. To appropriate can seem sympathetic while also remaining categorically racist. As Coombe observes, "Romantic celebrations of insurrectionary alterity, long popular in cultural studies, cannot capture the dangerous nuances of cultural appropriation in circumstances where the very resources with which people express difference are the properties of others" (p. 10). The significance of cultural appropriation as a phenomenon is that it is felt by those whose cultures are stolen and undermined from.

IDENTITY AND FELT THEORY

Million's (2008) "felt theory" is a useful way to predict and understand the effects of colonial practices. She argues that narratives, witnessing and affect of Indigenous women should be valued in academia, law contexts, and beyond. Indigenous women's views are often undervalued because they are perceived to present history as largely emotive or affective. Million (2008) subverts this understanding by claiming that there is profound "truth in the emotional content of this felt knowledge: colonialism as it is felt by those whose experience it" (p. 272). While Million uses felt theory as it pertains to sexual and emotional abuse of Indigenous women, it is important to recognize that images of cultural appropriation, in which sexualization and primitivization of Natives (including but not limited to) women, have the capacity to conjure up very real emotions for Native viewers.

To ignore the past and long-standing history of genocide—sexual, physical and emotional abuse, racisms, and cultural erasures—is a goal of colonization. Settler colonialism is imposed upon Natives, thus their/our experiences around the phenomena should be considered paramount (Million, 2008). Felt theory contributes to theoretical understandings of cultural appropriation as it makes apparent the inadequacies in contemporary critical frameworks that frame these discussions.

From these theories or theoretical entry points we understand that cultural appropriation plays on historically created and perpetuated stereotypes in a globalized, hybridized society. But conspicuously missing is a meaningful consideration of how Natives feel about the appropriations, how Natives resist and speak back to them, and how cultural appropriation is a racist iteration of settler colonialism that is common in many terrains, including cyberspace and, more specifically, social media. Social media is a space in which Native people and allies inject their feelings, lived experiences, and emotional knowledge into their practices. Here they are able speak back to cultural appropriation as a "felt" attack on their cultures and identity.

IMAGING COACHELLA

This study uses textual analysis as a framework and method of interpretation in order to unpack "the ways in which members of various cultures and subcultures make sense of who they are, and of how they fit into the world in which they live" (McKee, 2003, p. 1). What textual analysis offers is a lens through which scholars not only speculate on the intended, preferred, meaning (encoding) by creators of texts, but also likely interpretations (decoding) of those forms of communication. Five images of millennial attendees at the 2018 CVMAF are analyzed as illustrations of the articulation of settler colonialism to answer these research questions:

1. Is woman Native Americanness re-presented in millennial music festivals such as Coachella?
2. What are the markers of woman Native Americanness in fashion and form at the 2018 CVMAF? (And, to that end, what cultural histories are undermined in the process of wearing them?)
3. Does social media activity created by indigenous millennials (and their allies) address, resist, and/or revise stereotypical or appropriative re-presentations?

Digital responses to cultural appropriations to the "Coachella look" are also discussed in terms of resistant memes, specific hashtags, and blogs.

CONSTRUCTED MARKERS OF
NATIVE AMERICAN APPROPRIATION

Headdresses are amongst the most blatant, and most immediately recognizable, constructed markers of Native American appropriation. Although this appropriation has been researched (White, 2017; Deloria, 1998; Keene, 2016), this "trend" has been recycled and rearticulated time and time again, especially by music festival subcultures (Cordes, 2018). That these cultural rip-offs with profound meaning to a small percentage of tribes are so prevalent at Coachella makes headdress appropriation deserving of continued attention. The CVMAF context affords a unique opportunity to look into how the millennial generation appropriates the headdress.

Headdresses

Headdresses displayed in the Instagram images have different shapes and embellishments, but a common quality is the arrangement of hundreds of feathers. The first image (which can be viewed at @soulandrhapsody, 2018; the authors encourage readers to follow the links provided on the reference page to the images described in this chapter) shows a headpiece resembling a headdress made of yellow feathers of a medium height, secured by a thin band made from a generically ethnic patterned material. On top of the band is a strand of goldish beads and on both sides yellow, green, and blue pompoms are placed. Long strands of a blue shade dangle from each side of the headpiece, wrapped with gold embellishments and more feathers which are fastened to the ends.

The image's accompanying text includes a description of the materials used: "In case you're curious, this set is made and hand embellished by me using vintage parts from Afghan Kuchi belts, bronze beading, tassels, poms, and feathers!" Some of the hashtags include #festivaltribe and #gypsysoul. This headdress is composed of various materials demonstrating sensibilities of mélange or cultural hybridity, and it is also an appropriation that can be described as transculturation, making it difficult to identity only one cultural origin point (Rogers, 2006). Using Afghani pieces, likely bulk-bought feathers, vague traces of Russian headpieces, and other seemingly craft-oriented materials to compose a tribal-inspired headdress draws on more than a few cultures. The hashtag, #festivaltribe, frames the appropriation as a marker of belonging into some iteration of festival culture, something of an illusion to neo-tribalism within a capitalist space. It also seems somehow appropriate to the Instagram poster to equate this with Native tribal cultures.

Another image (see deAnda, 2018) shows a couple facing one another, seemingly about to kiss with a loving gaze. The woman on the left is wearing a headdress that is more elaborate and markedly larger than those pictured in the other Instagram images. It features turquoise and white feathers fastened by thick sections of wound material. Dusty orange and black and white fabrics in a generic tribal print of geometric shapes decorate the band at the front of the headdress. The rest of her outfit is made from various shades of beige, giving this look an earthier, neutral and natural feel. It is vaguely reminiscent of buckskin material which harken to the Native American representations shown in Western films or images of ecologically stereotyped Native Americans.

At least one company's social media posts, rather than including Coachella-goers as models, focused on the headpieces themselves on Instagram to reach and sell to the millennial demographic drawn to these appropriations. Similar to the crafted, do it yourself (DIY) feel of the headpiece in the first described photo, @Thatthing.co (2018) posted an image with eight crafted headpieces of feathers, ribbons, fabric trimming, and flowers that are also sold on their website. Items like these, which are problematic to intellectual and artistic property rights, are sold on the medium that millennials use to share images, consume images, and buy the products needed to construct the "Coachella look."

The widespread commodification of headdresses has blurred the various significances they hold to a small percentage of tribal nations. In some Native American cultures, and at contemporary pow-wows, the shedding or dropping of even a single feather requires a blessing to proceed with the ceremony. At CVMAF, feathers litter the grounds, swept without regard by hired maintenance professionals before the festival resumes at around 11 a.m. the next morning. The headdresses themselves and the feathers that drop from them are not considered in any meaningful way in this spectacle setting.

Hair

Less discussed in conversations about cultural appropriation are the ways in which the women attendees of CVMAF wear their hair. Hair, for women of color, is a particularly political site of struggle (Patton, 2006). In the Instagram images (Muñoz, 2017; @vogue_boho, 2018), we noticed a distinctive hairstyle. The double-bun hairstyle, or what is sometimes referred to as the cinnamon bun, butterfly or squashed-bun hairstyle, is very often worn by CVMAF-goers. The first image is a close-up of a woman with her head tilted, donning the hairstyle, with flowers comprising the backdrop of the image. She is sticking out her tongue and gazing into the camera, giving both a suggestive and infantilized feel to the image. In the second image, two women are featured with the woman on the left wearing the distinctive hairstyle. Colored dreadlocks, hair pieces or extensions, and braids are also tied in to her hair to add a more artificial, sub-culturally tinged look to the stylization. The look, for some, became famous in popular culture with the release of the first *Star Wars* (1977) movie. Princess Leia donned the hairstyle intended to be fitting for outer space (read: more alien, less mainstream fashion). In a *Time* article devoted to the iconic look, director George Lucas is quoted as saying,

> In the 1977 film, I was working very hard to create something different that wasn't fashion, so I went with a kind of Southwestern Pancho Villa woman revolutionary look, which is what that is. The buns are basically from turn-of-the-century Mexico. Then it took such hits and became such a thing. In the new trilogy, the same thing applies, to try and do something timeless. I'm just basically having a good time. (Cagle, 2002, para. 15)

The article also asserts that Lucas had dreams of being an anthropologist as opposed to an illustrator, making this appropriation more particular. While he believed he was drawing inspiration from the Mexican Revolution (1910–1920), this hairstyle can be traced much further back and has deeper roots. In particular, Native women, from the Hopi and Tewa tribes for example, have historically worn their hair in this way. The style was highlighted in images from Edward Curtis' fraught photographic collection titled *The North American Indian* (1907–1930), specifically the images titled, "Hopi Maiden, 1922" or "A Tewa Girl, 1921." Some reference to these ties were featured in a Denver Museum of Art exhibit, "Star Wars and the Power of Costumes" as well as a number of online magazines (Cagle, 2002).

Leia's buns have covered and made invisible, or markedly less visible, how this is appropriative of more than a few Native cultures. Today's women Coachella festival-goers are appropriating a meaningful Native hairstyle in mass numbers, often decorated with glitter and colored hair extensions. The hairstyle has become part and parcel to subscribing to the "Coachella look." This appropriation is occurring knowingly or unknowingly by CVMAF-goers, whether they claim to be inspired by Princess Leia, or even other people, groups, and characters that have appropriated it since: Scary Spice of the Spice Girls, rave subcultures of the 1990s, cartoon characters in *Flash Gordon*, and other reference points which are actually merely simulacra.

War Paint

Another common marker of Native Americanness is war paint or facial adornment. While some Coachella festival-goers shown in images use make-up in patterns around their eyes and on their foreheads or essentially bedazzle their face with gems, the patterns with which they arrange them appear to be based on re-presentations of Native American war paint. War paint, sometimes worn in tribal contexts by warriors, chiefs, and medicine men, among others, were tied to spiritual beliefs, camouflage and daily aesthetics that are also widely appropriated in Hollywood contexts (Rosenthal, 2005). The facial war paint "look" harks to Native American re-presentation but also resembles South Asian bindis and other ornamentations with cultural and religious significance. For those Coachella-goers that draw from Native American cultures, they are rearticulating and feminizing a signifier of a warrior, which is framed as masculine in many Hollywood Western films, but is now appropriated in higher numbers by women at CVMAF.

The war paint appropriation at CVMAF is most evident in images (Muñoz, 2017; @vogue_boho, 2018). In the first image dotted lines arch over one woman's eyebrows in a metallic color. This look is also paired with the double-bun hairstyle. Moving down the image, she accessorizes with a choker-style necklace made of metals and fabric that draw similarities to Native jewelry. Her bra, which she wears as a top, is made with transparent material, white straps and daisies patches, which evoke a sense of the flower child. This combination of signifiers refers back to the free-spirited Native American stereotype associated with appropriations made by hippies of the 1960s. When hippies became disenchanted with various aspects of capitalism, war and work-a-day lifestyles, they turned to a romanticized escape by appropriating selected or perceived signifiers of Native American culture (think long hair, headbands, ecological tendencies) (Torgovnick, 1997). In the context of CVMAF, this appropriation is particularly ironic because of how commodified and consumerist the scene has become. This is antithetical to the stereotype tied to the anti-capitalism from which they are attempting to draw inspiration.

The second example includes a woman with patterns drawn in white and black around her eyes, on her cheeks and down her nose. Again, dots trace over her eyebrows, but additional V-shapes, horizontal lines, and squiggles are included. Gems of a pink shade decorate the areas directly under her eyes and are covered by her 1960s- and 1970s-inspired horizontal oval sunglasses. In addition to the facial painting appropriation, the poster of the image is again aware of the illusions to hippie subcultural style. This is evident in the encoding of the message attached to the image. Hashtags such as "#hippiesoul, #gypsyinspo and #hippylife" explicitly link the hippie subculture, which is now also an entrenched millennial trend, with Native American culture. The hashtag gypsy seems to be interpreted by these millennials as free-spirited, travelling people, which conflates ethnic and cultural groups from other continents, particularly Europe, with the mis-represented stylization of Native Americans.

The preceding descriptions suggest that millennials attending CVMAF appropriate Native Americanness, and in doing so fall into various trapping of Native American appropriations of past subcultures as well as cultural hybrids. While these looks saturate the fashion landscape at CVMAF and become hypervisible through their posting, re-posting and viewing on Instagram, they are not simply accepted without opposition. The following section describes social media responses to these types of cultural appropriations.

#DONTTRENDONME:
SOCIAL MEDIA RESPONDS TO COACHELLA

While the previous analysis has described some of the cultural appropriations that are found at Coachella, we also observed how social media proves to be a useful space in which more culturally informed members of this generation confront and challenge appropriation. They are able to speak back to felt racist attacks on their cultures that tend to erase, or at least not meaningfully consider, the histories of where those cultural markers are derived.

One way in which cultural appropriation is addressed is through the deployment of specific hashtags. Hashtags are used in social media for two main reasons: (1) to describe any such content in the image, and (2) to allow that image to be visible in the search areas that use the same hashtag; a virtual encyclopedia or myriad of possible like-images (Sinha, 2005). #DontTrendOnMe, #NativeAppropriation, and #Nochella or #Nochilla were used on Facebook, Twitter, and Instagram to protest Coachella and cultural appropriation around the time of the festival. #DontTrendOnMe and #NativeAppropriation were most explicitly directed at appropriation and frequently used to call out those who were perpetuating the trend. #DontTrendOnMe suggests that fashion trends should not disrespect Native American nations, that culture is not a craze that can come in and out of style, and that it is taken personally. #Nochella and #Nochilla are hashtag responses that are more general to Coachella. These encourage or express disenchantment with one or more aspects: ticket prices, venue, music, rules, consumerism, and widespread appropriation.

Another example of Native and ally social media activism or resistance is the wide dissemination of resistant memes. Gil (2018) defines memes as cultural symbols or ideas that are spread virtually, especially through social media platforms by 20-something millennials. These memes tend to be humorous, contain myths, and typically include image and text. Memes that include rhetoric of cultural appropriation are hereafter described.

One meme, for example, is a clear parody and depicts a class photo-style picture featuring a highly offensive mascot with widespread arms complete with fringes, feathers and symbols, and at the bottom the words: "WHITE GIRLS AT COACHELLA" ("White Girls at Coachella," n.d.). This mocks the perpetrators and calls out how silly as well as offensive it is viewed as by Native Americans and allies. It is intended to shame appropriators through humor. Another popular meme ("No, it's cool," n.d.) shows two white women dressed in hipster fashion, complete with headdresses, holding red solo cups. The words, "No, it's cool. It's not like your ancestors killed them or anything" accompany the image. This sarcastic message ties cultural genocide, actual genocide, and cultural appropriation into one cohesive message. Both of the memes served to call out or embarrass the most common perpetrators of the trend, white women, while explicitly tying settler colonialism to genocide in both cultural and literal senses.

As Debord (1967) might have argued, the mass spreading of these representations, corrective or otherwise, serves to pacify the masses. It is a labor performed by the broad base of social media users. Memes, however, are far more capable of resistance than they may seem on the surface (denotative) level. One just needs to replay the power of social media in shaping the 2016 American presidential elections to consider this (Ross & Rivers, 2017). In the case of memes speaking back to cultural appropriation, they tend to carry myths, defined in the sense of great truths, through a medium consumed regularly by millennial audiences. They connect people with the same view and disrupt those with opposing views in the repeating, re-posting and engagement with messages. Through felt theory, we can also frame them as emotive, politically charged acts rather than vacuous, useless ones.

Lastly, blogs are social spaces intended to encourage the spread of ideas and dialogue and are often written in an accessible style (Kaplan & Haenlein, 2010). While memes or hashtags are useful and powerful, more in-depth and emotionally charged reactions to appropriation on social media use the blog form. Here Native American feminists in particular disrupt re-presentations of Native American women as romanticized and sexualized, educate readers on the plurality of tribes and cultural nuances, and underscore implicitly and explicitly the felt experiences of having one's culture time and time again disrespected and appropriated.

For example, Adrienne Keene, Cherokee, Native scholar and EdD, created the *Native Appropriations* blog in 2010 and has maintained it since to call out flaws in dominant cultural logic surrounding costuming in subcultural practice and to discuss (mis)representations of Native peoples. The blog focuses on stereotypes, cultural appropriations and activism, including a petition against the Washington Redskins football team name and mascot. Keene tackles a range of topics from descriptions of *Pocahontas* on Netflix to an Apache pizza joint in Ireland to headdress art decorating Valentino shoe boxes. In sum, she makes a case that "representations matter" in an accessible writing style that calls out and calls for these insidious appropriations to be addressed.

Jessica Metcalfe, Turtle Mountain Chippewa, Native scholar and PhD, created another blog, *Beyond Buckskin* (2009), to address similar issues. Her blog, however, focuses on empowerment and celebrates Native artists and designers by providing a list of Native-owned business online for others to support. This encourages financially backing Native American cultural producers as opposed to mainstream companies that see culture as simply trends to profit off. She also provides resources to report businesses that falsely suggest that their items are authentic. This is illegal and can be reported to the Indian Arts and Crafts Board ("Should I report," n.d.).

After being continuously asked by blog visitors about the politics of cultural appropriations, Metcalfe created an area that aggregated the most helpful online articles about the topic. These blogs have also led to the author being asked to write for a wider audience in feminist media outlets including *Jezebel*, *Bitch Magazine*, and *Ms. Magazine*, thereby spreading viewpoints and messages about Native American cultural appropriation as it is felt by herself and others. This blog and website is more geared toward authenticity and genuine appreciation of support for Native arts and demonstrates how there are ways to purchase and wear products in culturally appropriate settings. By doing so, we can recognize and honor the Native American designers of high fashion as opposed to those who steal artistic property. In one post, "RETROSPECTRUM!: A Style Mixer," she engages a sense of futurity by asking, "What would fashion history look like if Native American designers were consistently represented in mainstream style magazines, department stores and fashion shows?" Perhaps this would help remedy cultural misunderstanding that leads to the types of appropriation we see at the CVMAF.

RECLAIMING "DIGITAL" TERRAINS TO RESIST APPROPRIATION

While those who appropriate claim that adhering rhinestones on their faces in a certain pattern or hot glue-gunning feathers into a faux war bonnet is a benign act that simply allows them to look the part or fit into the scene, appropriation actually sheds light on significant racial conditions. The main markers or signifiers of Native Americanness at CVMAF include headdresses, war paint, general tribal prints, jewelry and tribally specific hairstyles. The work that these appropriations perform is to empty these signifiers or markers and to refill them with millennial ideations of coolness capital, divorced from their cultural significance. At CVMAF we see sacred headdresses rearticulated into a seemingly meaningless mess of colors, feathers, tassels, and war paint into a mere facial bling. The histories and meanings of these are not recognized by the appropriators who are coming at the "costumes" from a place of privilege.

When cultural items are appropriated, they serve as exclusionary rhetoric for the culture being undermined. The festival is attended by more than 80 percent white people, who, via privilege, assume authority to re-present others rather than participate in creating a space welcoming for people of all races. By creating a false spectacle of cultural aesthetic diversity, white people thereby get to play and party while other racial groups are mocked, excluded and further colonized. These appropriations serve to remind many Native Americans and allies of the ways Native American culture is undermined, reproduced and commodified. Debord (1967) explains how spectacles commodify leisure as well as the ingredients that make a scene a signature staple of culture. In particular, millennials are "trying on" Native Americanness as a trend in order to fit into something less meaningfully subcultural but more spectacle-ized, backed by big brands, big money, and celebrity culture.

Our final research question asked this: Does social media activity created by Indigenous millennials (and their allies) address, resist, and/or revise stereotypical re-presentations? We argue that social media is a useful terrain for decolonial views to speak to and against racist performances of Native American identity in the digital age. These responses tend to (1) call out settler colonialism as the underlying problem, (2) hone in on most egregious and widespread appropriations like headdresses, (3) match medium to medium tactics (e.g. creating an Instagram meme to address racist Instagram image, and (4) inject principles of felt theory in addressing issues and perpetrators. Identifying and pushing back to disparage white settlers "playing Indian" (Deloria, 1998) is important in the larger scope of decolonization because it refuses to allow settlers to feel comfortable in their racist performances (Tuck & Yang, 2012). Given that repatriation of Native land is often at the core of Native and ally projects, it is doubly symbolic that some are taking to, reclaiming, and creating the "digital" terrains of cyberspace to resist appropriation.

We suggest that non-Native American festival attendees have an ethical responsibility to educate themselves about cultural appropriation in a multipronged way by engaging in an educational process. They should visit blogs such as those detailed in this chapter, interact with Native American peoples attuned to their perspectives as opposed to those constructed by cultural outsiders, and support Native art and fashion instead of mainstream retailers. Millennials should also challenge appropriation by setting new culturally appropriate trends and finding something meaningful from their own cultures to draw upon. Resistance demonstrated through social media is just one piece of a larger method of addressing these racist performances.

Textual analysis is but one method to analyze communication. McKee (2003, p. 72) states that scholars using textual analysis ask, "What *is* the likely interpretation: context, context, context." This requires analysis that is informed not only with knowledge of what the preferred meaning might be but also what negotiated and resistant ones would yield. This varies, depending on the audience, as Hall observes (1973). Furthermore, as McKee writes,

"What makes us 'educated,' in our 'educated guesses at the likely interpretations of a text,' is our knowledge of relevant intertexts" (2003, p. 73). There are many other ways to read photographs as cultural texts. Future research could present these images to a number of subjects and either qualitatively or quantitatively gather responses.

While popular culture online magazines as well as fashion websites discuss cultural appropriation, a glaring problem is that after almost two decades of Coachella's existence, as well as a longer period of music festivals beginning around the 1960s, the trend is still so prominent that millennials believe it is not even problematic anymore. There are shortcomings to these articles that recast the same arguments and do not adequately consider the "felt" emotionally charged responses and feelings that these trends and images conjure up for Native American women in particular. While appropriators see it as a benign practice, appropriation undermines the historical truths that Native Americans were, and still are, facing cultural assimilation and genocide; it erases histories and meanings while tainting them with new meanings—that a headdress equates to coolness or being the it-girl, brings Instagram likes and social media adoration, or is a staple symbol of partying. Festival-goers and hipsters should not have free reign to wear headdresses and other cultural items while Native Americans endure the ramifications of centuries of forced erasure of their items of cultural significance. In this vein, felt theory contributes an understanding that these are profound truths or myths that speak deeply to colonial legacies of "playing Indian."

We suggest that future research and popular press on the topic consider felt theory, take steps to include the standpoints and opinions of those that are offended, and evaluate the specific harms that flow from them. Additionally, since these types of cultural appropriations have been common at many festivals, including Woodstock, Burning Man, Lightning in a Bottle, Sasquatch and more, and may continue in generations beyond millennials, we suggest that they continue to be analyzed. This will allow for continued attention, provide a view into how the trend is evolving and insights into how appropriations speak to our cultural realities. By sentimentalizing their performances with various moves-to-innocence (e.g., that they are appreciating cultures or promoting multiculturalism) these millennials are perpetrating similar injustices of past generations.

What strikes us as different and overlooked is that Native American tribes, in addition to being considered a racial category, are also members of sovereign nations. This is an important distinction because appropriations and re-presentations ignore Native American nations' own national laws on artistic and intellectual property and their perspectives. They self-grant the authority to try on identities of nations they know little to nothing about. It is a matter of international communication and must be framed as such. In the process of appropriation, we lose even more cultural truths when nationhood is considered. Images of the homogenized, festivalized, bohemian Native American tend to make others believe that the 573 federally recognized tribes, and numerous unrecognized tribes, also are not worthy of recognition and respect. Rather than accept the sovereignty of nations and federally recognized or unrecognized tribes, popular culture celebrates knock-offs of a played-out version of the festivalized Native American as a truth as opposed to the truths of living citizens of tribal nations confined within the borders of their colonizers.

While research has shown that Native American women tend to be re-presented as the binary of princess or the squaw, or an overlapping of the two, at CVMAF they are especially represented as hypersexualized. This is evident by the pairing and overlapping of appropriations with skintight dress-es, crop tops, nipple-coverings, and mini-skirts. These Coachella-goers make stylistic choices which hark only to the sexualized, available princess frame.

The common close-to-nature stereotype is invoked through beige and brown clothing, feathers, and desert backgrounds, which draws some similar-ity to hippie styles. But there is also something new happening; there is simultaneously a closeness to the artificial, synthetic, and oddly futuristic. As most of the Instagram images we analyzed showed, neon colors, gemstones, double-bun hairstyles, and plastic beads, tied tightly to rave and hippie sub-cultures and futuristic psychedelia, are now intermixing and overlapping with markers of Native Americanness. In this regard, it seems that millenni-als are rearticulating the Native American in their imagination—as groovy, exotic, and aesthetically superior—and taking it upon themselves to imagine Indigenous futurity and the future of Native American representation. They created a distinct look that can perhaps be typified as disjointed Native American *costumes* on acid.

Indigenous futurism, however, is based on the ability of sovereign nations to project *their* ideas of a future-state, often something markedly less coloni-al; it can be fantasy, it can be imaginative, it can be radical (Dillon, 2012). But when CVMAF millennial attendees and other subcultures create versions of what Native Americanness is in the present and future they limit or at least undermine the possibilities of how we as Native American people will sur-vive, resist, represent and self-identity. Though we, as well as those that have taken to social media terrains to resist cultural appropriation at CVMAF, are deeply disappointed that these appropriations have continued and been morphed by millennials, we also find here an opportunity for intervention. Millennials and future generations, conceptualized as awakened, may actual-ly finally wake up to the racial harms they enact with more education and attention to the felt experiences of others.

REFERENCES

@thatthing.co. (2018, May 1). Ohmagoodness! We're giving you a SNEAK-PEAK LOOK at these beautiful feather headdresses. [Instagram]. Retrieved from https://www.instagram.com/p/BiPAEgonzhR/?taken-by=thatthing.co.

"Appropriate." (n.d). *Oxford dictionaries*. Retrieved from https://en.oxforddictionaries.com/definition/appropriate.

Battan, C. (2016). The appeal of the Coachella way of life. *The New Yorker*. Retrieved from https://www.newyorker.com/culture/cultural-comment/the-appeal-of-the-coachella-way-of-life.

Butler, M. (2018). "Guardians of the Indian image": Controlling representations of indigenous cultures in television. *American Indian Quarterly, 42*(1), 1–42.

Cagle, J. (2002, April 21). So what's the deal with Leia's hair? *Time*. Retrieved from http://content.time.com/time/arts/article/0,8599,232499,00.html.

Coombe, R. J. (1998). *The cultural life of intellectual property*. Durham, NC: Duke University Press.

Cordes, A. (2018). Festivalizing of Native Americanness and postmodern cultural appropriation at Burning Man. Manuscript submitted for publication.

Curtis, E. S. (1907–1930). The North American Indian. *Northwestern University Digital Library Collections*, 2004. Retrieved from: http://curtis.library.northwestern.edu/curtis/toc.cgi.

de Anda, E. [@erubeydeanda]. (2018, April 16). Just love…#coachella2018@marioruiz… [Instagram]. Retrieved from https://www.instagram.com/p/BhnGeHEDCpR/?taken-by=erubeydeanda.

Debord, G. (1967). *The society of the spectacle*. London: Bread and Circuses Publishing.

Declaration on Human Rights. (September 13, 2007). Working group on indigenous populations, accepted by the United Nations General Assembly, *Declaration on the Rights of Indigenous Peoples*, archived June 26, 2015, at the Wayback Machine; UN Headquarters; New York City.

Deer, S. (2015). *The beginning and end of rape: Confronting sexual violence in Native America*. Minneapolis: University of Minnesota Press.

Deloria, J. P. (1998). *Playing Indian*. New Haven, CT: Yale University Press.

Dillon, G. L. (Ed.). (2012). *Walking the clouds: An anthology of indigenous science fiction*. Tucson, AZ: University of Arizona Press.

Dimock, M. (2018, March 1). Defining generations: Where millennials end and post-millennials begin. Pew Research Center. Retrieved from http://www.pewresearch.org/fact-tank/2018/03/01/defining-generations-where-millennials-end-and-post-millennials-begin/.

Gil, P. (2018, June 3). What is a meme? *Lifewire*. Retrieved from https://www.lifewire.com/what-is-a-meme-2483702.

Greene, R. (1975). The Pocahontas perplex: The image of Indian women in American culture. *The Massachusetts Review, 16*(4), 698–714.

Hall, S. (1973). Encoding/decoding. In *Culture, media, language: Working papers in cultural studies, 1972–1979* (pp. 128–138). London: Hutchinson.

Hall, S. (1997). *Representation: Cultural representation and signifying practices*. London: Sage.

"History." (n.d.). *Coachella*. Retrieved from

Johnston, C. B. (2000). *Screened out: How the media control us and what we can do about it*. Armonck, NY: M. E. Sharpe.

Kaplan, A. M., & Haenlein, M. (2010). Users of the world, unite! The challenges and opportunities of social media. *Business Horizons, 53*(1), 59–68.

Keene, A. (2010, June 2). Headdresses and music festivals go together like pb and…racism? Native Appropriations. Retrieved from https://nam05.safelinks.protection.outlook.com/?url=https%3A%2F%2Fnativeappropriations.com%2F2010%2F06%2Fheaddresses-and-music-festivals-go-together-like-pb-and-racism.html&data=02%7C01%7C%7C910a6744fea14d55078908d70c65d1e0%7C7f3da4be2722432ebfa764080d1eb1dc%7C0%7C1%7C636991

503787906502&sdata=K0DaICFzf7zguBKYTJa0chIPF2W%2BqB%2Bjzri16PmxvdE%3 D&reserved=0.

Kellner, D. (2003). *Media spectacle.* New York: Routledge.

Khawaja, J. (2017). The kids are all white: Can US festivals live up to their "post-racial" promise? *The Guardian.* Retrieved from: https://www.theguardian.com/music/2017/jul/04/ music-festivals-race-white-black-coachella-afropunk.

"Legal Information Institute." (2018). *Cornell.* Retrieved from https://www.law.cornell.edu/ wex/appropriation.

Leonhardt, M. (2018, March 29). What it really costs to go to Coachella 2018. *Time.* Retrieved from http://time.com/money/5217998/cost-coachella-2018-beyonce/.

Marubbio, M. (2006). *Killing the Indian maiden: Images of Native American women in film.* Lexington, KY: University Press of Kentucky.

McCaskill, N. D. (2016, April 25). Poll: Millennials don't like Trump. *Politico.* Retrieved from https://www.politico.com/story/2016/04/poll-do-millennials-like-trump-222397.

McKee, A. (2003). *Textual analysis: A beginner's guide.* Thousand Oaks, CA: Routledge.

Merskin, D. (2010). The s-word: Discourse, stereotypes, and the American Indian woman. *Howard Journal of Communications, 2*(14), 345–366.

Metcalfe, J. (2009). About. *Beyond Buckskin.* Retrieved from http://www.beyondbuck skin.com/p/about_16.html.

Metcalfe, J. (2016, February 27). RETROSPECTRUM!: A style mixer. *Beyond Buckskin.* Retrieved from http://www.beyondbuckskin.com/2016/02/retrospectrum-style-mixer.html.

Million, D. (2008). Felt theory. *American Quarterly, 60*(2): 267–272.

Mitchell, J. (2018, April 24). Coachella 2018. How brands are tapping into the hybrid lifestyle of festival fans. *Forbes.* Retrieved from https://www.forbes.com/sites/julianmitchell/2018/ 04/24/coachella-2018-how-brands-are-tapping-into-the-hybrid-lifestyle-of-millennials/#c08 0f2f75a0d.

Morigeau, S., Whitford, L., Smith, B., Windy Boy, J., Stewart-Peregoy, S., Small, J., Smith, F., Peppers, R., Kipp III, G., & Webber, S. (2018, July 13). We are not Pocahontas: When Indians—especially Indian women—are used for props for a political agenda—call it out. *High Country News.* Retrieved from https://www.hcn.org/articles/indian-country-news-we-are-not-pocahontas.

Muksin, A. [@Anhikamuksin]. (2018, April 10). #throwback to a year ago where the Disney Baes went to #coachella. [Instagram]. Retrieved from https://www.instagram.com/p/ BhwTDVDHal2/?taken-by=andhikamuksin.

Muñoz, S. [@mpozefashion]. (2017, April 12). BE INSPIRED!! Coachella 2017 Trends and Fashion Inspo…[Instagram]. Retrieved from https://www.instagram.com/p/BSw8z_NFE GF/?hl=en&taken-by=mpozefashion.

"No it's cool, it's not like your ancestors killed them or anything." (n.d.). Retreved from http:// visualstudying.blogspot.com/2012/04/no-its-cool-its-not-like-your-ancestors.html.

O'Leary, A. (2019, April 12). What is Coachella? *Mirror.* Retrieved from https:// www.mirror.co.uk/3am/celebrity-news/what-coachella-full-run-down-7785765.

Patton, T. (2006). Hey girl, am I more than my hair: African American women and their struggles with beauty, body image, and hair. *National Women's Studies Association Journal, 18*(2), 24–51.

Pettas, M. (2016, April 17). A brief history of the Coachella Valley Music and Arts Festival. Retrieved from http://www.coachella.org/about-us/history.

Rogers, R. A. (2006). From cultural exchange to transculturation: A review and reconceptualization of cultural appropriation. *Communication Theory, 16*(4), 474–503.

Rosenthal, N. G. (2005). Representing Indians: Native American actors on Hollywood's frontier. *Western Historical Quarterly, 36*(3), 328–352.

Ross, A. S., & Rivers, D. J. (2017). Digital cultures of political participation: Internet memes and the discursive delegitimization of the 2016 US Presidential candidates. *Discourse, Context & Media, 16*, 1–11.

Schmidt, B. (2015). Boutiquing at the raindance campout: Relational aesthetics as festival technology. *Dancecult Journal of Electronic Dance Music Culture Culture, 7*(1), 35–54.

"Should I report a potential violation." (n.d.). *Indian Arts and Crafts Board.* Retrieved from https://www.doi.gov/iacb/should-i-report-potential-violation.

Sinha, R. (2005, September 27). A cognitive analysis of tagging. Retrieved from http://rashmi-sinha.com/2005/09/27/a-cognitive-analysis-of-tagging/@soulandrhapsody. (2018, April 28). ADVENTURES IN CALI • If you caught our story yesterday you may have seen our gorgeous gal@tawz... [Instagram]. Retrieved from https://www.instagram.com/p/BiH-NaLMFcsL/?taken-by=soulandrhapsody.

Torgovnick, M. (1997). *Primitive passions.* New York, NY: Random House.

Tuck, E., & Yang, K. Y. (2012). Decolonization is not a metaphor. *Decolonization: Indigeneity, Education & Society, 1*(1), 1–40.

UNESCO. (n.d.). UN declaration on the rights of indigenous peoples (UNDRIP) related to cultural and linguistic diversity. Retrieved from http://www.unesco.org/new/en/indigenous-peoples/cultural-and-linguistic-diversity/undrip-clt/@vogueboho. (2018, July 4). DM for credit [Instagram]. Retrieved from https://www.instagram.com/p/Bk0Ceo8nBfe/?taken-by=vogue_boho.

White, F. (2017). Fashion and intolerance: Misappropriation of the war bonnet and mainstream anger. *Journal of popular culture, 50*(6), 1421–1436.

"White Girls at Coachella." (n.d.). Retrieved from https://www.viralswarm.com/2015/04/white-girls-at-coachella/.

Chapter Eleven

(Un)covering *International Secret Agents*

Constituting a Post-Network Asian American Identity through Self-Representation

Vincent N. Pham and Alison Yeh Cheung

On July 29, 2011, the venerable *New York Times* brought the phenomenon of Asian American YouTube stars to the mainstream public's attention. In an article titled "For Asian American stars, many web fans," *NYT* reporter Austin Considine highlighted what was already known among most Asian American audiences and media scholars—that mainstream media lacked Asian American representation and Asian Americans took up YouTube as a platform to share their stories. The article marked a turning point in YouTube's evolution as a platform utilized by marginalized groups, when mainstream media—news outlets and the entertainment industry alike—recognized the power and reach of digital and social media platforms. It signaled to the public that Asian American audiences existed and, importantly, they flocked to YouTube.

While long overlooked, Asian American audiences have recently caught the purview of advertising agencies and media companies. A study by IPSOS MediaCT, commissioned by Facebook, argued that markets should "embrace the diversity of background, make online a destination, and showcase culturally relevant content" (Facebook IQ, 2015). In recognizing the importance of Asian American media audiences, the Nielsen Company in 2018 issued its sixth report on Asian American consumers titled "Asian Americans: Digital Lives and Growing Influence." It is clear from reports like these that Asian American millennial audiences are being recognized by the same forces that once seemed to work against their presence in media.

As we near 2020, we now have a generation of viewers who have grown up watching such YouTube stars. These Asian American millennial audiences are well-versed with a participatory culture, moving to and from various media platforms to engage with media makers and find desired content. They are familiar with the impact and importance of YouTubers, which are equal to (or even more than) the airing of *Fresh off the Boat*, the first Asian American sitcom since 1994 by a mainstream television network. Yet, what does this idea of a millennial audience mean for Asian Americans who have cultivated an Asian American independent media space? How do such representations on YouTube respond to mainstream ones of old? And what is the impact of social media platforms connected to YouTube for Asian American audiences, who have been deemed as some of the world's most digitally connected (Spooner, 2001).

In this chapter, we turn our attention to the very platform that cultivated Asian American millennial audiences—YouTube. We focus our attention on a prominent player in the Asian American YouTube mediasphere, International Secret Agents (ISA), and their Youtube channel, ISAtv. Although relatively young and already changing, ISA and ISAtv is a collaboration started by arguably the two most influential Asian American popular culture purveyors—long-standing and well-accomplished YouTubers Wong Fu Productions and the electronic pop-rap group Far East Movement. We situate and explore ISA as a media organization by briefly contextualizing its efforts within a long-standing history of Asian American media-making that has longed for "self-representation" in response to mainstream media representations. We then turn our attention to the content and circulation of ISAtv. We look at what representations are present and how they are circulated through different aspects of the ISAtv platform. Drawing on and building upon Lisa Lowe's (1996) conception of Asian American identity, we argue that ISAtv simultaneously constitutes and speaks to a geographically dispersed Asian American millennial audience and locates its endeavors and possibilities within the necessity of community-based spaces, particularly Los Angeles. In doing so, they posit that the future of Asian American millennial audiences depends on self-representation encouraged and cultivated through ISAtv and its network of Asian American YouTubers. In this chapter, we attend to these tensions within Asian America made evident through the content creation of ISAtv, which seeks to create and connect to an Asian American millennial audience while negotiating its diversity and changing nature. In the next section, we first conceptualize the idea of a post-network Asian American millennial audience by situating it within the history of Asian American media representation.

CONCEPTUALIZING A POST-NETWORK ASIAN AMERICAN MILLENNIAL AUDIENCE

Asian Americans remain largely unseen in mainstream media. According to the Center for African American Studies (2017) at UCLA, black and Latino racial minorities have gained a level of exposure that Asians still lack; next to white, black and Latino characters, Asians still receive the least screen time. When Asians are given the opportunity to appear in mainstream media, they often appear in the stereotyped roles that replay the racist traditions of the yellow peril, the perpetual foreigner, the model minority and the exotic being (Ramasubramanian, 2011; Zhang, 2010; Ono & Pham, 2009).

Despite these limitations, there have been surprising developments and an increase of Asian American representation in mainstream media in the 2010s. Asian males have historically been portrayed as asexual and undesirable, yet Steven Yeun played Glenn Rhee, one of the popular AMC program *The Walking Dead*'s most beloved characters, and Vincent Rodriguez III played the lead romantic interest on the CW network's *Crazy Ex-Girlfriend.* Meanwhile, Mindy Kaling played the lead in her popular series *The Mindy Project,* which ran from 2012 to 2017. A watershed year for the emergence of Asian American representation on network television was 2015; in February, ABC aired *Fresh Off the Boat,* the first sitcom to feature an Asian American family in twenty years, followed it in September with the crime mystery drama *Quantico,* featuring Asian American actress Priyanka Chopra as lead, and concluded the year with the multi-camera sitcom *Dr. Ken* based on physician-turned-actor Ken Jeong's experiences as a doctor.

Asian American media representation also concurrently occurs outside mainstream television. Historically, film festivals, often niche Asian American specific ones, were the domain of exhibiting up-and-coming work from Asian American directors and filmmakers. The Center for Asian American Media's CAAMFest spotlighted local well-accomplished directors like H. P. Mendoza (*Colma, Fruit Fly, I am a Ghost* and *Bitter Melon),* and the Pacific Arts Movement's San Diego Asian Film Festival brought to light unknown first-time filmmakers like Patrick Wang (*In the Family*). More mainstream film festivals, like Sundance, also played a role in cultivating buzz for Asian American filmmakers. Justin Lin, of *The Fast and Furious* franchise, received his mainstream movie deals after his solo directorial debut, *Better Luck Tomorrow,* rocked the 2002 Sundance Film Festival (Ramanathan, 2018). Jennifer Phang's 2013 PBS FutureStates short film *Advantageous* was developed into a full-length feature film that won the U.S. Dramatic Special Jury for Collaborative Vision from the 2015 Sundance Film Festival and was released exclusively to Netflix (Yoshida, 2015). Justin Chon (from the *Twilight* series and *21 & Over*) wrote and directed the film *Gook* in honor of the 25th anniversary of the Los Angeles Riots, which won the NEXT Audience Award at the 2017 Sundance Film Festival (McNary, 2017). While the luxurious romantic comedy *Crazy Rich Asians* and John Cho's suspenseful thriller *Searching* were surprise hits in the summer of 2018, *To all the boys I've loved,* a coming-of-age film, was an on-demand Netflix sensation soon after (Fang, 2018).

Although independent film festival spaces hold their niche place in media consumption and on-demand streaming services are part of our daily consumption, the broader media environment has now shifted toward privileging audience agency in content selection, production and consumption. First, audiences shifted to a convergence culture that prizes participatory actions, prioritizing consumer agency where they are encouraged and empowered through new technologies and cultural norms to seek out content and make connections amongst formerly disparate areas. It is simultaneously "a top-down corporate-driven process and a bottom-up consumer-driven process" (Jenkins, Clinton, Purushotma, Robison & Weigel, 2006, p. 18). For television, it is no longer the mass medium for a broad audience as it was in the past but is rather now in what Amanda Lotz calls a "post-network era," where the audience, not the television network, has the ability to customize content they want to engage and consume, cultivate the community around that, and in effect control their own viewing experiences. For example, subscription video on-demand (SVOD) services are replacing traditional television as they continue to increase in popularity (BI Intelligence, 2016). In 2015, 8.4 million U.S. households and 57 percent of U.S. broadband households subscribe to at least one over-the-top content (OTT) service that provides online video streaming, but do not pay for TV service (Arolovitch, 2015). According to the Pew Research Center, 61 percent of young adults (those between 18 and 29) watch television with streaming services on the internet (Rainie, 2017). These trends are attributed to the increase of "cord-nevers," or the generation of youth who grew up with access to "any content at any time on any device," and "cord cutters," or those "who at one point had cable, but then opted for an internet connection as their pathway to video content" (Arolovitch, 2015, p. 16).

Millennial audiences are at the center of these "cord-nevers" and "cord cutters" and Asian American millennial audiences are deemed as some of the most tech-savvy and desirable for ad agencies (Arolovitch, 2015; Horrigan & Duggan, 2015). Characterized as between the ages 18–34, the Nielsen Company in 2018 described millennial Asian American audiences as willing and able to function within two cultures (i.e., "ambicultural," a service mark of EthniFacts, LLC.). Also, according to the Pew Internet Research Study, Asian Americans were characterized as having a "mastery of online shopping," or solely used the internet to shop (Perrin, 2016). While the study alludes to YouTube stars like Michelle Phan and Ryan Higa, it primarily focuses on the capital-producing potential of Asian American audiences through their use and consumption of digital content. For example, Nielsen says that "Asian-American Millennials (ages 18–34) spend the majority of their digital time (51 percent)—and more time than Asian Americans of other generations—on apps and the internet on a smartphone. They also spend more time than older Asian Americans on watching video on their smartphone and using game consoles" (Nielsen, 2018, p. 19). The study recognizes the strength and potential of the millennial generation, recognizing that "this younger generation is one of the main reasons Asian Americans are leaders in everything from technology usage and media consumption, to e-commerce" (2018, p. 13).

YouTube is the flashpoint technology and platform for this post-network and convergence culture era. As a digital platform, it functions as a post-television alternative due to the role that its community members place as both creators and consumers (Tolson, 2010). Jenkins et al. (2006) explain that YouTube contributes to a participatory culture due to its accessibility and dissemination of original work, which allow virtual users to build social connections. As a participatory form of media, YouTube functions as a post-television alternative (Tolson, 2010). Since its founding in 2005, the video-hosting website initiated a newfound agency over production and consumption (Salina, 2008). The platform provides a space for the stories of "ordinary people" because it relies on user-generated content, allowing any individual to participate in its virtual community. A central part of YouTube is that it cultivates peer-to-peer connections and a "culture of related blogs, social networking sites, and mass media coverage" (Balance, 2012, p. 139). YouTube functions as "an alternative avenue of cultural production" or a DIY (do-it-yourself) form of cultural production as a forum of civic engagement and form of viral media (Balance, 2012, p. 141).

Asian American millennial audiences are well-suited to a post-network media environment that privileges audience agency. Lacking mainstream media representation, they flocked to YouTube to create their own representations and share it with a borderless community of Asian Americans and others interested in Asian American stories. For Asian Americans in places without a strong Asian American presence and that lacked Asian American film festivals, digital spaces connected geographically dispersed communities through shared YouTube channels and content. And for those in the centers of Asian American cultural production like Los Angeles, YouTube stars enacted what Aymar Jean Christian (2018) describes as an alternative network of "open TV," deployed by often marginalized groups using "independent web tv production and distribution that is digitally native, on-demand, and peer-to-peer" that did not rely on the mainstream legacy networks of Hollywood for representational success (p. 4).

However, ad agencies and media companies' attention to Asian American millennial audiences often overlook cultural producers and the very media environments that cultivate Asian American millennial audience viewing practices. In short, such studies risk essentializing Asian American millennial audiences within static demographic categories, so the conception of an Asian American millennial audience cannot be divorced from the idea of Asian American culture nor the origins of the pan-ethnic term "Asian American."

As many have noted, the pan-ethnic unity that "Asian American" as a category was built upon as a strategy to address civil rights has been undercut by diversity in class division, nationality, history and culture within the category. Nevertheless, "Asian American" continues to be used to organize populations according to racial status. In her discussion of abjection, Karen Shimakawa (2002) asserts that it is in the tension between anti-Asian racialization and political coalition-building where the productive potential of Asian American abjection is realized. She explains that "what characterizes Asian Americanness as it comes into visibility . . . is its constantly shifting relation to Americanness, a movement between visibility and invisibility, foreignness and domestication/assimilation" (p. 3). Though Asian Americans remain in the tension of having limited yet growing representation in media, it is within this tension that Asian American millennial audiences have cultivated a cultural identity.

To complicate and consider an idea of an Asian American millennial audience, we draw on Lowe's conception of Asian American identity and culture as couched in heterogeneity, hybridity and multiplicity. In her (1996) landmark book *Immigrant Acts*, Lowe stresses that Asian American culture is characterized by "heterogeneity, hybridity, and multiplicity" (pp. 66–67). These ideas emphasize the differences within the term "Asian American" (i.e., heterogeneity), the impact of uneven power relations on cultural production (i.e., hybridity), and the social relations of groups on multiple axes of power (i.e., multiplicity) that all together "help us reconcile the material conditions of Asian Americans against the dominant constructions of Asian Americans" (p. 67). She focuses on cultural debates, literature and film, as these are "accessible, 'popular,' and commonly held" and is concerned with identity based on politics and not the politics of identity (p. 75). Thus, digital spaces permit scholars to attend to another space that is accessible and popular for Asian American millennial audiences. Such digital spaces respond to the needs of the audience seeking a space for cultivating cultural identity even *while* it simultaneously shapes them through its vision of what is possible to represent and the possibilities of Asian American culture and related cultural identity.

In shifting to the digital environment, we can more clearly see how the politics of identity and an identity built on politics are both possible. Instead of an either/or of the politics of identity versus an identity built on politics, we focus on the Asian American millennial audience and the content geared towards them on digital platforms like YouTube. This points to the possibility of an identity based on the changing politics of (self-)representation, especially since the history of Asian American representation is predicated on an identity that is excluded from the material conditions of representation. In the next section, we turn our attention to ISAtv and how it constitutes Asian American millennial audiences through its content directed to such audiences. In doing so, we argue that such representations illustrate the heterogeneity, hybridity and multiplicity of Asian American millennials through the way in which their work simultaneously constitutes and speaks to a geographically dispersed Asian American millennial audience and locates their endeavors and possibilities within the necessity of community-based spaces, particularly Los Angeles. We then turn our attention to the content and circulation of ISAtv; that is, what representations are present and how are they circulated through different aspects of the ISAtv platform? We argue that ISAtv serves as content creators and curators for Asian American millennial audiences and positions Asian American cultural production as an ahistorical act, one born out of sheer determination, merit and talent. In the following section, we trace ISAtv's projects, both online and offline, to examine Asian American self-representation and Asian American millennial audiences.

CONTENT CREATORS AND CURATORS FOR ASIAN AMERICAN MILLENNIALS

International Secret Agents (ISA) was founded as a collaboration between Wong Fu Productions (WFP) and Far East Movement (FM). WFP was formed in 2003 at University of California San Diego when college friends Wesley Chan, Philip Wang and Ted Fu began making videos together. Music group FM began performing in 2003 with members Kev Nish (Kevin Nishimura), Prohgress (James Roh) and J-splif (Jae Choung, who eventually left the group due to personal reasons), and eventually DJ Virman (Virman Coquia), who joined the group in 2008. In 2010, FM became the first Asian American group to reach the number one spot on the *Billboard* Hot 100 chart with its single "Like a G6." WFP's official website lists 2007 as "the beginning of a long-term partnership of projects and endeavors [with FM], primarily the 'International Secret Agents' concerts" (Wong Fu Productions).

ISA initially played the role as a curator of Asian American media arts, starting "as a simple concert series aimed at empowering and uniting the Asian Pacific American community [and] has since grown into a thriving brand and entertainment platform" (International Secret Agents, n.d.-a). On its webpage, ISA states that it is "the premiere platform for celebrating Asian Youth Culture and its global influence . . . [and] strives to provide a destination to elevate Asian Pacific American stories, entertainment, community, and culture" (International Secret Agents, n.d.-a). Through its concert series, ISA intended on being a "hub for Asian American Culture, Talent, Entertainment, & Lifestyle" (International Secret Agent, n.d.-b).

On its surface and in its original conception, the concert series is an act of self-representation geared toward Asian American audiences. In an interview prior to ISA's first concert, Philip Wang from WFP explained their motivation for the concert:

> We wanted to show the young people that there are Asian Americans that are really talented . . . they should be seen, that there is talent out there. I feel like if we can show them while they're younger, we can maybe spark something in them, and it might inspire them to do something as well. (A_RONTV, 2008)

The concert series served to inspire and cultivate (through the act of being seen) by providing an Asian American audience the possibility of a future filled with Asian American performers and creators. In many ways, this is not altogether different than ISA's digital content. However, that digital content is distributed nationally and through mediated screens of the laptop, tablet or smartphone. The concerts, on the other hand, are affective experiences located in a particular place and community and attempt to physically connect audiences with popular Asian American cultural producers as well as Asian international stars. Indeed, the concerts featured many Asian American YouTubers as well as American and international celebrities. For example, notable YouTube singer AJ Rafael and K-pop artist Jay Park (who is from Seattle but established his career in Seoul) were invited to perform at ISA LA 2010, and TV personality Nick Cannon was also invited to join the stage that year (Nguyen, 2010). As Balance (2012) argues, these concerts "capitalize on a niche audiences' emotional attachment to performers" (p. 142). Having YouTube stars appear at the concert pulled them from their mediated stardom into the neighborhood space where the audience resides and reinforces the affective attachments and its affective economies that retain ISA's position as Asian American culture creators.

The curatorial acts of ISA via the concert series asserts that Asian Americans *must* be seen and heard. Yet, the concert series locates itself as a unique phenomenon, independent of the history of Asian American independent media production and cinema that also acted in service of self-representation and exhibiting Asian American media makers. Its novelty is its act of being "new" and exciting for audiences. By organizing and hosting a concert of selected Asian American performers (with occasional guest stars outside of Asian America), ISA centers LA's San Gabriel Valley and engages in a grassroots connection to and cultivation of community. Importantly, the act of organizing the concerts illustrates a do-it-yourself ethos, arguing for the viability of Asian American audiences in the capitalistic terrain of media representation. Whereas mainstream media's dismissal of Asian American audiences as not existing and not viable, the ISA concert series provides an alternative idea: "If you build it, they will come."

Although the concerts were the start of ISA's success, ISAtv, the organization's YouTube channel, began to play a more prominent role in shifting toward community-based messages. ISA's concert series were suspended in 2012, but in September of 2012, ISAtv posted its first segment advocating for a community cause in partnership with the Asian American Education Institute and the Jubilee Project to encourage viewers to vote by teaming up with fellow Asian American YouTubers to share the message (ISAtv, 2012b; ISAtv, 2012c). While ISA invested into its local community, the organization addressed an international audience and encouraged submissions from around the world. In October 2014, ISA held The Mobile Mix sponsored by AT&T, which called viewers to vote on their favorite remix of the song "Write It in The Sky" by Asian American YouTuber Kina Grannis (ISAtv, 2014b). On June 16, 2015, ISA initiated its own project and announced Project I.D., calling fans to share their identity with the organization by submitting one- to two-minute videos so that they could learn about the "unique personalities that make up [their] ISA audience around the world" (International Secret Agents, 2015).

Though submissions were accepted from across the nation, contest judges were largely based on the west coast. That same year, ISA held another competition with Toyota in November called The Ride Up to present "an opportunity for aspiring talents across the nation to take their career to the next level" (International Secret Agents, 2016b). Participants submitted entries for one of three categories: music, acting and dance, and were paired with an industry professional who would become a mentor if selected. All of the mentors, Ki Hong Lee (acting), the Kinjazs (dance), and Jun Sung Ahn (music), were based in Los Angeles. In 2016, ISA held its second annual ISA Digital Film Shootout in April and hosted the IDENTITY LA Music Festival with Councilmember David Ryu on May 6, 2017, to celebrate Asian Pacific American Heritage Month (International Secret Agents, 2017a; International Secret Agents, 2017b). In each project, ISA worked within its local network to feature Asian American figures. By emphasizing figures based in their local area as "industry professionals," ISA localized Los Angeles as the source or authority of cultural production. This emphasis with Los Angeles as the locale is reiterated through the recaps of the concert series and the charity events on the ISA website, which were shared with non–San Gabriel and non–Los Angeles area audiences.

In August 2014, ISA updated its website and listed FM and WFP as making up the ISA team. The description on its About page was updated to its current version, which explains the organization as "comprised of two core elements: ISAtv + ISA Live" (International Secret Agents, 2014). ISAtv encompasses its digital content including interviews, music videos and game shows, while ISA Live encompasses concerts, film premieres and charity events. In the next section, we turn our attention to some of ISAtv's content and how it constitutes and shapes Asian American millennial audiences.

ISATV: CENTERING ASIAN AMERICA

ISA launched its new website in July 2011, moving from concert production and media-event promotions to an "all-encompassing entertainment portal for news, original programming, and frequently updated blog content" (International Secret Agents, 2011). Since its founding in 2012, ISAtv posted approximately 440 videos over its first six years of existence. ISAtv serves as an important gap for audiences who may not see themselves as part of Asian American culture, despite the channel's association with Asian American identity, given their association with FM and WFP. ISAtv's videos are organized into eight different playlists: Recent Uploads from ISAtv; isaKIDtv w/ Hudson, Ian, and Forrest; We are ISAtv: Elevating Asian Pacific American Culture, Lifestyle, and Entertainment; ISA Music; ISA! Variety Game Show Season 2; the Dating Challenge Show! w/ Jeffery Fever + Jun Curry Ahn; aka Dan: Korean Adoption Documentary Series; 2 Girls, 1 Lab w/ Linda Dong + Gina Darling; and Angry Asian America Season Two w/ Phil Yu (Angry Asian Man) + Jenny Yang.

By teaming up with established YouTube stars such as KevJumba (Kevin Wu) to do collaborative videos, ISAtv advanced its role in creating and curating content and situated the channel as a hub for Asian American audiences. In this section, we turn our attention to ISAtv's content and how it centers Asian Americans in ways that illustrate the heterogeneity of Asian America even as it constructs differential relations among Asian Americans and to other racial groups. It is through thematic content and Asian American representation in relation to such content that destabilizes an essentialized idea of Asian American identity.

ISAtv demonstrates creative agency over cultural expression by highlighting Asian American identity positionality in its content. One of its first original shows was a weekly series called *ISA Weekly Rewind*, which reported updates on "some of the hottest stories in pop culture and ISA news . . . according to us" (ISAtv, 2012a). Its first episode discussed ongoing events like Earth Day and the music festival Coachella, while centering the events around Asian American figures; for example, the episode featured skits about Earth Day by nigahiga and Wong Fu Productions, and tweets about Coachella from Asian American YouTubers KevJumba and Timothy DeLaGhetto. By curating stories on the most current popular events and figures, ISA familiarizes viewers with content that helps support its goal of celebrating and empowering Asian American youth and creatives. This act of curation, within a weekly update show, reinforces *who* are the major players in the YouTube online space, even as it reconnects them with other audiences.

Second, the content of ISAtv emphasizes Asian Americans as "creators" and "creatives" worthy of attention. As a popular digital platform, YouTube provides a space through which users can engage in creative cultural practices (Douglas & Poletti, 2014). Thus, other series began showing up that emphasize creative practices in ways that were deemed "Asian American" and also not at all related. These shows varied in content. They included the pseudo-fashion show *The Most Awesomest Fashion Show,* hosted in joking demeanor by KevJumba; *Step by Step,* dance tutorials by various Asian American dance troupes or choreographers; *The Makeshift,* craft tutorials by Wong Fu Productions's Wesley Chan; and *Secret Stage,* musical performances in non-concert spaces. These shows illustrate the varied interests and, more importantly, expertise of Asian American creators.

One notable ISA series was *aka Dan.* Written and directed by Dan Mathews, who also works for ISAtv, this autobiographical documentary traces his Korean adoption story, his discovery of a twin brother, and his return to Korea and reunion with his twin brother (ISAtv, 2014a). The four-part documentary (with an additional nine parts for additional content) situates the Korean adoptee story via Mathew's experience as central to the Asian American experience. Although Korean adoptee documentaries have been a staple of Asian American independent media, particularly Deann Borshay Liem's groundbreaking documentary *First Person Plural* (2000), Mathews's account had the support of ISAtv and the distribution power of YouTube. Although *aka Dan* had a small showing in Asian American independent festivals, its reach and release in webisode format on YouTube extended the reach of the story for those who follow ISAtv or the various YouTube networks associated with ISAtv. Through such series, ISA centers its content on Asian American cultural expressions and stories not typically captured by traditional media and that operate outside the geographic boundaries of film festivals.

While the content of transnational adoptee stories, expert dancers or musicians might align with some stereotypes of Asian Americans, ISAtv's Asian American variety show entitled *ISA!* seemed to eschew these stereotypes for absurdist takes on Asian American culture. The show was essentially a takeoff of Asian variety shows: As ISAtv explained, "Take two teams of your favorite celebrities competing in ridiculous challenges, mix in comedy & live musical performance, and you've got our brand new variety special on ISAtv" (International Secret Agents, 2013a). *ISA!* featured Asian American (digital/local) celebrities, a live audience and viewer participation through

Google Hangouts (Kristina, 2013). The first show was taped at YouTube Space Los Angeles and featured guests such as actress Arden Cho (*Pretty Little Liars*), YouTubers David Choi and Jen (FromHeadToToe), and dancer and choreographer Mike Song (International Secret Agents, 2013b). In gathering prominent Asian American figures, the variety show, which draws from the Asian television genre, demonstrates a cultural space through which identity and performance interact. Connections among different Asian American figures "reveal the development of transmedia branding across Asian American popular culture—a project that serves to create hubs of Asian American participatory culture that can be mobilized for different kinds of action" (Lopez, 2016, p. 141).

Although this transmedia branding across Asian American YouTube stars is not unique, the constellation of participants on the shows is intriguing in how it constructs racial relationality. The second season of *ISA!* had the staple Asian American participants, such as the well-known Fung Brothers and Ki Hong Lee from Netflix's *Unbreakable Kimmy Schmidt*. But it was the participation of white YouTube stars—Meghan (Strawburry17), Joey Graceffa, and Niko (Corridor Digital)—that is striking. In the game show, Asianness is foregrounded, stylistically through the Japanese-inspired game show format with Asian American topics and with the presence of young, aspiring Asian Americans. Whiteness is present but as the minority in the background with white Youtube stars, *ISAtv* inverts the typical representational landscape of shows; instead of Asian Americans as token characters, white people are the minority. However, it does not seem "weird" or subversive. Rather, the *ISA!* show illustrates multicultural and multiracial camaraderie as normal, of how it is as if one is hanging out with "friends" as an everyday occurrence. It is within this dynamic, of Asian American YouTube stars crossing over and collaborating with white YouTube stars, that the absence of blackness and black physical presence is striking.

ISAtv's digital content revels in centering Asian American representation on its own terms. However, in representing Asian American creators relationally, whiteness is physically present while blackness is not. Rather, blackness appears only in ways that Asian American cultural producers draw from—whether hip-hop culture or b-boy dancing. Thus, ISAtv's representational politics of its digital content reveals the possibility and perils of content directed toward an Asian American millennial audience. Through their digital content, they illustrate Asian America's heterogeneity, bringing attention to the diverse interests, stories and expertise that Asian American cultural producers bring to mainstream culture. But these stories and their content, particularly in *ISA!*, illustrate the limits of Asian American representational politics independent of its relationality with other racial groups. Whether the absence of black YouTubers and social media stars occurs is function of ISAtv's failure to network with them, or because of its intentional branding toward Asian American audiences, or because of simple oversight, this absence of interracial mingling belies the experience of Asian American communities in racially diverse areas. For ISA, its content represents facets of Asian America without making evident its relationality with other non-white racial groups even as it draws upon their cultural influences. In doing so, ISA promotes an idea of an insular "Asian America" even though its influences are not.

EMPOWERING A NEW GENERATION

FM and WFP created ISA after recognizing the obstacles faced by Asian American artists in mainstream media. The organization began with a focus on Asian American artists breaking into mainstream media and sought to provide opportunities to showcase their craft. By highlighting these artists and demonstrating Asian American involvement in the arts, ISA aimed to inspire and encourage Asian American youth to become artists and creators themselves. Using YouTube as a digital platform under the direction of WFP, ISAtv engaged pop culture while featuring Asian American voices through its original content and brought recognition to the role that Asian Americans can and do play in mainstream culture. The organization has been able to engage both mainstream and independent artists due to the founders' networks; FM navigates the line between mainstream and indie media due to its mainstream exposure and independent label, while WFP is established in YouTube and has been involved with independent and major productions. Their partnership situates ISA in a way that allows it to access enough resources and acquire funding to hold concerts, festivals and programs for a niche population. ISA has also established transnational relationships by working with K-pop stars and other Asian celebrities. As for community involvement, most of ISA events, aside from its concert series, were held in cities in the San Gabriel Valley, an area that is heavily populated by Asian Americans. By engaging Asian American youth in these areas as well as other parts in the nation, they aspire to empower a generation of Asian Americans to thrive in the arts despite mainstream media's barriers.

More importantly, ISA and ISAtv highlight the limits of visibility politics of creation, curation and representation in a YouTube space. Balance (2012) illustrates how Asian American YouTubers rely on the affective economies of audience attachment and investment to performers engaging in representational politics. While this empowers audiences to revel in the enjoyment of Asian American creative visions, it is also juxtaposed against the structural aspects that limit cross-racial and intersectional representations. Such unimagined possibilities become further relegated to niche audiences and markets instead of a larger more expansive notion of "Asian America." However, the platform of YouTube and its audience engagement allows for a re-envisioning of Asian American social relations and representations. Herein lies the potential of the interplay of ISA, WFP and FM and their Asian American millennial audiences; the continuing connection, constant communication and evolving conversation between audience and creators allows for creative storytelling and representations that may benefit both sides. One example of such evolution in stories and representations is the presence of mixed-raced Blasians (i.e., black and Asian) and interracial dating present in WFP's limited series, *Yappie*. While this is not a wholly new topic or story, its extended attention by WFP is a new development in its previously East Asian–centric stories.

While ISA does not describe itself as a media organization, its goal of advancing Asian Americans in the arts is frequently demonstrated by its role as a platform that connects artists from the mainstream, independent and local community. The organization not only incorporated programs that other Asian American media organizations have held, but also used emerging media technologies to advance its cause. By establishing its presence as a social media platform, ISA found other forms of exposure, developed an audience around the nation (and the world), and worked with new forms of viewer engagement. While this chapter examines the digital expansion of ISA as a media organization, future research would do well to continue to investigate the role of Asian American youth in pop culture. ISA's focus on Asian American youth demonstrates its hope for the future of Asian American representation. In 2015, ISAtv released a promotional video entitled "We are ISAtv—Join the Movement!" describing itself as a place for lifestyle, pop culture and Asian Pacific American news, issues and identity (ISAtv, 2015b). One of the many online comments to the video demonstrated an enthusiastic response to the call: "You have no idea how much I wanna be part of this! I just don't know what to put in the e-mail. Do I attach a CV? LOL!" (Jomar, 2015). As demonstrated by this comment and by ISA's growing audience, the organization is effectively working toward its goal of empowering a generation of Asian American youth and providing exposure for Asian American artists. ISA has shown that Asian Americans can and do play a role in cultural production, and it will continue to advance its role in the arts by maintaining its digital presence online while engaging the Asian American community offline.

REFERENCES

A_RONTV. (2008, September 16). Pt.2—International Secret Agents concert [Video file]. Retrieved from https://www.youtube.com/watch?v=o9N_CYinCMg.
Arolovitch, A. (2015). Streaming: The new normal? *Broadcasting & Cable, 145*(25), 16.

Bai, S. (2016, June 15). ISA announces winners of inaugural digital film contest. Retrieved from http://www.nbcnews.com/news/asian-america/isa-announces-winners-inaugural-digital-film-contest-n592966.

Balance, C. B. (2012). How it feels to be viral me: Affective labor and Asian American YouTube performance. *Women's Studies Quarterly, 40*(1), 138–152.

BI Intelligence. (2016, March 4). How subscription video on demand services like Netflix are contributing to the demise of pay-tv. Retrieved from http://www.businessinsider.com/viewers-are-changing-the-way-they-watch-content-here-are-the-winners-and-losers-2015-10.

Center for African American Studies at UCLA. (2017). *2015 Hollywood diversity report: Setting the record straight.* Retrieved from http://bunchecenter.ucla.edu/2017/02/new-2017-hollywood-diversity-report/.

Christian, A. J. (2018). *Open TV: Innovation beyond Hollywood and the rise of web television.* New York, NY: New York University Press.

Douglas, K. & Poletti, A. (2014). Rethinking "virtual" youth: Young people and life writing. In A. Bennett & B. Robards (Eds.), *Mediated youth cultures: The internet, belonging and new cultural configurations*, pp. 77–94. New York, NY: Palgrave Macmillan.

Facebook IQ. (2015, March 5). "Digital Diversity: A closer look at Asian Americans in the U.S." *Facebook.* Retrieved from https://www.facebook.com/iq/articles/digital-diversity-a-closer-look-at-asian-americans in the us.

Fang, M. (2018, August 22). "With the success of 'Asian August,' it's your move, Hollywood." *Huffington Post.* Retrieved from https://www.huffingtonpost.com/entry/asian-august-crazy-rich-asians-to-all-the-boys-ive-loved-before_us_5b7bf41ce4b0a5b1febee76f.

Gorham, B. W. (1999). Stereotypes in the media: So what? *The Howard Journal of Communications, 10*, 229–247.

Horrigan, J. B., & Duggan, M. (2015, December 15). One-in-seven Americans are television "cord cutters." Retrieved from http://www.pewinternet.org/2015/12/21/4-one-in-seven-americans-are-television-cord-cutters/.

International Secret Agents. (2017b). IDENTITY LA: A concert & celebration for Asian Pacific American heritage month. Retrieved from http://isatv.com/blog/identity-la-a-concert-celebration-for-asian-pacific-american-heritage-month/.

International Secret Agents. (2017a). ISA Digital Film Shootout 2017. Retrieved from http://isatv.com/blog/isa-digital-film-shootout-2017/.

International Secret Agents. (2016b). The Ride UP mentorship program. Retrieved from http://isatv.com/blog/enter-today-the-ride-up/.

International Secret Agents. (2016a). Digital film shootout. Retrieved from http://isatv.com/blog/digital-film-shootout/.

International Secret Agents. (2015). Join Project I.D. Retrieved from http://isatv.com/blog/join-project-i-d/.

International Secret Agents. (2014). Meet the team. Retrieved from https://web.archive.org/web/20140803002511/http://isatv.com:80/about/meet-the-team/.

International Secret Agents. (2013b, March 27). Contestants announced for ISA! Retrieved from https://web.archive.org/web/20130928024101/http://isatv.com/entertainment/contestants-announced-for-isa/.

International Secret Agents. (2013a, March 14). Be a part of the live studio audience for ISA! Game show special—limited seats available! Retrieved from https://web.archive.org/web/20130324173752/http://isatv.com:80/entertainment/isa-game-show/.

International Secret Agents. (2012). ISA charity basketball game recap and stats! Retrieved from http://isatv.com/blog/entertainment/youtube-stars-align-for-isa-charity-basketball-game/.

International Secret Agents. (2011). About. Retrieved from https://web.archive.org/web/20110712103716/http://isatv.com:80/?page_id=181.

International Secret Agents. (n.d.-b). About. Retrieved from https://www.facebook.com/pg/internationalsecretagents/about/.

International Secret Agents. (n.d.-a). About. Retrieved from http://isatv.com/about/.

ISAtv. (2016, July 6). YouTubers playing basketball—ISA charity basketball game 2016 [Video file]. Retrieved from https://www.youtube.com/watch?v=TkgOblwWiVI.

ISAtv. (2015b, January 12). We are ISAtv—join the movement! [Video file]. Retrieved from https://www.youtube.com/watch?v=52wLPIM9eIs.

ISAtv. (2015a, June 23). YOUTUBERS PLAYING BASKETBALL—ISA! Charity Basketball Game 2015 [Video file]. Retrieved from https://www.youtube.com/watch?v=zFMkbHLIL1I.

ISAtv. (2014b, October 20). Help Kina Grannis remix a song!—The Mobile Mix [Video file]. Retrieved from https://www.youtube.com/watch?v=mPra_hQC-Zg.

ISAtv. (2014a, March 13). Korean adoptee reunites with identical twin brother!—"aka DAN" Korean adoptee doc pt. 3 [Video file]. Retrieved from https://www.youtube.com/watch?v=sWPcPbzlOLk.

ISAtv. (2012c, October 31). #TakeAction and vote: TURNING 18 ft. AJ Rafael [Video file]. Retrieved from https://www.youtube.com/watch?v=zHStfcMbSyc.

ISAtv. (2012b, September 26). ISAx Jubilee Project—#TakeAction campaign—(Don't) VOTE [Video file]. Retrieved from https://www.youtube.com/watch?v=BPjfURWBkQk&t=95s.

ISAtv. (2012a, April 24). Philip Wang gets a Hologram—ISA WEEKLY REWIND Ep. 1 [Video file]. Retrieved from https://www.youtube.com/watch?v=fmAIJCvNs_I.

Jenkins, H., Clinton, K., Purushotma, R., Robinson, A., & Weigel, M. (2006). *Confronting the challenges of participatory culture: Media education for the 21st century*. Chicago, IL: MacArthur Foundation.

Jomar. (2015). Re: We are ISAtv—Join the movement! [Video file]. Retrieved from https://www.youtube.com/watch?v=52wLPIM9eIs.

Kristina. (2013, April 3). I was in the ISA! game show. Retrieved from https://web.archive.org/web/20130409043421/http://isatv.com:80/entertainment/i-was-in-the-isa-game-show-through
-google-hangout/.

Ling, S. (2012, October 20). History of Asians in the San Gabriel Valley. Retrieved from http://imdiversity.com/villages/asian/history-of-asians-in-the-san-gabriel-valley/.

Lopez, L. K. (2016). *Asian American media activism: Fighting for cultural citizenship*. New York, NY: New York University Press.

Los Angeles 09—premier show. (2009, July 28). Retrieved from http://internationalsecreta-gents.com:80/events/los-angeles-08.

Lowe, L. (1996). *Immigrant acts: On Asian American cultural politics*. Durham, NC: Duke University Press.

McNary, D. (2017, April 19). "Sundance Next Audience award winner 'Gook' picked up by Samuel Goldwyn." *Variety*. Retrieved from https://variety.com/2017/film/festivals/sun-dance-winner-gook-samuel-goldwyn-1202034031/.

Nguyen, M. (2010, September 24). International Secret Agents LA 2010: An action-packed night of sneak attacks. Retrieved from http://asiapacificarts.usc.edu/article@apa?international_secret_agents_la_2010_an_action-packed_night_of_sneak_attacks_15673.aspx/.

Nielsen Company. (2018, May 8). Asian Americans: Digital lives and growing influence. Retrieved from https://www.nielsen.com/us/en/insights/reports/2018/asian-americans-con-sumers.html.

Ono, K. A., & Pham, V. N. (2009). *Asian Americans and the media*. Malden, MA: Polity Press.

Perrin, A. (2016, February 18). English-speaking Asian Americans stand out for their technolo-gy use. Retrieved from http://www.pewresearch.org/fact-tank/2016/02/18/english-speaking-asian-americans-stand-out-for-their-technology-use/.

Rainie, L. (2017, September 13). About 6 in 10 young adults in U.S. primarily use online streaming to watch tv. Retrieved from http://www.pewresearch.org/fact-tank/2017/09/13/about 6 in 10 young-adults-in-u-s-primarily-use-online-streaming-to-watch-tv/.

Ramanathan, L. (2018, Aug. 15). The story of 'Better Luck Tomorrow,' a movie with an Asian American cast long before 'Crazy Rich Asians' Washington Post. Retrieved from https://www.washingtonpost.com/news/arts-and-entertainment/wp/2018/08/15/the-story-of-better-luck-tomorrow-a-movie-with-an-asian-american-cast-long-before-crazy-rich-asians.

Ramasubramanian, S. (2011). Television exposure, model minority portrayals, and Asian-American stereotypes: An exploratory study. *Journal of InterculturalCommunication, 1*(26), 4–22.

Salinas, C. (2008). *WhoTube? Identification and agenda-setting in new media.* Paper presented at the National Communication Association: unCONVENTIONal, San Diego.

Shimakawa, K. (2002). *National abjection: The Asian American body on stage.* Durham, NC: Duke University Press.

Spooner, T. (2001, December 12). "Asian-Americans and the Internet." Pew Research Center: *Internet & Technology.* Retrieved from http://www.pewinternet.org/2001/12/12/asian-americans-and-the-internet/.

Tolson, A. (2010). A new authenticity? Communicative practices on YouTube. *Critical Discourse Studies, 7*(4), 277–289.

Wong Fu Productions. (n.d.). About. Retrieved from http://web.archive.org/web/20170427024357/http://wongfuproductions.com:80/about/.

U.S. News & World Report. (n.d.). Alhambra high. Retrieved from https://www.usnews.com/education/best-high-schools/california/districts/alhambra-unified/san-gabriel-high-1665/student-bodymark.

U.S. News & World Report. (n.d.). Mark Keppel high. Retrieved from https://www.usnews.com/education/best-high-schools/california/districts/alhambra-unified/mark-keppel-high-1664/student-body.

Yoshida, E. (2015, May 19). "The excellent Sundance sci-fi film *Advantageous* is coming to Netflix." *The Verge.* Retrieved from https://www.theverge.com/2015/5/19/8624233/netflix-sundance-advantageous-jennifer-phang.

YouTube. (n.d.). About. Retrieved from https://www.youtube.com/yt/about/.

Zhang, Q. (2010). Asian Americans beyond the model minority stereotype: The nerdy and the left out. *Journal of International & Intercultural Communication, 3*(1), 20–37.

Chapter Twelve

"Being Black at Southern Miss"

The Mythology of the African American True Believer

Marcus J. Coleman

"A lot of students have a strong sense of entitlement and it's definitely a detriment to our self-esteem as far as . . . being black and being humans . . . next to people that sometimes still don't consider us to be on the level that they are. . . ."

—Quote from "Being Black at Southern Miss"
YouTube Video (McGowan, 2015)

On December 29, 2015, a graduate student in the Mass Communication and Journalism program at the University of Southern Mississippi (USM) published a four-minute and thirty-three second video titled "Being Black at Southern Miss" that went viral—6,000 YouTube views and countless shares on social media platforms. The video sparked discussion for many, on-campus and off-campus. As a faculty member, I was happy to see students express themselves without infringement from the university, and I was alarmed that the institution was not living up to its responsibility to all of its students. As an alum, which colors my perspective on student life at the university, I was incredulous to the claims being made by the students regarding their experiences because they did not match the memories that I carry from my time at USM. So I will not disguise my bias, but it should be seen as a window into a perspective of generations of African American alum from USM. Over time, I have learned that my perspective on USM is myopic, given the experience of African American students who attended USM in previous decades.

Minchin and Salmond (2011) tell the story of one of the first African Americans to attempt enrollment at USM, Mr. Clyde Kennard. Mr. Kennard was a WWII veteran and an attendee of the University of Chicago who wanted to return home to Mississippi to be closer to family. It is safe to say that Mr. Kennard was a patriot and a true believer in American values, which is evidenced by his insistence on finishing his college degree at "Mississippi Southern," now known as USM (Wanzo, 2009). As recorded in the Mississippi Sovereignty Commission papers, both black and white community members, including Governor J. P. Coleman, attempted to dissuade Mr. Kennard from applying to USM (Mississippi Department of Archives and History, SCR ID # 1-27-0-37-1-1-1). Even so, Mr. Kennard was persistent in his efforts, so much so that Mr. Kennard made his case for entry to USM in the *Hattiesburg American* via three letters that he wrote to the editor on December 6, 1958, September 25, 1959, and January 23, 1960. In addition, I retrieved Kennard's letter to the then Admissions Director, Aubrey K. Lucas, from the Mississippi Department of Archives and History's digital archives, regarding his intention to apply to "Mississippi Southern" on September 2, 1959. Unfortunately, Mr. Kennard was denied entry to the university in 1955, 1956 and 1959. Tragically, Mr. Kennard was targeted by local dissenters, framed for a crime, and sentenced to jail in Parchment (Mississippi's federal prison). While Mr. Kennard was in prison, he was diagnosed with stomach cancer and was eventually released for treatment. Shortly after his release, he passed away, in July of 1963.

All too often, the story of denial of African American entry into predominantly white institutions are told as anachronism, but I teach students who encounter, in real time, similar Civil Rights–era events often written about as historic and proliferated during Black History Month. Similar to Mr. Kennard's efforts, one of the ways to battle exclusion is by exposing asymmetrical treatment via public appeals. Below, I unpack the penultimate statement by focusing on the *relational interactions of publics* via *myth*.

Myth (*muthos*) and symmetry help us impute meaning to human sensuous activity (Barthes, 1973). Myth is (re)produced via signs that function via polysemy, metaphor and metonym; moreover, those signs help create historical tales that bring order to an entropic world (Welsh & Asante, 1981; Grossberg, 1992). Similarly, symmetry is historical and encompasses the past, present and future, particularly a future that is knowable due to the oftentimes generalizable actions of humans (Hall, 2001). From this perspective, I discuss the use of public appeals by millennials to overcome subversive racial practices. In this chapter, I assess the use of African American mythoforms as a way of decomposing the *relational tension between publics* to illustrate the function of myth. To do so, I first analyze the appeals made in Clyde Kennard's correspondence in 1958, 1959 and 1960. I then move to a text from 2015, "Being Black at USM," which was produced by millennial students at the University of Southern Mississippi.

MILLENNIALS, PUBLICS AND
THE BLACK PUBLIC SPHERE

First, a note about millennials and their use of social media. In contrast to the Baby Boom cohort, whose membership is defined by substantial changes in the U.S. birth rates, the millennial cohort is a generation largely defined by shared experiences. Generation X, those in between the millennials and Boomers, were born between 1965 and 1980 and are often characterized as skeptical, independent, savvy and entrepreneurial loners. Millennials are on track to be the most educated generation to date, especially women. Pew Research Center found that 27 percent of female millennials had completed at least a bachelor's degree at ages eighteen to thirty-three compared to 21 percent of millennial males. However, the percentages for millennial women and men are considerably higher than for both Generation X and Boomers. Millennials are also much more engaged online. To highlight the saturation of technology use among millennials, I reference a Pew Research Center (2018) study that states,

> More than nine-in-ten Millennials (92 percent) own smartphones, compared with 85 percent of Gen Xers (those who turn ages 38 to 53 this year), 67 percent of Baby Boomers (ages 54 to 72) and 30 percent of the Silent Generation (ages 73 to 90), according to a new analysis of Pew Research Center data. Similarly, the vast majority of Millennials (85 percent) say they use social media.

It is safe to say that social media for millennials is a trusted and often-utilized communication channel.

The *public* is discussed here via two prominent scholars, Dewey (2012) and Arendt (1958). To start, Dewey (2012) defines a public as "all of those who are affected by the indirect consequences of transactions to such an extent that it is deemed necessary to have those consequences cared for" (p. 15). To his credit, Dewey's conception of the public sufficiently allowed for extensions and revisions for how and why people form publics, namely a characterization of the public sphere (Habermas, 1989), rethinking the public sphere (Fraser, 1992), explicating the black public sphere (Dawson, 1995), explicating the public screen (DeLuca & Peeples, 2002) and categorizing the black public sphere by motivation (Squires, 2002). Thus, the vague motivation for the formation of a public points to myriad reasons for why people join with others who possess similar interests to address common concerns.

Conversely, Arendt (1958) characterizes the public realm as essential to human existence, but incapable of sustaining humanity, helping people relate to each other, or even demassifying people based on common interests. Arendt's characterization of the public extinguishes opportunities to extend the exploration of the public into interdependent publics acting together to address direct and/or indirect consequences, in other words, interest groups, political parties, and so on, outside of public adoration. As such, Dewey's conception of the public is central to this project.

Further, Dewey (2012) conceptualizes the state as an arbiter in relation to the consequences of human associative action, direct and indirect, particularly to protect those who are disenfranchised, such as children, elderly and historically oppressed groups. In doing so, Dewey makes a tacit assumption that recognition of one's being is inevitable and unavoidable. There has been considerable work done since that time to overcome this assumption (Fraser, 1992; Dawson, 1995, 2003; Squires, 2002). Similarly, public deliberation research, this piece included, assumes that the improvement of human communication will ultimately lead to a more informed and responsible participatory citizenry.

Habermas's (1989) initial discussion of a bourgeoisie public sphere was limited to white males who assembled as private individuals to deliberate in public spaces (*öffentlichkeit*). In these public conglomerates, private citizens come together face-to-face, in public spaces, to discuss their concerns comprising a public sphere. The idea of bracketing identities is posited, thereby creating environments of mutual respect for the subject positions of others and their various social positions (Fraser, 1992). Fraser's (1992) "rethinking" of the public sphere recognizes that there have always been multiple publics, which creates room for alternative publics to function and even agitate the bourgeoisie public sphere.

Fraser (1992) also addresses dubious assumptions that accompany Habermas's public sphere theory, such as the ability to bracket identity; the value of a multiplicity of publics for democracy; the outright move toward a common good in lieu of private issues and interests; and, lastly, the distinct separation between civil society and the state. These assumptions collectively function to make room for *subaltern counterpublics*, which Fraser (1992) defines as "parallel discursive arenas where members of subordinated social groups invent and circulate counter-discourses to formulate oppositional interpretations of their identities, interests, and needs" (p. 123). Here, the black public sphere emerges, recognizing that communication is cultural and that organizational space is necessary.

Dawson (1995) helps to conceptualize a black public sphere, illustrating the overlapping, yet divergent, approaches taken within black communities toward social activism and issues that comprise a black political agenda. To describe the necessity for exploring black public spheres, Dawson (2003) states,

> Societies which are marked by racial apartheid are not only likely to develop separate public spheres, but those spheres themselves become the bases for the articulation of divergent, often conflicting, group interests. The subordinate

group, in particular, is likely in bourgeois democratic societies to perceive ideology through the lens of whatever social cleavage is the basis of its historical oppression, whether its members believe their oppression to be based on religion, class, or (in the American case) race (p. 53).

Black public spheres highlight counterpublics created for and by African Americans. Often, as in other social movements, theorists are simultaneously activists, community organizers, financiers, family members, for example, Clyde Kennard. Those various subject positions are indeed *relational*, but they are constituted in opposition/antagonism/resistance to a normative rationale of domination.

Further, Squires (2002) posed a foundational criticism of Dawson's conception of black public spheres. Squires claims that Dawson conflates the organization of a sphere with its success as a sphere, but it is a tempting assumption. The organization of a sphere does not assure its success or its sustainability as a sphere. Also, one may not be able to assign internal homogeneity to a sphere (Squires, 2002). (History is brimming with examples of coalitions that have worked together to achieve enfranchisement, e.g., the Socialist Democratic Party, the American Communist Party, the Black Panthers in concert with the Young Lords.) Even so, neither of the above-mentioned researchers assess the relational elements of public spheres to each other. In essence, publics are people in conversation bound by reason (Carey, 1996). Although, publics are conceptualized as communicative and socially relational, they are rarely ever assessed as such.

DIALECTICAL MYTHOFORM
AND AFRICAN AMERICAN MYTHS

Within black public spheres, as in other culturally specific spheres, cultural identity is constructed via memory, fantasy, narrative and myth that function to unconsciously organize our experiences. As such, African American communication practices have typically been shaped via resistance to domination and in response to imposed social, political and economic hardship (Welsh & Asante, 1981; Asante, 2004; Hecht, Jackson & Ribeau, 2003). Asante (2004) claims that myths function as fundamental patterns by which we subconsciously organize our experiences. Conversely, myths also operate on a conscious level and maintain our symbolic life at a phenomenal level.

Asante (2004) asserts that unique to the mythoforms of members of the African Diaspora is that cultural identity formation springs from a resistance to colonization, hegemony and all other forms of domination from those outside the culture of origin. Welsh and Asante (1981) assert,

A significant function of the African American myth in discourse is the demonstration of control over circumstances as opposed to control over nature. It is the heroine's or hero's mission, sometimes messianic in nature, to surmount any obstacle in the cause of peace, love, or devotion to family. African American myths are set in the inexact past, unless, of course, they are historic, legendary myths, such as that of Harriet Tubman. (p. 389)

There are two primary mythology types among African American myths, *suffering* and *suckling*. Suffering myths rest on an implicit assumption that suffering precedes redemption (Asante & Welsh, 1981). Conversely, suckling is described as the "mother-earth" category that is tantamount to *caring*. Though the suckling myth is typically tied to Harriet Tubman's action as a liberator of more than three hundred slaves, it is not exclusive to females, but it is feminine in character (Asante & Welsh, 1981).

The hero and heroine myths that are common to African American mythology typically include John Henry to denote strength; Stagalee to emphasize the radical impulse to resist domination; Harriet Tubman to focus on the linked fate nature of racial uplift; the trickster as a virile logical/interpretive manifestation of phenomenology; and also Christian personification such as the story of Job.

There is considerable work done to expose the relational topoi that underlie publics. As established above, mythology is part of the theoretical labor necessary to assess the relational elements of publics. Specifically, the framing nature of mythoforms, which help characterize the relationship of African Americans to their respective communities. To make a more explicit link between the mythoforms and the relational characterizations of publics, I adopt Coleman, Harris, Bryant, and Rief-Stice's (2018) use of relational metaphors *tumultuous* and *guardian*. Coleman et al. (2018) qualitatively evaluate African American participants talk about attachment to nation. A *tumultuous* relationship is described simply as one partner taking advantage of the other. This precarious situation involving relational conflict leaves the disadvantaged partner disgruntled, yet not to the point of breaking up. Rather, the disadvantaged partner works toward making the relationship better and more viable (Burgoon & Hale, 1984). A *guardian* approach to relationship is regarded as a leadership approach to community. Proponents acknowledge that one may not be recognized, but still provides unconditional love, such as caring, while still offering necessary critique (Burgoon & Hale, 1984).

There is kinship between Coleman et al.'s *tumultuous* and *guardian* relationships and the *suffering* and *suckling* mythological traditions of African Americans. The creation of Coleman et al.'s categories are reflective of their exclusively African American participants who historically order their society through the established mythoforms embedded within African American cultural identity (Asante, 2004). Even though there is kinship between the two African American mythological genres and the relational metaphors presented, there are also distinctions. There is a melancholic character to the tumultuous metaphor, while there is a true-believer element to the guardian metaphor. As Wanzo (2009) writes,

> Many African American thinkers have addressed their belief in US citizenship and their anger and melancholy at the nation's failure to fulfill its promises. Yet, despite the failure of the US to create equality for all of its citizens, the black patriot still has a melancholic attachment to its possibilities and takes pride in the black citizen's role in working toward equality and justice." (p. 342)

Both, suckling and suffering, genres of African American mythology are melancholic, and neither include a true-believer characterization. As such, I pose two questions in the analysis that follows. How are relational characterizations deployed in relation to each other in public appeals related to race at USM? How do mythoforms influence relational characterization of publics related to race at USM?

DIALECTICAL RELATIONSHIPS
AND GENERATIONAL WHITE SUPREMACY

This project uses both an inductive and a deductive approach to conduct a qualitative case study. In part one, I retrieved Clyde Kennard's letters to the editor of the *Hattiesburg American* for December 6, 1958, September 25, 1959, and January 23, 1960. In addition, I retrieved Kennard's letter to the then Admissions Director, Aubrey K. Lucas, from the Mississippi Department of Archives and History's digital archives, regarding his intention to apply to "Mississippi Southern" on September 2, 1959 (Mississippi Department of Archives and History, SCR ID # 1-27-0-29-1-1-1). After doing so, an inductive constant-comparative method (CCM) (Baxter & Babbie, 2004) was used to ensure that the themes were apparent and that significant exemplars were not overlooked. In part two, deductively, I use the theoretical perspective derived from assessing the writings of Mr. Kennard to frame the transcript of "Being Black at Southern Miss" video.

Three types of coding are used during the constant comparison method: open, axial and selective (Boeije, 2009; Wahyuni, 2012). Open coding is described as the disaggregation of the text; axial coding is described as the categorization of data; and selective coding is described as identification of emergent themes from the systematically categorized data. CCM helps answer three essential topics: the variation between elements, the objectives of different types of categories, and the varying types of comparisons as they relate to each other (Boeije, 2002). This method helped me to identify some commonalities between texts. During open coding, I identified a common appeal to the public. Next, during axial coding, it was apparent that Kennard's persuasive appeals were embedded within a perspective that focused on persistently asymmetric racial publics. In the process of selectively coding, in accordance to our frame of relational characterization, Kennard's writings provide a frame of a dialectical relationship between publics. After assessing Mr. Kennard's writings, I categorized the utterances from the "Being Black at USM" using the dialectical relationships gleaned from the Kennard writings.

Using Owen's (1984) criteria, themes were identified based on recurrence (e.g., the same thread of meaning was present in two or more places) and repetition (e.g., reiterations of key words or phrases used within each transcript). The findings below outline the takeaways from this analytic approach.

Clyde Kennard Takes on White Sovereignty in Mississippi

As a WWII veteran, Mr. Kennard served in the military after military units had been desegregated in 1948 and he, like Medgar Evers, returned home to Mississippi with an assertion of racial symmetry and race pride. From this perspective, we see Mr. Kennard employ a dialectical use of relational characterizations, tumultuous and guardian, in his public appeals. Regarding the question—"How are relational characterizations deployed in relation to each other in public appeals related to race at USM?"—dialectics is the theoretical framework that emerged from assessing the writings of Mr. Kennard related to his admission to USM. Relational dialectics is a foundational theory of communications studies that asserts communication is a constitutive mechanism between relational partners, not merely a reflection of the state of play between individual interlocutors (Baxter, 2004). Regarding the question— "How do mythoforms influence relational characterization of publics related to race at USM?"—Mr. Kennard recognizes the suffering of the African American Mississippians at the hands of white Mississippians, yet using a true-believer guardian approach, he asserts that the relational approach, in other words white supremacy—described by hooks (2004) as the interlocking political systems of apparatuses that help sustain, uphold and perpetuate prudent values imputed to a phantasmagoric whiteness—of white Mississippians is misguided and illogical.

Through his op-eds and his letter to Admissions Director Lucas, Clyde Kennard laid bare his idea of the *tumultuous* relationship between publics, for example, integrationists and segregationists. Kennard (1958) states in his letter to the editor, "Mixing," if we are ever to attain the goal of the first class citizenship, we must do it through a closer association with the dominant (white) group. . . . Now it is the "getting closer" attempt by the Negro group that has aroused . . . a temporary animosity between the two groups. (p. 2-A)

Kennard directly takes on white supremacy. Particularly, Kennard asserts that a mythical white supremacy is the dialectical tension that characterizes the relationship between the integrationists and segregationists.

Mr. Kennard reasoned that dominant/subordinate dialectical tension of a mythical white supremacy has no essence and that its form is contingent on revisionist history. Mr. Kennard (1958) writes, "We hold these truths to be self-evident" as he quotes from the Declaration of Independence, "that all men are created equal. How different that statement is in spirit from the one which says: Before I see my child go to school with a Negro, I will destroy the whole school system." He asserts that the nihilistic relational approach, in other words white supremacy, of the supposed dominant (white) group toward their black counterparts indeed rested upon a system of codes that must constantly be open to scrutiny. Further, Mr. Kennard's attempt to enroll at Mississippi Southern College and his ability to appeal to the public in such a reasoned manner versus the coordinated vitriolic effort of the Mississippi Sovereignty Commission to deny his enrollment helps confirm the *myth* of white supremacy.

Mr. Kennard also rejected assertions of inferiority and otherness, which is indicative of a *guardian* relational perspective, when he wrote to the the the Admissions Director regarding his intention to apply to "Mississippi Southern." On September 8, 1959, Kennard lays out five arguments commonly used by segregationists to discourage integration. Kennard asserts that segregationists rationalize their stance toward segregated education as such: allowing whites and blacks to go to school together would eventually lead to a mixing of the races, miscegenation, which would destroy the races; second, the "low moral habits" of blacks would discourage whites students from associating with black students; thirdly, white students are so much more scholastically advanced and having to compete with black students who are naturally less capable would hamper the little development possible when left in a segregated setting; fourthly, black teachers would end up unemployed due to the increase in competition with white teachers; and last, segregationists argued that equal facilities and teachers should lead to equitable outcomes in a segregated society. A theme of Mr. Kennard's five points is the sense of entitlement on behalf of segregationists at the expense of integrationists, inherent to the myth of white supremacy.

The resultant dialectical tension is assuaged using a coping strategy commonly employed to mitigate dialectical tension, reframing/recalibration. In the "School Mixing" op-ed that Mr. Kennard wrote in 1960, he argues,

> If we decided to be realistic about the whole thing, and employ people according to merit, would it not be much more sensible and certainly more economical to permit the lawyers, doctors and engineers who are to be working on the same staffs just after graduation to go to the same schools where they could learn to respect and appreciate each other? (1960)

In this quote, we see that Mr. Kennard acknowledges the dominant/subordinate dialectic that exists, but he seeks to reframe the dialectic as a relationship that can be co-mutual and based on merit, not racial bias. Mr. Kennard juxtaposes the stance of the United States government and the Constitution to the stance of the Southern states related to the status of African Americans as citizens. That juxtaposition allows Mr. Kennard to make plain that the myth of patriotism and the myth of white supremacy are at odds. As it was then, it can be confidently stated that there is currently no systematic impartial arbiter of scholastic merit at Southern Miss. Consequently, we continue to experience asymmetry manifested as racial bias toward African American students and faculty.

Next, I apply the relational dialectical frame used by Mr. Kennard to the "Being Black at Southern Miss" video. Additionally, I assess the use of African American mythoforms. Therefore, this part of the analysis uses a deductive qualitative approach to assess the public appeal of the African American millennials in the video.

"Being Black at USM" — Millennials and Relational Tensions

I watched and transcribed, verbatim, the four minute and thirty-three second video titled "Being Black at Southern Miss." After doing so, I applied the relational dialectic framework derived from the analysis of Clyde Kennard's public appeals to the "Being Black at Southern Miss" video. The findings below outline the takeaways from this analytic approach.

Through a lens of integration versus segregation, the "Being Black at USM" video, made by students regarding their status at the University of Southern Mississippi, displays tension between *tumultuous* and *guardian* relational characterizations. The video begins with an African American female student being asked a question by an individual who is off screen, "How does it feel to be black at Southern Miss?" and she answers immediately, "It feels revolutionary, yet suppressing at the same time." The student expresses both suckling and suffering in the same utterance. She goes on to state that she feels that upon her entry into a classroom, which is typically populated with a majority of non–African Americans, she needs to "change a little bit . . . to politically be correct in the classroom." Another African American female student details how voting happens at USM. She asserts that during elections for Miss USM or the Homecoming court, there is racially polarized proselytizing and voting. Again, we see the framework of segregation and integration in contemporary times, but at the same institution, the University of Southern Mississippi.

Later in the piece, the same woman states, "I should be able to speak my mind and share my ideas and opinions as a black person and as a black woman, um . . . from an African American culture here in the United States of America. . . . Based on my experiences that I have brought to Southern Miss . . . it should make Southern Miss greater, it should make the classroom greater, I shouldn't have to change my identity . . . I should be able to add to the identity of the university." So, resisting or conforming to the desires of the dominant (white) group are ultimately the two options the student sees as viable for her in this relationship. Thus, the presence of dialectical mytho-forms result in a proliferation of possible and/or contested meanings to utterances common to asymmetrical interactions, which may result in inhibited mutual understanding thereby influencing the relational dialectical approach employed by publics.

Another student is asked about the disadvantages of being black at Southern Mississippi. The African American female student answers concisely, "Opportunity." She intimates that there is strong competition for opportunity between students, but that the non–African American students have a "strong sense of entitlement" that has a detrimental effect on the self-esteem of black students. Where resistance or conformance is the previous framework used, self-concept is highlighted from this student. Self-esteem is self-evaluation of yourself, which can be triggered from your interactions with others. Ostensibly, if the non-black student expresses a sense of deservedness of opportunity, it may manifest in her interactions that there is a lack of deservedness of opportunity for black students. For example, another black female student recalls being asked how she obtained an internship, apparently from a non–African American student, who assumed that she is exceptional or underserving of an internship due to race. Again, the proliferation of contested meanings of utterances from their peers leaves the students uncertain of how to approach their ongoing relationships.

Next, an African American male student from Texas contextualizes his feeling of being in the minority by contrasting the ethnic diversity that he sees in his native Texas to the lack of ethnic diversity present at USM, in other words, integration. Even so, he mentions that he does not feel a sense of alienation daily. We see this student give voice to the unevenness of publics at Southern Miss, but he also asserts that it is not a defining characteristic of his experience. As such, he seeks to compartmentalize, integrate, his experience within a set of experiences that is not defined by the myth of white supremacy.

Regarding the question of how relational characterizations are deployed, through the lens of the relational dialectics, African American millennial students seemingly shine light on the polysemy of signifiers regarding how students approach their relational engagements at USM. In reference to the question of how mythoforms influence relational characterization of publics related to race at USM, we see the students seeming to assume a similar true-believer status to Mr. Kennard, which undergirds exigence for making the video. Also, similar to Mr. Kennard, the suffering apparent in the utterances of the African American millennial students is indicative of a larger set of social relational tensions.

THE AUDACITY OF ASSERTING SYMMETRY

The myth of white supremacy functions as a defense against symmetry. It seems that millennial black students at USM are frozen in a place of inferiority and inherently a threat to a higher order. The constant reifying of mythical conceptions of white supremacy exist within structures, such as ideological apparatuses and in colloquy, that support the motivation to signify the relationship between African American and non–African American using the asymmetrical relational dialectic of dominant/subordinate. From this dialectic, myriad negative relational topoi stream forward such as: abusive, neglectful, authoritarian, lacking empathy, and so on (Burgoon & Hale, 1984). As an implication, we see the "Being Black at Southern Miss" video as commentary on the current relationship between African American and non–African American, which is supposedly based on merit, display a continued racial bias toward white supremacy.

To explain, motivation and polysemy are hallmarks of assessing signification of the historical association of signifiers and the signified. Motivation is undergirded by a feeling of loss and the need to protect and/or restore (Ehninger, Gronbeck, & McKerrow, 2000; Gresson, 1995). From this, the need to protect or to restore becomes paramount. Polysemy, as the proliferation of multiple meanings that may emanate from a syntagmatic chain of signs, leads us to a motivated sequence that may end with varying outcomes. Thus, the myth of white supremacy, which highlights the dominant/subordinate relational dialectical tension, exposes the desire of a public motivated to maintain and/or increase its dominance for fear of loss. In order to stave off loss of domination, a public may move to secure its position by denial or limitation of opportunity to other publics, such as asymmetry. Conversely, but simultaneously, those of the perceived subordinate public assert symmetry by employing a dialectical strategy that includes use of the *suffering* mythoform within a *tumultuous* relationship, for example, book of Job, while simultaneously displaying the *caring* characteristic of a *guardian relationship*, for example, Harriet Tubman. Resultant of the employment of the aforementioned dialectical strategy, by African Americans, a mythoform that has not been well researched in our present conception of African American mythoforms, the black patriot who is a true believer, such as Mr. Clyde Kennard, emerges.

The assumption of and even the audacity of asserting symmetry is what undergirds this project. The appeals discussed in this piece, decades apart, are ostensibly discussions about an assumed symmetry. The millennial students and Mr. Kennard are true believers in the promises of the United States. The millennial students made the video at a time when the president of the United States was an African American man, Barack Obama, while Mr. Kennard was a WWII veteran who had also been admitted to and who had succeeded at one of the best predominantly white schools in the nation, the University of Chicago.

There are obvious differences in the context of the appeals of the young people above. Of course, Mr. Kennard was not a millennial, but he was still a young man, thirty-two, when he wrote Dr. Aubrey Lucas about his desire to attend Mississippi Southern in 1959. To add, his first attempt to enroll at Mississippi Southern was when he was twenty-eight. Another similarity between Mr. Kennard and the black millennials students is their strategy of using a public appeal to foment deliberation about the relationship of black students to USM. This approach indeed led to discussions on campus and off campus, evidenced by the amount of social media exposure of the "Being Black at Southern Miss" video.

Unfortunately, Mr. Kennard never attended the Mississippi Southern College, USM. The cultural climate of overt racism is not the same due to myriad citizens who labor and continue to labor toward a "more perfect union." Regardless of the differences apparent between millennials in the "Being Black at USM" video and Mr. Kennard, they are alluding to similar prejudices, such as asymmetry, that operate as deep-seated myths by non-blacks that help lead to *disenchantment/alienation* by African Americans.

This work is limited in scope to a case study of African American millennials at the University of Southern Mississippi, but there are other examples of "Being Black" videos from other predominantly white institutions. (See, for instance, "Being Black" videos from Harvard, Columbia, Georgia, UCLA, USC and Stanford.) The array of videos, as public expressions, speaks to a desire to belong, in a larger context, for the true-believer guardian. Mr. Clyde Kennard's public appeals at a time when and in a state where the paucity between white and black was stark, unavoidable and seemingly insurmountable helps us to create a lens through which to view the mythoforms and the relational approaches at work for millennials. The millennial generation is the most highly educated, most likely to enjoy shared activities, tech savvy, entrepreneurial, and has the highest saturation of social media use. Even so, using social media as a vehicle for airing grievances remains a necessary method of combating white supremacy. As such, tumultuous and guardian relational approaches are paramount to achieving togetherness in our time.

REFERENCES

Arendt, H. (1958). *The human condition*. Chicago: The University of Chicago Press.

Asante, M. K. (2004). *The Afrocentric idea*. In Ed. Ronald L. Jackson II, *African American communication and identities*. Thousand Oaks, CA: Sage, 16–28.

Burgoon, J. K., & Hale, J. L. (1984). The fundamental topoi of relational communication. *Communication Monographs, 51*(3), 193–214.

Barthes, R. (1973). *Mythologies* (London: Paladin, 1973).

Baxter, L. A. (2004). A tale of two voices: Relational dialectics theory. *Journal of Family Communication, 4*(3-4), 181–192.

Baxter, L. A., & Babbie, E. (2004). *The basics of communication research*. Canada: Thomson Wadsworth.

Boeije, H. (2002). A purposeful approach to the constant comparative method in the analysis of qualitative interviews. *Quality and quantity, 36*(4), 391–409.

Boeije, H. (2009). *Analysis in qualitative research*. Thousand Oaks, CA: Sage Publications.

Carey, J. W. (1996). The Chicago School and mass communication research. In E. E. Dennis & E. A. Wartella (Ed.), *American communication research: The remembered history,* 21–38. New York: Routledge.

Coleman, M. J., Harris, T. M., Bryant, K. L., & Reif-Stice, C. (2018). A cultural approach to patriotism. *Journal of International and Intercultural Communication,* 1–19.

Dawson, M. C. (1995). *Behind the mule: Race and class in African-American politics*. Princeton, NJ: Princeton University Press.

Dawson, M. C. (2003). *Black visions: The roots of contemporary African-American political ideologies*. Chicago: University of Chicago Press.

DeLuca, M. K., & Peeples, J. (2002). From public sphere to public screen: Democracy, activism, and the "violence" of Seattle. *Critical Studies in Media Communication, 19*(2), 125–151.

Dewey, J., & Rogers, M. L. (2012). *The public and its problems: An essay in political inquiry*. University Park: Penn State Press.

Fraser, N. (1992). Rethinking the public sphere: A contribution to the critique of actually existing democracy. *Between borders: Pedagogy and the politics of cultural studies,* 74–98.

Gresson, A. D. (1995). *The recovery of race in America*. Minneapolis: University of Minnesota Press.

Grossberg, L. (1992). *We gotta get out of this place*. New York: Routledge.

Habermas, J. (1989). The structural transformation of the public sphere. *Polity, 7*(8).

Hall, S. (2001). Encoding/decoding. In M. G. Durham & D. M. Kellner (Eds.), *Media and cultural studies: Keyworks,* 137–145. Chichester, West Sussex: Wiley-Blackwell.

Hecht, M. L., Jackson, R. L., & Ribeau, S. A. (2003). *African American communication: Exploring identity and culture*. Mahwah, NJ: Routledge.

hooks, b. (2004). *The will to change: Men, masculinity, and love*. New York: Simon and Schuster.

Kennard, C. (1958, December 6). Mixing. *The Hattiesburg American*, p. 2A.

Kennard, C. (1959, September 25). The race question. *The Hattiesburg American*, p. 6A.

Kennard, C. (1960, January 23). School mixing. Mississippi Department of Archives and History, Sovereignty Commission Archives, SCR ID # 1-27-0-58-1-1-1. Retrieved from: http://www.mdah.ms.gov/arrec/digital_archives/sovcom/result.php?image=images/png/cd01/002203.png&lotherstuff=1|27|0|58|1|1|1|2145|#'.

McGowan, J. (2015, December 29). *Being Black at USM* [Video file]. Retrieved from https://youtu.be/8ij9meUxgbM.

McKerrow, R. E., Gronbeck, B. E., Ehninger, D., & Monroe, A. H. (2000). *Principles and types of speech communication*. New York: Longman.

Minchin, T. J., & Salmond, J. A. (2011). *After the dream: Black and White southerners since 1965*. Lexington: University Press of Kentucky.

Mississippi Department of Archives and History. Sovereignty Commission Archives SCR ID # 1-27-0-37-1-1-1. Retrieved from: http://www.mdah.ms.gov/arrec/digital_archives/sovcom/result.php?image=images/png/cd01/002145.png&otherstuff=1|27|0|37|1|1|1|2090|.

Mississippi Department of Archives and History. Sovereignty Commission Archives SCR ID # 1-27-0-29-1-1-1. Retrieved from: http://www.mdah.ms.gov/arrec/digital_archives/sovcom/result.php?image=images/png/cd01/002090.png&otherstuff=1|27|0|29|1|1|1|2041|.

Owen, W. F. (1984). Interpretive themes in relational communication. *Quarterly journal of Speech, 70*(3), 274–287.

Pew Research Center. (2018). Social media use in 2018: Demographics and statistics. Retreived on January 15, 2019, from: http://www.pewinternet.org/2018/03/01/social-media-use-in-2018/.

Squires, C. R. (2002). Rethinking the black public sphere: An alternative vocabulary for multiple public spheres. *Communication Theory, 12*(4), 446–468.

Wahyuni, D. (2012). The research design maze: Understanding paradigms, cases, methods and methodologies. *Journal of Applied Management Accounting Research, 10*(1), 69–80.

Wanzo, R. (2009). Wearing hero-face: Black citizens and melancholic patriotism in truth: Red, white, and black. *The Journal of Popular Culture, 42*(2), 339–362.

Welsh, K., & Asante, M. K. (1981). Myth: The communication dimension to the African American mind. *Journal of Black Studies, 11*(4), 387–395.

Chapter Thirteen

Making Meaning of the Messages

Black Millennials, Film and Critical Race Media Literacy

Jayne Cubbage

Students in a course titled Media Literacy in a Diverse Society at a historically black university in a Mid-Atlantic state (where the author served as an adjunct instructor) were required to complete an analysis of three films that explored themes of racial dynamics with a focus on millennials. Given that the class was held during the spring 2018 semester, which saw the release of the blockbuster hit *Black Panther*, students were already eager to further dissect the important and poignant messages in this film. Drawing on previous discussions of the film, which ventured beyond mere entertainment for many of the students with its talk of nation building, liberation, wealth generation and, of course, the all-important "good vs. evil" (not to mention the costumes and the cinematography), students were asked to write a review of another movie they had seen in recent months, and that assignment led to the final class project, a group assignment (Cooper, 2009).

In a discussion of that assignment, students were asked to name a few movies in recent years that held similar themes to *Black Panther* or, at the very least, made audiences think about issues that are important to people of color. Accordingly, the students identified two additional films, *Get Out* and *Dear White People,* to examine for their final projects. The class was divided into three groups, and each group was assigned one film to present to the class. During their presentations, the groups were instructed to discuss three main themes: messaging to black millennials, media literacy themes and their own take as a group on the movie, including how they would change the ending of each if they were the director of the film.

Using critical race media literacy theory (Agodzo, 2016; King, 2017; Kohnen & Lacy, 2018; Yosso, 2002), this essay explores the themes of race and millennials as well as their understanding of contemporary film and targeted messaging in films directed at black millennials. As such, the purpose of this chapter is to use my class as a way to understand and reveal the number of ways that black millennials process information and messaging in films targeted toward their group, particularly those issues related to race and social justice. The primary importance of exploring such pedagogy, especially within a media literacy framework, is to highlight and to stress the need for added discussion of race within media literacy education.

These concepts and their importance are discussed in the work of various media literacy scholars (Kellner & Share, 2007; Stuckey & Kring, 2007; Yosso, 2002) who express the value of critical and variant approaches to media interpretation. From a pedagogical and sociological perspective, the predominate themes, which are applicable to black millennials yet are not fully representative or designed to be a monolithic approach, are outlined in the work of Rogowski and Cohen (2015). They cite social media, employment, social justice, education, healthcare, political inclusion and political efficacy as strong concerns of this generation. Further, news articles by and about black millennials (Allen, 2019; Sharp, 2014; Simmons, 2017) echo similar themes and reinforce the notion that black millennials are adept at social media and are keenly aware of rampant cultural appropriation.

Mainstream cinema is one of the few forms of mainstream media that black millennials can look to if they want to see their viewpoints expressed and find a form of both self-expression and cultural recognition. While black filmmakers have struggled since the advent of filmmaking to gain control of the black image and to steer the dominant culture from appropriating and profiting from stereotypical caricatures of black people, there has been *some* progress (Reich, 2016; Rhines, 2003). Films in the 2010s, as opposed to the Blaxploitation era of the 1970s, have more fully representative characters that properly reflect the vast tapestry of black life in America. Some of those films have even garnered mainstream support and have been wildly popular (Everett, 2014; Seymour, 2001).

One well-known example is the film *Black Panther*, which, although a creation of Marvel Comics and distributed and produced by Disney and the brain trust of two white, Jewish men, was directed by Ryan Coogler (Feige & Coogler, 2018), an African American, and featured a predominately black cast. The blockbuster hit garnered over $1.35 billion dollars in domestic and foreign box office sales and was re-released in August 2018 due to ongoing demand for theater showings in addition to its scheduled release on pay-per-view television and DVD (McNary, 2018). Another mega hit, which garnered box office gold and even an Oscar nod and other cinematic acclaim for the director, Jordan Peele (Blum & Peele, 2017), is the staid yet poignant "soft horror" film *Get Out*. This movie surpassed box office estimates and made over $254 million in sales globally (The Numbers, 2017).

A third film, *Dear White People*, released in 2014 with much less fanfare, did not have the blockbuster success as *Black Panther* and *Get Out*. Its themes were distinctly about the experiences of black students at predominately white universities, depicting the experiences of black students at a fictitious Ivy League institution, Winchester University, who were trying to find their place and to learn how to navigate the world of white dominance. Reviewers felt the movie fell far short of what it could have accomplished, and its global box office net of $5.4 million was far less than *Black Panther* or *Get Out* (The Numbers, 2018). Yet the themes (and provocative title) of *Dear White People* do in fact carry much weight and speak, if however haltingly, about a common experience in the black community and among black millennials—how to get along with "wipeepo" while away at college and in society in general. Accordingly, the less than stellar performance at the box office notwithstanding, the movie provided much fodder for discussion, and the film was spun off into a Netflix original series for a broader and more extensive take on the experiences of black students at Winchester University.

Each of these movies has several commonalities. They are each directed by an African American director. Each film features a theme of racial identity, and each discusses and addresses the issue of justice and equity. Given the age of each of the directors, the films can be seen as primarily targeting black millennials. Justin Simien directed *Dear White People* at age 25, and Ryan Coogler directed *Black Panther* at 32. Jordan Peele, director of *Get Out,* is the elder of the three at 40. To his credit, Peele adroitly negotiates the fine line that many Gen X/Millennial "cuspians" do so well by appealing to both groups. For Peele, *Get Out* has stark resonance for millennial audiences, with high instances for resonance for both Gen Xers and Boomers (Henderson, 2017).

Given the high levels of appeal for millennials for each film, it was a logical step to include each of them as a part of an assignment for a media literacy class. This class was held during the spring semester in 2018. The class is a general education class and students from various majors across the university curriculum were enrolled for a total of twenty-five students. Although the university is classified as a historically black university (HBCU), the demographics of the class were diverse, if minimally so. While the predominant number of enrollees were African Americans having been born in the United States, a number of the students indicated that they were from African nations such as Nigeria, Sierra Leone and Ghana. Two students hailed from the Middle East, one from Saudi Arabia and another from Yemen. One white student, from Sweden, was also enrolled. A number of students who appeared to be black pointedly classified themselves as Hispanic or Latinx, and others cited mixed ethnicities and racc. Other students said they were of Caribbean origin, either as émigrés or whose parents were immigrants from the islands.

Regarding identity politics, most students, no matter their ethnic origin, identified with "the struggle" and strongly identified with their status as black millennials; they were also clear in their sense that, as people of color, they are in fact marginalized members in American society. All of the students were "traditional" students (between the ages of 18 and 25) and classified as undergraduates.

During the course of the semester, the students in the course explored a number of components of media literacy, which is officially defined as the ability to access, analyze, evaluate, produce and act upon media messages (Hobbs, 2010a; National Association for Media Literacy Education (NAMLE), 2007). In this exploratory course, we analyzed several media genres, including television, radio, newspapers, the internet and film. Assignments are given to the students and are designed to not only teach them about the manner in which the media work, but to also examine the way media messages impact communities of color and other marginalized segments of society. In addition to discussion of the primary tenets of media literacy in this class, all assignments and discussions are predicated upon three premises: First, they are asked to examine the primary purpose and theme of each message—who created it and for what audience. Second, students consider the economic elements of each media message and genre—who paid for it and how much did it cost. Finally, students discussed their feelings or beliefs about the messages; if they responded that they didn't like it or had a problem with a message, we explored "what can be *done* about it?"

When the blockbuster hit *Black Panther* was released in theaters in the United States and globally in February of 2018, the students saw the film and were excited about the themes portrayed, the characters, the emancipatory potential, as well as the cinematography and costumes. The film's release was timed well to set up the final group assignment, and the class was asked to divide themselves into three groups, based upon student preferences, to analyze one of three films, *Black Panther*, *Dear White People* or *Get Out*. As noted previously, each film was selected because of its high attention to millennial themes—social media, social justice, political inclusion and political efficacy—and because each film featured an African American director.

This assignment required that the students assess movie reviews of their films from *The New Yorker*, *The New York Times*, *Variety* and *Rotten Tomatoes* and write a group paper on what the reviews stated about the film and whether or not the group agreed with the reviews, essentially asking the students to explore the differences between the reviewers' opinions of the film and their own opinion. The exercise itself was designed to acculturate students to the process of reviewing a film.

In addition to the paper, the students were required to prepare a twenty-minute presentation on their group's film that would provide an overview of the group's ideas and opinions about the film. For the PowerPoint presentation, students were required to distribute speaking roles among the group, allowing each member to discuss various points, to open the presentation with a clip of the film and to include a question and answer session at the end. The assignment was designed to allow students to consider the intersections within the pedagogy of media literacy education, such as race, gender and socioeconomic background, and it presented an important opportunity for enhanced focus on media literacy through the lens of popular film. Next, using textual analysis, I will examine the students' responses in order to answer the following questions: 1) How do black millennials interpret and respond to messages in movies which are targeted to their demographic? 2) What themes in movies targeted to black millennials are most resonant with students? 3) What do black millennials think directors who have targeted them in their movies leave out of their respective films?

CRITICAL RACE MEDIA LITERACY

The theoretical component of this chapter is critical race media literacy (Agodzo, 2016; King, 2017; Kohnen & Lacy, 2018; Mills, 1997; Yosso, 2002). The concept is an offshoot of both critical race theory (CRT) and critical media literacy. The premise of critical race media literacy theory is that the exploration of media literacy without the full understanding of how media serve as a conduit of racism and white supremacy is a discussion that is short sided, particularly when the subjects are persons of color and who are learning how to navigate their way a through media-saturated, digitized society. Additionally, theorists argue that students form marginalized groups must learn to name the ways in which they are oppressed in order to facilitate a proper pathway to liberation and to knowledgably face down the power elite (hooks, 1994; Yosso, 2002). Other media literacy scholars, such as Kellner and Share (2007), suggest an examination of "who gets to say, what to whom and why and how?" Without these discussions, there is a mere repetition of existing hegemonic themes that only reinforce the status quo and the practices and priorities of the dominant culture.

Media literacy is typically defined by many scholars including, Aufderheid and Firestone (1993), Hobbs (2010a) and the National Association of Media Literacy Education (2007) as the ability to access, analyze, evaluate, produce and act upon media messages. Further, NAMLE along with other media literacy advocacy institutions urge media consumers to consider, along with the business mandates of most media, the authorship of media messages, how those messages may be interpreted by different audiences, what is missing from media messages and what the purpose of such messages is.

In addition to media literacy, Kellner and Share (2007) advocate for critical media literacy. They argue that media literacy alone is not enough and that while media consumers may learn to access, analyze, produce, evaluate and act upon media message, they must also engage in all of these processes with an even greater critical eye in order to understand the various inner workings of media systems, how these processes impact their lives and the quality of the information they receive—*or don't* receive—along with the appropriate action necessary to facilitate change. Critical media literacy leads to discussion of critical race theory and media literacy as related and interconnected concepts.

Critical race theory is defined by scholars (Delgado & Stefanic, 2001; Hiraldo, 2010) as the examination and impetus to change the imbalanced and racialized impact on marginalized groups in society. More specifically, CRT unabashedly addresses disparities that are a result of social dominance of one group over another. Stated specifically and referencing the social and racial dynamic in the United States under the systems of white supremacy and capitalism, CRT not only examines and discusses vast structural inequalities (i.e., social, economic, educational and political inequalities), it serves to eradicate the impact of existing inequalities through the use of five tenets: counter storytelling; the permanence of racism; whiteness as property; interest conversation; and the critique of liberalism (Hiraldo, 2010, p. 54). Through this process, Delgado and Stefanic (2001, p. 3) assert that CRT questions the very assumptions and foundations of liberal order.

Similarly, critical race media literacy, as detailed in the work of Kohnen and Lacy (2018, p. 104), which sites the work of King (2017), Mills (1997) and Yosso (2002), asserts that because media create a racial contract, in which the "dominant culture" appoints societal roles and avows a position of authority with an assumed priority for themselves, while at the same time ascribing inferior and second-class status to non-whites, media must be examined with this social construct in mind. With regard to adding critical race media literacy to educational settings, Agodzo (2016) argues that the concept and theoretical frame is useful in raising the "critical consciousness of students with regard to challenging prevailing racial deficit ideologies and discourse" (p. 25). She argues further in favor of its incorporation into the media literacy dialogue and as a part of multicultural curriculum, stating, "Critical race media literacy, as demonstrated by Yosso (2002), can provide a helpful pedagogic framework for educators in bringing a social justice orientation to issues of race and racism in today's globalized classrooms" (p. 30).

Collectively, each concept allows for the full exploration of race as a structural barrier and filter, and the manner in which media systems, which are platforms and conduits of dominant culture narratives, can be examined by members of marginalized groups who in coming to a full understanding of their own condition and the premise under which these constraints have materialized can forge a path of liberation for themselves and others. While this is a seemingly ambitious notion to undertake during the course of an undergraduate media literacy class, it is a necessary tool in establishing the pathway to emancipation from oppressive systems. For groups and students who are keenly aware of their otherness and the notion that they are indeed oppressed, a language of expression along with solid documented examples of hegemony, defined as the political, cultural and economic dominance of one group over another (Lull, 2011), are apt for this and similar works.

In addition to themes of liberation and literacy, the notion of black film studies and criticism is also important for this work. Film studies scholars underscore the historic struggle of African Americans to gain inclusion into the elite image-based system of Hollywood, but they also recognize an increase in the number of black films that do provide a balanced representation of the African American community; however, they argue that more improvement is needed (Everett, 2014; Reich, 2016).

Other film scholars (Cranmer & Harris, 2015; Stuckey & Kring, 2007) point to the utility of film and film criticism as an effective means of interpreting both racialized messages and gaining increased critical media literacy skills, particularly in educational environments. Stuckley and Kring (2007, p. 25) write, "Movies can also be a particularly useful tool for developing critical media literacy in education settings; they help students learn how to analyze the ways in which gender, race, ethnicity, class, and sexual orientation . . . are portrayed in film." Cranmer and Harris (2015) add that by employing critical race theory to analyze film and their relation to societal phenomena that "film can be an effective tool for social justice by uncovering and highlighting implicit social injustices" (p. 154). It is in that spirit that this textual analysis of my students' responses to three films proceeds.

MILLENNIAL ANALYSIS OF THREE FILMS

Black Panther

Group 1—the group that analyzed *Black Panther*—shared a number of viewpoints regarding the issues addressed in the film and how they related to black millennials. They wrote,

> *Black Panther* addresses many issues regarding the concerns of Black Millennials in America, such as inequality. The film begins with a scene of black youth playing basketball at a local park, except the basketball net was replaced by an actual basket symbolizing poverty in black communities. Additionally, Erik Killmonger (portrayed in the film by actor Michael B. Jordan) was uti-

lized to personify the common negative energy black youths have towards social inequality in their communities. Ryan Coogler references the mass incarceration rates and the lack of resources in communities as well.

Group 1 also spoke of the technological advancement portrayed in *Black Panther* as well as the prospect of an independent black state:

> This film is filled with a projection of possibilities. The current generation is defined with technology amidst frequent innovations and creativity. The film entails fictitious entities such as advanced sky locomotives that may suit the current rage of technology. The current generation may therefore borrow a leaf from these fictions and fabricate a real design into being. Apart from technology, the film addresses current themes such as power. The quest for power has led to many conflicts even in the current generation, thus making it an important issue of concern.

They also shared that they particularly enjoyed the portrayal of Killmonger in the film and that they felt his character closely resembled that of Malcolm X. Of the character Killmonger, they stated:

> Growing up, he learned more about his native country through notes his father left behind. Realizing [he was abandoned by his own people], he made it a mission to someday go back to Wakanda and take what he deserved. His underlying purpose was to help those in poverty around the world using Wakandian technologies. Earlier in the movie we find that the Wakandians are an isolated people and do not want to share. The thing about Killmonger that resonates with the group is that his aggressive personality resembles that of Malcolm X. The two individuals resemble each other because they didn't care if they had to use violence to get what they wanted. Also, they didn't strive for African Americans to be equal to Whites. They wanted Black superiority.

Overall, the students who presented on *Black Panther* were delighted with the movie. While they expressed some reservation about the use of the Everett K. Ross (portrayed by actor Martin Freeman) character, he seemed more like "a Marvel add-on," and they stated that they would have liked to have seen more development of a few other characters. For instance, the students felt like they were left hanging and wanted more from the character Nikia (who was played by the actress Lupita Nyong'o), and they said she was "underused" despite being listed as a main character and that her part "showed a great deal of promise at the beginning of the movie." They added that they felt Nikia was outshined in her role by the other more dominant characters in the movie such as Shuri (portrayed by the actress Letitia Wright), T'Challa's sister and scientist, and Okoye (who was played by actress Danai Gurira), head of the Wakandian army.

Once the students' presentation was completed, they were instructed to open the floor up to the entire class and the instructor and lead a discussion on the film. The response was resounding. Students in the audience as well as students in the presentation discussed multiple aspects of the movie and everyone wanted to express their opinion about the movie. Upon restoring order, the discussion centered around several talking points, applying the themes in *Black Panther* to African Americans. Asked if it was possible for there to be an independent black nation, the students said "yes." Wealth and income inequality also featured prominently in the discussion. Some students initially responded that they didn't think Wakanda should open its doors to others as had been originally planned in the film. Others were relieved when T'Challa/Black Panther (played by Chawick Boseman) changed his mind and actually decided to go back to Oakland where Killmonger had come from to fund a few programs for inner-city youth.

As the instructor, I asked, "Do you think that is enough?" Some students emphatically stated, "YES!! What else do you think they should DO???" I replied, "Wakanda is one of the wealthiest nations on EARTH—", another student interjected "Wakanda is *THE WEALTHIEST* nation on Earth—!" "Ok," I responded. "Wakanda is the WEALTHIEST NATION on EARTH, and you all think it is ACCEPTABLE to open the equivalent of a Boys and Girls Club to help the less fortunate? What about *income equality*?" Another student emphatically countered, feeling challenged: "Those kinds of programs *DO* help people. A lot of people get their start there and go on to do good things in their life," to which I replied, "Yes, that is correct, I am simply asking all of you to think about whether that is ENOUGH?" This statement caused a strong division in the class, with some stating that people need to work for their own money, and that no one should give *anyone, anything*. Others felt that there should be a gradual sharing of wealth once others were educated and given more financial literacy.

The discussion also netted comments from African students about "phony African accents" and cultural suggestions from the movie that made too many assumptions about the continent of Africa as a whole and its people, particularly the cultural practices and language and speech patterns.

Dear White People

Group 2 conducted their presentation on the film *Dear White People*. The group's presentation proved to be most creative, featuring a reenactment of the film's primary theme, "If you could tell White people, or '*wipeepo,*' one thing, what would that be?" Students from Group 2 opened their presentation with a skit of their own: As they sat in a semicircle at the front of the class, each member of the group spoke their truth to whites, which included statements that counter the existing narrative that is believed to reflect the opinion of black millennials in general, such as clarification of ethnicity, the fact that they do in fact have a two-parent household, that society is not post-racial because a black president was elected recently, and that they do actually have "real hair" among other similar statements. One chilling statement noted that one student struggled with self esteem based on the opinions of whites about her. A white student in the class interjected humor into the presentation by stating that she doesn't even patronize a certain coffee shop which had experienced a racial insensitivity in recent days.

This comment incited widespread chuckles among students, given that it was made by the lone white person in the class in the aftermath of a recent racially charged event at a famous national coffee chain (Stevens, 2018).

Regarding journalistic reviews of the film, the students in Group 2 appeared to think the reviews were at least fair. They didn't have strong opinions of the reviewers' statements one way or the other and highlighted three sample statements from each of the reviews of the film. One review from *The New Yorker* wrote that "*Dear White People* doesn't risk controversy—rather it stimulates controversy" (McNary, 2018). Another cited a review that stated that director Mark Simien "serves harsh medicine with remarkable charm and good humor." A third review, in *Variety*, stated: "Meanwhile, en route to its explosive 'African-American-themed party' climax, which owes something to recent history and something to *Do the Right Thing*, the story wanders in a few less-than-productive directions."

The students said that both the movie's title and even some of the less-than-favorable reviews merely served as bait for would-be filmgoers to be inticed to see the film. They think the reviews were "successful" overall. Regarding the issues in the film that were related to millennials, Group 2 actually agreed with the reviewer in *Variety* that *Dear White People* evoked themes similar to those in *Do the Right Thing*, but they felt that the themes were, indeed, "half cooked." They stated that some of the themes simply needed to be explored further such as the interracial dating and the power structure on college campuses.

The themes in *Dear White People* that addressed concerns or issues specific to black millennials noted by Group 2 were natural hair styles and the importance of portraying women and men in their natural state, rather than having them appear different than what they really are. They noted the variety of themes that were centered around sexuality, sexuality identity and discrimination in the film, noting that this is a particularly salient topic for black millennials today, and they were satisfied that this topic was even addressed in the film. They also pointed out issues of racial identity in the film and discussed the concept of needing to choose a side in today's politically fractured environment.

After the group presentation, other students were then polled about which elements their group found lacking or issues that were not covered in the film. They responded by stating that the movie lacked clear and properly defined role models for the students on campus to learn from. They also noted that Dean Fairbanks (portrayed by actor Dennis Haysbert) was not "black enough" and appeared to be a "sell out," as he was portrayed as not really being interested in helping or hearing about the plight of black students in the film. Students also suggested that there could have been more instances in the film where the characters displayed a healthier dose of "self love." One said, "You didn't really see a lot of self love, each person really kind of struggled with who they are."

Further, they noted that Samantha White, the biracial lead character and host of the radio program "Dear White People" (portrayed by Tessa Thompson), appeared to be confused about her racial identity and as the lead female character in the film the students felt that her character and her subsequent identity confusion sent a conflicting message to audience members about who black women are. Students in this group also spoke about the missing climax scene in the film, where all of the issues and characters converge in a flash point to foster resolution by the end of the film. Finally, the group noted that even though the movie was situated on a college campus, there needed to be some treatment of police brutality in the film. Students stated that campus police are notorious for engaging in heavy-handed tactics at campus parties and other events when students of color are in attendance, as opposed to such gatherings with whites, who typically enjoy a lack of police presence.

Students also stated that it was shortsighted for the director to avoid inclusion of the recent killings of African Americans by police as this film was released in 2014 in the aftermath of several highly publicized killings. Further, they noted that if they could change anything about *Dear White People*, they would have developed stronger rallying themes in the movie that tackled deeper issues beyond "dorm rights and a blackface party."

On the other hand, Group 2 heaped praise upon their favorite character, Lionel Higgins (portrayed by Tyler James Williams), who they described as a hero because of his stand against the scene at the blackface party. They also noted that throughout the movie Lionel didn't want to necessarily pick sides, but after encountering blatant racism, this character ultimately recognized his blackness and he understood clearly which side he was on.

During the class discussion of *Dear White People*, the strongest sentiment expressed by the class was about the issue of interracial dating. Black millennials subscribe to the notion in many cases that "you love who you love" and that while race *does* matter, they don't see why love choices should be limited. They further expanded their views on black college life and the experiences at predominantly white institutions (PWIs) versus those at HBCUs. Many students expressed relief that they attended an HBCU rather than a PWI. Students also noted that the series on Netflix appeared to treat many of the issues that were missing from the film. Just as with Group 1, the ensuing class discussion was racoucious and lively. Students again were delighted to share their thoughts about the film and the various elements of the issues discussed.

Get Out

As noted previously, when polling students on their preferred movie to discuss for the final group assignment, an overwhelming majority chose *Get Out*. As such, students had to be moved from this group in order to create a more balanced number of students in the other groups. Group 3 opened their presentation by showing a trailer of the film. The trailer highlighted the primary scene from the movie, which depicts the moment that Chris (portrayed by Daniel Kaluuya) realized that he was in a mental and physical fight for his life as he struggled to avoid permanent placement into the "sunken place." Once the trailer ended, students sat in reflective silence for a moment before Group 3 proceeded with the presentation. After discussion of the actors in the film, the group's discussion turned to the journalistic reviews that each group was assigned to read and review collectively.

Overall, the students stated that they thought the reviewers (from *The New York Times*, *The New Yorker*, *Variety* and *Rotten Tomatoes*) were largely fair. They noted that the reviewers were mostly favorable of the film and that they agreed with the major points of the reviews. The students said that there was a point of contention when it came to how each of the professional reviewers rated each film. The students also mentioned that while each reviewer wrote positive things about the film, when it came to assigning a score or an overall rating, the reviewers gave *Get Out* a less than perfect score in every instance (e.g., they cited one score which gave the movie an 8.3/10 and another review which scored it a 4.2/5), and the students saw this as contradictory and racially motivated. Of the critics' reviews they noted the racial disparity in the reviews and didn't feel that director Jordan Peele was given proper praise for the film because it was not ever rated perfectly despite the overall favorable opinions of the film. The students in this group found this troubling given that Peele is black and said they believed that he was glossed over in some respects.

The students cited *Get Out* director Jordan Peele and his reason for making the film in the first place, "to challenge the experience of being an African-American and to expose the lie of post-racial America" (Ramos, 2017). They also stated that film exposed the "identity crisis" which impacts both black and white communities, noting that whites often, as depicted in the film, want to benefit from the best of African American culture, and that they secretly want the physical features and characteristics (cultural, sexual, athletic) of blacks, while outwardly hating them. Regarding blacks or African Americans, they wrote of the benighted experience many find themselves in and how this leads to the process of a lack of awareness which was represented in the film as the "sunken place." The students themselves named this phenomenon "black oblivion" or "black ignorance." They also noted that they were pleased with how realistic the events in the film were because, in their words, themes depicted in the film truly reflected current issues relating to race in the United States today.

The group identified themes in *Get Out* that were directly related to many occurrences in society today, such as the prevalence of racism, "liberal racism" and white supremacy. However, Group 3 related that the primary concern for millennials that was addressed in the film related to the ongoing challenges faced by black millennials and their experiences in daily life in the United States. They firmly asserted and reaffirmed that black people in the United States are still subject to blatant racism, and they face several co-indignities such as cultural appropriation and lack of recognition of actual successes and their contributions to society and the world. They stated that these tactics are part of the overall strategy of the dominant culture to maintain a state of confused oppression and to denounce the hard work and style of black people.

Given the students' favorable opinion of *Get Out*, they did have a few comments on what they would have liked to see developed further in the film. First, they noted that the scene in the movie with Hiroku Tanyaka, the Asian character (played by Yasuhiko Oyama), was underdeveloped. They wanted more on the background on this character and felt that the viewer was left to determine what his role was in the film and how Peele interpreted the role of Asian Americans in the United States today. They also noted that the comment about the deer made by Rose's father, Dean Armitage (played by Bradley Whitford), who when told that Chris and Rose (portrayed by Allison Williams) hit a deer on the way up to the family home excitedly remarked, "It's one of thousands that is dead, but it's a start." Again, the students wanted a deeper explanation of this scene and particularly the comment. Astutely, they determined by guessing that black people are continually devalued and demeaned in U.S. society, while at the same time are "targeted for destruction and demise." The idea was that animals may receive better treatment than black people in some cases. This analysis is apt in that the theme of the deer is represented in the film by Chris and his expression in the "sunken place," which is also akin to that of one who is looking like "a deer *frozen* in the headlights."

Despite these concerns about the film, the students gave kudos to their favorite character, Rod (played by Lil Rel Howrey), who they cited as being that proverbial "friend in need" who displayed the keen characteristics of loyalty *and* devotion to his "Boy" or "Boi," a quality these (mostly) black millennial students asserted that they *prize highly*. Of Rod they stated that he was a "ride or die" kind of friend who would stay with you until the end and never let you down. They noted that throughout the film Rod kept checking on Chris and, when he believed his friend was in trouble, he went to find him. Additionally, they stated that even though Chris was benighted or "asleep," he eventually "woke up" and that he "slowly started to figure out that something was wrong." Their final comment about characters in the film caused a resonant chuckle among the class about the plight of black characters in any horror film and their "kill status" or longevity in the script. They wrote that Chris's ability to survive for the duration of the film amounted to a cinematic anomaly for black characters.

Regarding what Group 3 would actually change about the ending of the film, they creatively titled a section of their presentation "I'm in the Chair" and named three alternative endings for the film. In Scenario 1, Chris figures out early on who Rose and her parents are and leaves. However, Rose is able to convince Chris that she was hypnotized by her parents into doing these deeds. Chris believes her and ultimately Rose goes on a killing spree unbeknownst to Chris, but he is the only person who will be able to stop her—if he ever finds out what she is up to. In Scenario 2: Upon arrival to the Armitage home, Chris gets a weird "vibe" from the family and decides to leave. As he tries to leave and once outside the home, he discovers that he is being followed—everywhere he goes. Since he can't seem to "shake them," he decides to "join them," and after trying to tell others about the family "secret," since he is not ultimately believed, he endeavors to fight them from "the inside." In Scenario 3, once Chris begins to see and understand what is happening with Rose and her family, they convince him that he is mistaken and that everything is indeed "ok." But Chris knows he is NOT mistaken and begins to "go crazy" and decides to leave. Rose goes out after him and she is able to call him and states that she was hypnotized by her parents, too. Before he can end the call, she "clinks a spoon on a tea cup and the screen goes black."

Again, as with the other two films, the class discussion about *Get Out* and the presentation for Group 3 was lively. Students were eager to discuss themes from the film and how they relate to the millennial generation first and foremost, then to the African American community and to society at large.

FILM, BLACK MILLENNIALS
AND CRITICAL RACE MEDIA LITERACY

For *Black Panther*, the themes were technology, black wealth, black superiority and independence, and social justice black power. In *Dear White People*, the resonant themes were natural hair, sexuality and discrimination. Identity issues among black students who try to assimilate at PWIs were also prevalent themes. The themes presented in *Get Out* included cultural appropriation, friendship, loyalty and black ignorance. The students related to these themes easily and identified them in the film due to their resonance and perhaps given the directors of each these movies were black millennials themselves. Generally, students in the class responded positively to messages and seemed to accept the notion that the increased number of films targeted to their group was normal and acceptable. They stated that they were particularly concerned with the authenticity of messages, which are presented in each film and are keen on whether they accept or resonate with themselves personally or among their peers.

For *Black Panther*, the students appeared to want to see more discussion of equality and the differences among poorer and wealthy blacks. For *Dear White People*: There were not enough proper role models, no real climax scene of the movie, and the blackface party was a bit of a letdown and not a proper way to discuss the issues necessary in the film. The students also felt that the issue of police brutality was missing and not treated in the film despite being a central issue impacting African Americans in daily life. Although *Get Out* was well received, the students expressed concern over their ability to interpret some of the messaging in the film surrounding racialized comments or characters who were neither black or white.

Black millennials are heavy media users. In the media they consume, they are keenly aware of messages that are targeted toward them directly. They, like many other media audience segments, feel and take in the components of the messages they find resonant, and also as in the case of others, they reject and aptly interpret themes that are not of their liking (Kohnen & Lacy, 2018; Yosso, 2002). This is reflected in the work of Stuckey and Kring (2007, p. 25), who write: "Movie viewers often discuss characters with whom they relate, and their comments often reflect parts of their own narratives." Because the three films reviewed as part of the assignment were black themed and featured African American directors, these films were seen as highly favorable by the group of students, who were mostly black. While they viewed most of the themes in the films as favorable, there were aspects of each film that each of the groups and their peers named as either confusing, troubling or odd, and they each expressed ways in which they would either change or redirect the ending or other components of each film. This suggests active media consumption because they are thinking about the way a movie or film could have been played differently in each instance. Though this assignment was for a class, the students were eager to provide their own interpretation of each film and state their opinion about the themes present and about their experience as persons of color in the United States today.

This process is the beginning of critical media literacy and in the instance where race is a central part of a film's theme and/or when the audience is of color, critical race media literacy. Both media literacy and critical media literacy are important foundations for the media-consuming audience, and critical race media literacy scholars (Agodzo, 2016; Yosso, 2002) posit that as race serves as the backdrop for the entire social, political and economic structure in the United States, to engage in critical consumption of any media product, particularly those with a heavy dose of race-based themes and non-white characters, which are also targeted to audiences of color and others, failure to incorporate the themes of critical race media literacy is shortsighted and would amount to an ineffective discussion on media literacy.

Because this study was conducted informally and was formed as a basis for a class assignment, it is in no way reflective of a consensus on critical race media literacy, black film criticism and media literacy in general. What it does reflect, however, are the opinions and perspectives of the students in the class, Media Literacy in a Diverse Society, and their interpretation of the themes and targeted messages to black millennials in *Black Panther*, *Dear White People* and *Get Out*. On the other hand, each film provided an opportunity to delve deeper into the concepts of critical race media literacy, media literacy and film criticism within the context of both the group assignment and the course itself. Further studies on this topic can replicate this work and expound upon it by creating a larger group of students to discuss not only film, but also other media content that is salient and relevant to black millennials and to create a database of information on this particular segment of the media-consuming audience.

REFERENCES

Agodzo, D. (2016). "Burying their heads in the sand": Critical race media literacy & Surrey School District teachers. *Multicultural Education, 24*(1), 25–30. Retrieved from: https://www.thefreelibrary.com/%22Burying+their+heads+in+the+sand%22%3a+critical+race+media+literacy+%26...-a0491611089.

Allen, R. (2019, January 5). The American dream isn't for black millennials. Newyorktimes.com. Retrieved from: https://www.nytimes.com/2019/01/05/opinion/sunday/american-dream-black-millennials-homeownership.html.

Alverman, D. E., & Hagood, M. C. (2000). Critical media literacy: Research, theory and practice in "new times." *The Journal of Educational Research, 93*(3), 193–204. doi: 10.1080/00220670009598707.

Aufderheid, P., & Firestone, C. (1993). *Media literacy: A report of the national leadership conference on media literacy.* [Report] Queenstown, MD: Aspen Institute.

Blum, J. (Producer), & Peele, J. (Director). (2017). *Get Out.* United States: Universal Pictures.

Cooper, C. (2009). *Movie/film review lesson plan.* Retrived from: http://www.smalltowncritic.com/downloads/.

Cranmer, G. A., & Harris, T, M. (2015). "White-side, strong side": A critical examination of race and leadership in *Remember the Titans. Howard Journal of Communications, 26*(2), 153–171. doi: 10.1080/10646175.2014.985807.

Delgado, R., & Stefanic, J. (2001). *Critical race theory: An introduction.* New York, NY: New York University Press.

Everett, A. (2014). Black film, new media industries, and BAMMs (Black American media moguls) in the digital media ecology. *Cinema Journal, 53*(4), 128–133. doi: 10.1353/cj.2014.0038.

Feige, K. (Producer), & Coogler, R. (Director). (2018). *Black Panther* [Motion picture]. United States: Marvel Studios/Disney Pictures.

Henderson, J. M. (2017, February 25). Why millennials get *Get Out*. Forbes.com. Retrieved from: https://www.forbes.com/sites/jmaureenhenderson/2017/02/25/why-millennial-audien ces-get-get-out/#12e47c4e2ef2.

Hobbs, R. (2010a). Digital and media literacy: A plan of action. Washington, DC: The Aspen Institute. Retrieved from: https://www.aspeninstitute.org/events/digital-media-literacy-plan-action/pdf.

hooks, b. (1994). *Teaching to transgress*. New York, NY: Routledge.

Kellner, D., & Share, J. (2007). Critical media literacy: Crucial policy choices for a twenty-first century democracy. *Policy Futures in Education, 5*(1), 59–69. doi:10.2304/pfie.2007 .5.1.59.

King, L. (2017). The media and black masculinity: Looking at the media through race[d] lenses. *Critical Education, 8*(2), 31-40. Retrieved fromhttp://ojs.library.ubc.ca/index.php/ criticaled/article/view/186224.

Kohnen, A. M., & Lacy, A. (2018). "They don't see us otherwise": A discourse analysis of marginalized students critiquing the local news. *Linguistics and Education, 46*, 102–112. Retrieved from: https://doi.org/10.1016/j.linged.2018.07.002.

Lull, J. (2011). Hegemony. In G. Dines & J. M. Humez (Eds.), *Gender, race, and class in media: A critical reader* (pp. 33–36). Los Angeles, CA: Sage.

Marvel Studios. (2018) Synopsis. *Black Panther*. Retrieved from: https://www.marvel.com/ blackpanther#/synopsis.

McNary, M. (2018, August, 4). Box office: *Black Panther* to cross $700 million in North America. *Variety*. Retrieved from: https://variety.com/2018/film/news/box-office-black-panther-north-america-1202895427/.

Mills, C. W. (1997). *The racial contract*. Ithaca, NY: Cornell University Press.

Mithaiwala, M. (2017, August, 4). *Get Out* is the most profitable movie so far in 2017. Screenrant.com. Retrieved from: https://screenrant.com/get-out-profit-2017-comparison/.

National Association for Media Literacy Education (NAMLE). (2007). Core principles of media literacy education in the United States. Retrieved from: https://namle.net/publica-tions/core-principles.

Ramos, (2017, October 22). *Get Out* director Jordan Peele on Black identity & the "White savior." DeadlineHollywood.com. Retrieved from: https://deadline.com/2017/10/jordan-peele-get-out-film-independent-forum-keynote-speaker-diversity-inclusion-1202192699/.

Reich, E. (2016). The power of black film criticism. *Film Criticism, 40*(1), 1–3. http:// dx.doi.org/10.3998/fc.13761232.0040.126.

Rhines, J. (2003). Black film/Black future. *The Black Scholar, 33*(1), 47–53. https://doi.org./ 10.1080/0006426.2003.111413203.

Rogowski, J. C., & Cohen, C. J. (2015). *Black Millennials in America*. Retrieved from: https:// blackyouthproject.com/wp-content/uploads/2015/11/BYP-millenials-report-10-27-15-FINA L.pdf.

Seymour, G. (2001, April 2). We've gotta have it, Black filmmakers seize the moment. *The Nation*. Retrieved from: https://www.thenation.com/article/weve-gotta-have-it/.

Simien, J. (Director). (2014). *Dear White People*. United States: Roadside Attractions.

Simmons, S. (2017, February 5). Who are Black Millennials? *The Philadelphia Tribune*. Re-trieved from: http://www.phillytrib.com/news/who-are-black-millennials/article_40dea0a2-fa10-5acc-ba72-c59c219a9136.html.

Sharp, D. (2014, August 8). 10 things the media won't tell you about Black Millennials. Theroot.com. Retrieved from: https://www.theroot.com/10-things-the-media-won-t-tell-you-about-black-millenni-1790876688.

Stevens, M. (2018, April 15). Starbucks C.E.O. apologizes after arrest of 2 Black men. New-yorktimes.com. Retrieved from: https://www.nytimes.com/2018/04/15/us/starbucks-phila-delphia-black-men-arrest.html.

Stuckey, H., & Kring, K. (2007). Critical media literacy and popular film: Experiences of teaching and learning in a graduate class. *New Directions in Adult and Continuing Educa-tion, 2007*(115), 25–33. doi: 10.1002/ace.264.

The Numbers. (2018). *Dear White People*. Thenumbers.com. Retrieved from: https://www.the-numbers.com/movie/Dear-White-People#tab=summary.

Turchiano, D. (2018, June 21). *Dear White People* Renewed for Season 3 at Netflix. Variety.com. Retrieved from: https://variety.com/2018/tv/news/dear-white-people-season-3-re-newal-1202854249/.

Yosso, T. J. (2002). Critical race, challenging deficit discourse about Chicanas/os. *Journal of Popular Film and Television*, *30*(1), 52–62. https://doi.org.10.1080/01956050209605559.

Index

About the Contributors

Robert D. Byrd, Jr. is an assistant professor of journalism in the Department of Journalism and Strategic Media at the University of Memphis. His research focuses on queer representations in media, specifically the intersections of race, sexuality, gender, class and ability.

Christopher P. Campbell is a professor in the School of Communication at the University of Southern Mississippi. He is the author of *Race, Myth and the News*, the editor of *The Routldege Companion to Media and Race* and the co-author and co-editor of *Race and News: Critical Perspectives*.

Alison Yeh Cheung is a doctoral student in the Department of Communication at the University of Utah. Her research draws on rhetorical and cultural studies theories and methods to analyze transnational Asian American subcultural media and industry.

Loren Saxton Coleman is an assistant professor in the School of Mass Communication and Journalism at the University of Southern Mississippi. Her work focuses on how black communities exercise conditioned agency via media practice, with particular emphasis on structures of race, class, gender and space. She is co-editor of *Media, Myth and Millennials*.

Marcus J. Coleman is an assistant professor of communication and interdisciplinary studies at the University of Southern Mississippi. His research interests include voting identification legislation, patriotism and civic engagement. Prior to accepting his current position, he served as the senior research analyst for the Washington, D.C. Department of Behavioral Health and a Research Fellow in the Civic Engagement and Governance Institute at the Joint Center for Political and Economic Studies.

Ashley Cordes (Coquille) is an assistant professor of indigenous communication at the University of Utah. Her research lies at the intersections of communication, digital media and Indigenous studies and is attuned to issues of social power and decolonization. Cordes' work can be found in *Television & New Media* and *New Media & Society*, and in *Nuu-wee-ya Naa-'a*, an Athabaskan language book. She has a professional background in multiplatform journalism, holds an American Philosophical Society Digital Knowledge Sharing Fellowship, and serves as chair of the Culture and Education Committee of the Coquille Indian Tribe.

Jayne Cubbage is an assistant professor in the Department of Communications at Bowie State University, where she teaches courses in the graduate program in organizational communication. Her research interests include media audiences of color, media literacy and social networking.

Celeste González de Bustamante is an associate professor in the School of Journalism at The University of Arizona and an affiliated faculty member of the UA Center for Latin American Studies and the Department of Mexican American Studies. She is the author of *"Muy buenas noches": Mexico, Television and the Cold War* and the co-editor of *Arizona Firestorm: Global Immigration Realities, National Media, and Provincial Politics*.

Natalie Hopkinson is an assistant professor in the graduate program in communication, culture and media studies at Howard University. A former staff writer, editor and cultural critic for the *Washington Post* and *The Root*, she is the author of three books: *Deconstructing Tyrone* Press, *Go-Go Live* and *A Mouth is Always Muzzled*.

Cheryl D. Jenkins is an associate professor in the School of Communication and associate director of the Center for Black Studies at the University of Southern Mississippi. She is co-author and co-editor of *Race and Media: Critical Perspectives* and a former journalist.

Nadeen Kharputly is a visiting assistant professor at Washington and Lee University. She is currently at work on a manuscript that interrogates the responsibilities placed on contemporary Muslim-American writers and artists who represent their communities in their work.

Jessica Maddox is an assistant professor of digital media technology at the University of Alabama. Her research examines the intersection of visual communication, digital media, and popular culture in order to analyze how images fit into digital cultures. Her work has received awards from the International Communication Association and the Association for Education in Journalism and Mass Communication, and it has been published in *Critical Studies in Media Communication, Feminist Media Studies* and *The Journal of Popular Culture*.

Debra Merskin is a professor of media studies in the School of Journalism and Communication at the University of Oregon. Her research focuses on intersectionality as it applies to race, gender and identity. She is the author of *Media, Minorities and Meaning: A Critical Introduction, Sexing the Media: How and Why We Do It*, and *Seeing Species: Re-presentations of Animals in Media & Popular Culture*.

Vincent N. Pham is an associate professor in the Department of Civic Communication and Media at Willamette University, where he researches the intersection of race, media and organizations as they engage in the politics of national belonging. He is the co-editor of *The Routledge Companion to Asian American Media* (2017) and the co-author of *Asian Americans and the Media* (2009).

Daleana Phillips is a doctoral student in the School of Communication at the University of Southern Mississippi. Her research draws on critical cultural theories and methods to examine media coverage on issues pertaining to immigration.

Jessica Retis is associate professor in the School of Journalism at The University of Arizona. She is the co-editor of *The Handbook of Diaspora, Media and Culture*. Her work has been published in academic journals in Latin America, Europe and North America.

Sharifa Simon-Roberts is pursuing a PhD in communication, culture and media studies at Howard University. Her research interests include the intersection of new media technology, television and digital streaming.